AQA BUSINESS COMMUNICATIONS SYSTEMS for GCSE

CAROLYN WORT
FIONA PETRUCKE

Orders: please con[illegible]) 01235 827720. Fax: (44) 01235 400454. Lines are [illegible] service. You can also order through our website www.hoddereducation.co.uk

If you have any comments to make about this, or any of our other titles, please send them to educationenquiries@hodder.co.uk

British Library Cataloguing in Publication Data
A catalogue record for this title is available from the British Library

ISBN: 978 0 340 986 028

First Edition Published 2009
This Edition Published 2009
Impression number 10 9 8 7 6 5 4 3
Year 2012, 2011, 2010

Hachette UK's policy is to use papers that are natural, renewable and recyclable products and made from wood grown in sustainable forests. The logging and manufacturing processes are expected to conform to the environmental regulations of the country of origin.

Cover photo © Slavoljub Pantelic/iStockphoto.com.
Typeset in 10 on 13pt Stone Sans by Phoenix Photosetting, Chatham, Kent
Illustrations by Oxford Designers and Illustrators
Printed in Italy for Hodder Education, an Hachette UK Company, 338 Euston Road, London NW1 3BH

Contents

Contents

Introduction

Welcome to the AQA GCSE in Business and Communication Systems. Before starting this course you will have had plenty of teaching in ICT, but the business contexts will be new to you.

This book is designed to be used by students of the AQA specification and covers the knowledge and skills you need to know for Unit 8, ICT Systems in Business, Unit 9, Using ICT in Business and Unit 10, Investigating ICT in Business.

All the ICT examples are based on Microsoft applications and Microsoft 2003 has been used throughout. If you are using later software or open source software the tools and facilities available should be similar.

You will be assessed by:

Unit	Form of examination	Length of time
8 ICT Systems in Business	Written paper 60 marks 40%	1 hour
9 Using ICT in Business	Computer-based examination 60 marks 35%	1½ hours
10 Investigating ICT in Business	Controlled assessment 40 marks 25%	8–10 hours research and planning 3–4 hours final presentation

How this book is organised

Each chapter starts off with a very short summary of what you will learn, taken from the sections in the specification and the examples that AQA give.

Getting started will give you a gentle introduction to the concepts involved using a context that you already know about. It is followed by a section called **What you need to know**, which sets out clearly and concisely the theory that you need to know. This is then followed by Activities, which are usually IT-based and fairly open-ended tasks.

The **Key words to learn** in each chapter are listed. Many of these words have a very specific meaning in Business or ICT.

Points for discussion are designed to get you thinking about the topic in more detail and can be used as extension tasks for more able groups of students. 'Give me five ...' is a revision tool and can be used as either a plenary or starter, provided that the basic topic has been covered.

Exam style questions are designed to give you practice in a range of shorter- or longer-style examination questions.

What is Business and Communication Systems?

In this GCSE you will learn about the importance to businesses of Business and Communication Systems to enable them to achieve whatever they set out to do. You will learn how ICT systems improve communication and affect the way people work, as well as the risks involved with using ICT. You will also learn about the importance of recruiting, retaining and rewarding people in work. You will improve your skills in a range of software applications and learn how they support each area of a business. The software with which you will be expected to be familiar is:

- word processing
- spreadsheets
- databases
- graphics
- presentation
- web authoring.

In addition to using the software for specific examination tasks, you will be asked to investigate ICT in a specific business situation and complete a practical exercise.

During this course you will learn many skills that you will use in further study on any Level 3 course or above. We wish you success for the future!

Acknowledgements

Fiona Petrucke

I would like to acknowledge once again the support and help that my husband, Paul Petrucke, has given me in preparing this book. His patience and help throughout has been tremendous.

However, my dear friend and colleague Huong Thai should also be acknowledged because her advice, support, suggestions and comments made the writing of this book so much easier. Many, many thanks.

Carolyn Wort

I would like to thank Phil Wort for checking advice throughout.

Every effort has been made to trace the copyright holders of quoted material. The publishers apologise if any sources remain unacknowledged and will be glad to make the necessary arrangements at the earliest opportunity. The authors and publishers would like to thank the following for permission to reproduce copyright photos:

Title page, © Slavoljub Pantelic/iStockphoto.com; p.4 uk retail Alan King/Alamy; p.8 Raf Makda/View Pictures/Rex Features; p.18 © Ingram Publishing Limited; p.20 OJO Images/Rex Features; p.25 Blend Images/Alamy; p.29 Tony Kyriacou/Rex Features; p.41 © Dmitriy Melnikov – Fotolia.com; p.50 © Photodisc/Getty Images; p.67 Fredrik Renander/Alamy; p.69 Action Press/Rex Features; p.73 © starush – Fotolia.com; p.83 Barking Dog Art; p.89 © Amazon.com, Inc; p.92 © Ingram Publishing Limited; p.94 Natalia Bull, Cool Bull Fitness; p.101 Oleksiy Maksymenko/Alamy; p.131 © Monkey Business – Fotolia.com; p.151 © kristian sekulic – Fotolia.com; p.154 www.PurestockX.com.

SECTION 1

ADMINISTRATION

1. Stakeholders
2. Business aims and objectives
3. Business administration and job roles
4. Business management and planning
5. Workplace organisation
6. The sustainable office
7. Health and safety at work
8. ICT data systems in business
9. Security of data

Chapter 1

Stakeholders

In this chapter you will learn:

- that there are different stakeholders in a business
- the importance to a business of its employees
- the importance to a business of its customers
- that different stakeholders impose constraints on a business.

Getting started

You may have just started this course in Year 10. Obviously you want to do well, but who else is interested in how you are doing?

Hopefully you have answered this question with: your parents or carers, other relatives, your friends, your teacher, your head teacher ... the list goes on and on. All of these people are stakeholders in you.

What you need to know

A stakeholder is a person or group of people who have an interest in a business. They want the business to succeed so that they can reap the benefits. They may also suffer if the business does not succeed. Just like your teachers if you do not succeed!

The interests of the stakeholders will not always be the same; in fact, they might be in direct conflict with each other. For example, employees may want as much pay as they can get, but this might conflict with the owners of the business who want the company to make as much profit as possible. They will not make as much profit if they pay their employees too much.

The main stakeholders

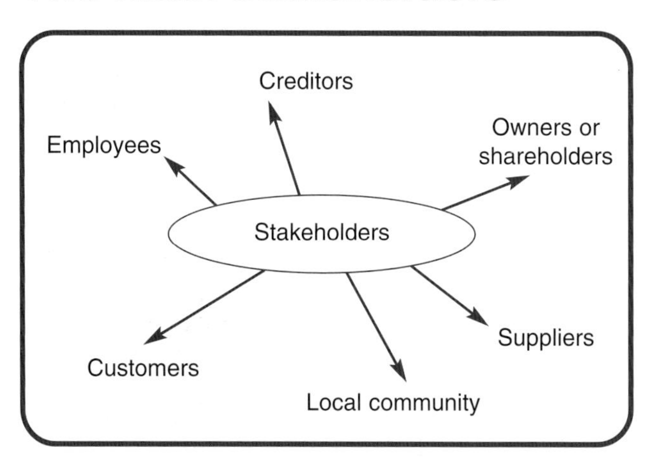

Employees

Why are employees interested in the success of the business?

If the business is not profitable then their job may not be secure. If they lose their job and find a new one in another area they might have to move house. So they want the business to be sustainable to give them security.

If the business is really successful, employees may receive bonuses or pay rises above the average that other businesses are giving.

If the business is successful then employees will feel that they have helped create that success. It will help them feel good about themselves and have more job satisfaction. It will also improve their status. It may also lead to them being promoted to a higher position within the business.

A successful business is more likely to invest in training its employees, so if they are not promoted then the training will improve their chances of being promoted in the future.

Customers

Why are customers interested in the success of the business?

A successful business is less likely to cut corners or buy cheap materials, so the quality of the product may be better. For example, a pair of jeans may be better made and less likely to come apart at the seams. Customers want to be satisfied with the quality of the product or service.

If the business is able to expand it may be able to charge less for the product because the costs of making the items are lower. This is called 'benefiting from economies of scale'. If a clothing factory buys one bale of fabric it may be charged £150, but if it buys ten bales of fabric it might only have to pay £120 per bale.

Customers want to be sure that they can keep buying the same goods. If a business is not successful and goes out of business then its products are no longer available. The customer would then have to go to the trouble of finding an alternative product, which can take time and effort. Think how annoying you would find it if your favourite chocolate bar was no longer available.

If the business is successful then it may be able to extend its range of products or services, making it easier for customers to find what they want. For example, a clothes shop may start selling accessories such as shoes and bags. This would make it easier for the customer to find a complete outfit for an occasion.

A successful business may have more to spend on employing staff, such as more assistants, customer services staff or personal shoppers. All of these people directly aim to make the experience of using the company easier for the customer and enhance the shopping experience.

Owners

Why are owners interested in the success of the business?

The profit (after tax) of the business belongs to the owners, so they get more money if the business is successful. They want the business to be profitable. The owners can also choose to retain the profit and reinvest it back into the business. This would enable the business to expand and potentially make even more profit in the future.

If the business is a limited company then the owners are known as shareholders. They invest in the business by buying shares, and they receive a share of the profits the business makes. If the business does not make a profit then the owners or shareholders do not receive any return for their investment. The more successful the business is, the better return the shareholders receive.

The local community

Why is the local community interested in the success of the business?

A successful business will usually employ more people. This is good for the community because it will offer job opportunities to local people, which means they will have money to spend in local businesses and will not have to travel far to work.

The business may support or sponsor local organisations. For example, a factory may sponsor the local football team by buying the kit in exchange for having the name of the business on it.

If a successful business wants to expand, the local council may be able to negotiate that it will grant permission to do so as long as the company provides additional resources for the community. These may be things like free car parking or the building of a community centre.

The business will pay business rates to the local council, which the council will use to provide services and to help improve the local area.

Some members of the community may wish the business to trade elsewhere because they dislike the noise, traffic or other aspect of the businesses.

Creditors

Why are creditors interested in the success of the business?

Creditors are people whom the business owes money to. If the business is doing badly and cannot afford to pay its creditors, they will lose out. If the business is doing well it may mean more business for the creditors. If a creditor is the bank and the business is doing well, the bank may get more business in the form of loans to enable the business to expand.

Suppliers

Why are suppliers interested in the success of the business?

Most suppliers have to wait some time before they are paid. If the business were to fail then they might never receive their money. This might then put their business into financial difficulties.

If the business is doing well then the suppliers will get more business and repeat orders. This will help them make a profit.

Let's go!

Activities

1 Look at the website www.bodyshop.co.uk and investigate its Community Trade programme.

a) What does the Body Shop mean by Community Trade?

b) Which stakeholders benefit from Community Trade?

2 Look at the website www.fairtrade.org.uk. Produce a presentation, using appropriate software, to persuade customers to purchase a Fair Trade product.

3 Research what Kellogg's (www.kelloggs.co.uk) sees as 'Our commitment'.

Which stakeholders do they state that they have a responsibility to?

4 Jamie Syrda is the organiser of a five-a-side football team in Holinside. He has been thinking about whether he might be able to get some sponsorship for the football kit for the new season. There is a large bakery, Breadco, in Holinside that employs several of the players' parents. One of the parents has suggested that he writes to the bakery and asks if they would be prepared to sponsor the kit.

The address of the bakery is Breadco, Elim Road, Holinside, Cheshire CH12 2JJ. Jamie Syrda lives at 4 The Laurels, Beech Rd, Holinside, Cheshire CH12 1EJ.

Compose a letter to the bakery from Jamie, asking if they would be prepared to sponsor the kit at a cost of £250 per year for three years. In exchange, Jamie is prepared to include the name Breadco on the shirts and to invite someone from the company to the team's awards ceremony.

Summary

- A stakeholder is a person or group with an interest in the business.
- Different stakeholders may want different things.
- Employees want the business to be sustainable so they can feel secure in their jobs.
- Customers want satisfaction, which is also important to the owners because they want their customers to keep on coming back for more of the product.
- The community may either want the business to do well so that more jobs are created, or they may not want the business to succeed if they think it makes the area a less pleasant environment to live in.

Key words

Stakeholder – a person or group of people who have an interest in how a business performs.

Creditors – people or organisations that are owed money by the business.

Customers – people who purchase goods or services from the business.

Customer service – this covers all aspects of how the customer is dealt with by the business. There may be a special department that deals with customer queries or problems.

Profit – the money left over from the sales of goods (revenue) or services after the business has paid all of its costs.

PROFIT = REVENUE – COSTS

Revenue – money coming into the business from sales.

Suppliers – people who supply goods or stock to the business.

Shareholders – people who invest by buying shares and become joint owners of a business. They receive a percentage of the profit the business makes in return for buying the shares.

Sponsorship – a way of publicising a business by giving money for a sporting or social event in exchange for publicity of some sort.

In Business

Surf to Go

Surf to Go is a surf school with branches on three popular surfing beaches in Cornwall. It was founded by Jason Dude in 2005, after he had moved into the area and found that there were not many surf schools in his part of Cornwall. As the owner, Jason wants the business to make a decent profit and to expand slowly.

Jason is the sole owner of the surf school and he employs 12 part-time seasonal staff. The staff he employs want to keep their jobs throughout the summer and many of them would like to come back and work for Jason next summer. Some are happy to work for little because they love the sport, but others are saving to go to university so need as much pay as possible.

The local community is pleased that Jason has started his business because it encourages people to stay longer in their area and support other local businesses. In particular the local coffee shops are doing well as parents often visit while their children are having lessons. The local community is also pleased that there are jobs for local young people during the summer holidays. It has given the area a much-needed boost.

To set up his surf schools Jason had to buy quite a large number of surfboards and wetsuits. If his business is more successful and expands he will have to order many more. This will please his suppliers who will have more business. If he needs a loan to buy this equipment he will create business for the bank.

People who come to Cornwall and use the Surf to Go school are pleased that his business is expanding as it gives them more chance to learn how to surf. They are hoping that he will start selling wetsuits too, so that they can buy their own rather than having to hire them for the lessons. They would also like him to open longer hours.

Points for discussion

1 Who are the stakeholders identified in the case study?

2 To what extent do they all want the same thing? Is there any conflict between them?

3 Are any of the stakeholders more important than the others?

Give me five

Give five reasons why different stakeholders want a business to be profitable.

Exam style questions

1 Levi Crump is planning on setting up a coffee bar in his local town of Welchurch. He plans to open his coffee bar six days a week from 9 a.m. until 5 p.m., offering a wide range of drinks and light meals. The site that Levi has found for his coffee bar is near to a residential area.

a) Explain what is meant by the term 'stakeholder'. (2 marks)

b) Give an example of a stakeholder in Levi's business. (1 mark)

c) Explain how there may be conflict between different stakeholders if Levi decides to stay open until 10 p.m. (5 marks)

2 Match the stakeholders to what they are most likely to want from a business.

Stakeholder	Wants
Owner	Prompt payment of money owed to him
Customer	More orders and top prices paid to him
Supplier	Sponsorship of local football team
Creditor	A secure job with good pay
Local community	Good range of stock at a low price
Employees	To sell a lot of goods or services at a high price to make more profit

(6 marks)

Chapter 2

Business aims and objectives

In this chapter you will learn:

- why the owners of businesses set objectives that they want the business to achieve
- the importance to a business of its objectives
- that businesses might have different objectives, depending on how long the business has been going or the preferences of the owner.

Getting started

Objectives are targets that are set. When you started doing this Business and Communications GCSE, what grade did you hope to achieve? Some of you will have set yourselves targets of an A* and others of you will have set yourself a target to pass – individuals' objectives are personal. The same applies to businesses – some want to make a massive profit whereas others are happy if they do not lose money.

What you need to know

Mission statements

A mission statement is a short phrase that is used to describe the purpose of or reason for the existence of a business or organisation. The mission statement usually fits in with the aims and objectives of the business.

Sainsbury's, one of the major UK supermarkets, describes its goal as:

'At Sainsbury's we will deliver an ever-improving quality shopping experience for our customers with great products at fair prices. We aim to exceed customer expectations for healthy, safe, fresh and tasty food, making their lives easier every day.'

Source: www.jsainsburys.co.uk

On their website, Boots say:

'Our purpose is to help our customers look and feel better than they ever thought possible.

Our customers are at the heart of our business. We're committed to providing exceptional customer and patient care, be the first choice for pharmacy and healthcare, offer innovative products "only at Boots", with great value our customers love.'

Source: www.boots-uk.com

Both companies have mission statements that are not easy to measure. They also talk about how much they are committed to their customers. Does that mean that they are not interested in making a profit?

Aims and objectives

The aims of a business are what it hopes to achieve as a result of its work. Aims cannot usually be measured, as they are quite general, such as 'to maximise profits'. The objectives are the activities or targets that the business sets itself in order to achieve the aims. Objectives, on the other hand, should have specific figures to achieve and dates by which they have to achieve them, so that the business can measure whether or not it has achieved them. Examples of objectives are 'to increase sales by 10 per cent by next year' or, 'to reduce the cost of raw materials by 5 per cent this year'. Both of these objectives will help the business to achieve the objective of maximising profits.

Maximising profits

To maximise profits means to make the most profit possible. To do this a business needs to keep its costs as low as possible and its revenues (income from sales) as high as possible. In order to make the maximum profit the business will need to be as efficient as possible, that is, to make the best use of the resources it has. A business needs to use its resources as efficiently as possible in order to reduce the costs. Increasing the number of sales and the price at which they are sold will also help to increase the profit, provided that the costs do not increase.

Maximising market share

A company's 'market share' is the percentage or proportion of the total market it has. For example, if one in five cups of coffee sold in the town of Whitchurch is bought at Kershaw's Café, then Kershaw's has a 20 per cent share of the market. One of the most important objectives used in business is to increase its market share. In 2008 it was widely reported in the media that almost £1 out of every £8 spent in the UK passes through Tesco checkouts. Tesco is the supermarket chain with the highest market share in the country, with 32 per cent of the market compared with Sainsbury's and Asda, both of which have a market share of around 16 per cent.

The *New York Times* reported in 2007 that in the soft drinks market, although Coca-Cola's market share had slipped it was still the world's favourite cola drink. Coca-Cola sells more than Pepsi in much of Europe and South America, but not in some of the Asian markets. In its 2007 Annual Report, Coca-Cola stated that its goal was to become more competitive and to accelerate its growth to create additional value for its shareholders.

Survival

At the end of 2008 and the beginning of 2009, because of a worldwide economic downturn, many businesses' main aim was to survive. 6 January 2009 saw the final closure of Woolworths stores, which had been popular in the UK since 1909.

The objective of survival was not confined to businesses operating in the UK. The BBC reported that Toyota was stopping production at all 12 of its Japanese factories for 11 days in February and March in an attempt to reduce their stock of cars that had not sold. Toyota had already planned to stop production in January for three days, but before 2009 it had not had to stop production since 1993, when it had ceased production for only one day.

Even in more favourable economic conditions many small or new businesses have survival as their main aim.

Breaking even

A new business or a business about to introduce a new product may have breaking even as its objective. Breaking even means that the total amount of money received from sales (revenue) equals the total costs. When a business breaks even it is not making a loss, and once the level of sales moves above the break-even point it can make a profit.

Growth

Businesses may grow as a result of trying to achieve any of the objectives discussed above. However, for a number of businesses growth is expressly stated as the objective as a means of increasing profit. Many businesses start out small and grow either from within, perhaps by opening up other branches, or externally by purchasing other businesses. The international chain Wal-Mart grew by buying Asda, and it also grows by increasing the number of stores it has.

Non-financial aims

Some owners of businesses do not seek to maximise their profit but to gain a better quality of life by being their own boss. The aim of their business, then, is likely to be to retain independence so that they can make all the decisions and not have to work for someone else. Being self-employed is seen by some people as preferable to and less stressful than a high-powered career in a large company and earning a larger salary.

Another aim might be to obtain a good reputation for service or quality of products. Businesses will gain more trade as their reputation improves, and they will also increase their status within their community. A good reputation will help the business get repeat business from its customers, which leads to brand loyalty and can result in the business having to spend less on advertising and promotion. This aim may also be written in terms of increasing customer satisfaction – clearly a business with satisfied customers will gain a better reputation.

Many businesses' websites now include a section on Corporate Social Responsibility. There is an increasing emphasis on stating the business aims in terms of responsibility to the community, the environment and the planet. Asda proudly declares on its website that it has pledged to send zero waste to landfill sites by 2010. This is a clear aim and success can be measured. It also says that the welfare of the planet is as important as its commitment to people and prices. It claims to consider the environmental impact of every part of its business, including helping suppliers to reduce the carbon emissions in manufacturing their products. (Source: www.about-asda.com, 20 January 2009)

Let's go!

Activities

1 Using a word-processing package, create a table with two columns, one labelled Aims and the other Objectives. Put each of the following under the correct heading in the table.

Produce more products than last year.

Launch a new product in June.

Provide a better service.

Reduce costs.

Reduce cardboard waste by 6 per cent this year.

Survive as a business.

Be environmental friendly.

Reduce costs by 5 per cent based on last year.

Expand the premises by next month.

Make a profit.

2 Most schools and colleges have a mission statement, which is often shown on the website or in the prospectus. Collect the mission statements from three similar schools or colleges and describe their similarities and differences.

3 Choose a business with a website which you are interested in and research its objectives. Create a presentation about the business and how it is trying to meet its objectives.

4 Word process a business letter to the owner of a local small business, explaining that you are studying BCS and are researching business objectives. Ask the owner to explain how the objectives of the business have changed over the years.

Summary

- An organisation's mission statement is usually a wide-ranging statement declaring the purpose of the organisation and broadly what it hopes to achieve. Usually it cannot be used to measure the success of the organisation and may include words such as 'customer delight', 'the world's favourite brand' and 'world-class reputation'.
- The aims of an organisation are usually more specific and may be expressed as, for example:
  - to maximise efficiency
  - to maximise market share
  - to maximise sales
  - to survive
  - to break even
  - to grow
  - to improve customer satisfaction
  - to improving the organisation's reputation
  - to increase repeat trade
  - to improve corporate social responsibility
  - to maintain independence.
- Business objectives are more specific than aims and are expressed in terms of a target with a date so that success can be measured. The major aim of new or small businesses is to survive. As the business develops, the aims often change to that of maximisation.
- Not all organisations exist to make a profit; some exist for the benefit of their members or society as a whole.

Give me five

Give five aims or objectives you think a local shop may have.

Key words

Break even – a business breaks even when the total costs of its product equal the revenue from its sales.

Efficiency – the best use of resources.

Market share – the amount of a market a business has, expressed as a percentage of the total market.

Maximisation – achieving the most of something that is possible.

Mission statement – a short phrase that sums up what a company believes in and what it wants to achieve.

Points for discussion

To what extent do you agree or disagree with the following statements?

1 'Despite what they may give as a mission statement, the only objective any business has is to maximise its profit.'

2 'All businesses need to grow to survive.'

Exam style questions

Sarah Collins and John Wilkiss decide to go into business together, and set up their own ice-cream-making business. They do not have much business experience, but Sarah has studied Business Studies and ICT and John has worked in an ice-cream factory.

1 Which of the following is not a business objective?

maximising profit break chart survival improving reputation (1 mark)

2 Explain what you think their main objective was when they *set up* their business. (4 marks)

3 Suggest three ways in which Sarah and John could try to increase their market share in the next couple of years. (9 marks)

4 Describe how Sarah and John might be able to find out if their customer satisfaction was increasing? (6 marks)

5 Describe how their objectives for the business might have changed after five years in business. (6 marks)

Extension activity

Wrexham Local Health Board works alongside the local authority in planning long-term strategies for dealing with issues of health and wellbeing in Wrexham. It also works closely with the local population, inviting input and feedback on local health-related matters, and consulting on any significant changes. It receives a substantial share of the NHS budget for Wrexham and is involved in planning and allocating heath services tailored to the local population, and then negotiating with hospital trusts, GP practices, dentists and other organisations to provide these services.

Public sector organisations such as Wrexham Local Health Board also have mission statements, although they are not expected to be profit making. The Wrexham Local Health Board states that:

'The role of a Local Health Board (LHB) is to improve the health of local people, plan the development of primary care and purchase health services to address the needs of its population.'

a) Explain why Wrexham LHB cannot have profit maximisation as its overall objective.

b) Suggest three different objectives that Wrexham LHB might set so that it can work towards its objective of improving the health of the local people.

c) Explain how they might measure their success in addressing the needs of the population.

d) Suggest ways in which the mission statement for Wrexham LHB may differ from that of a pharmacy in the area.

Chapter 3

Business administration and job roles

In this chapter you will learn:

- the role of administration
- how administration supports the business functions
- the range of job roles that exist in business.

Getting started

Your school or college is supported by a number of people who work as administrators. Increasingly, teaching unions have campaigned for administration to be done by people other than teachers so that they can concentrate on teaching and ensuring that you get the results you deserve. Administration tasks such as collecting dinner money, money for trips and typing letters are now usually done by office staff. Other administrative tasks, such as ordering exercise books and keeping financial records, are also done by specialist administrative staff.

What you need to know

The main business functions

In most businesses, where there are similar tasks that need to be undertaken these are grouped together as different functional areas. The usual functional areas of a business are human resources, finance, sales and marketing, production (if it is a manufacturing business), customer service and research and development.

- Human resources is the department concerned with the management of people. The human resources manager will usually be concerned with the hiring and firing of staff and training them.
- The finance department is concerned with keeping an accurate record of the movement of money within the business and predicting financial profits and losses.
- Sales and marketing are concerned with achieving the target for sales of the products or services.
- Customer services are concerned with keeping the customers happy.
- In businesses that make goods there will be a production function which is responsible for the product being made to a standard quality in a safe and efficient manner.
- For the business to survive there needs to be someone with a responsibility for research and development. Without improvement to products and services, competitors will eventually produce better products or give an improved service and take over their customers.

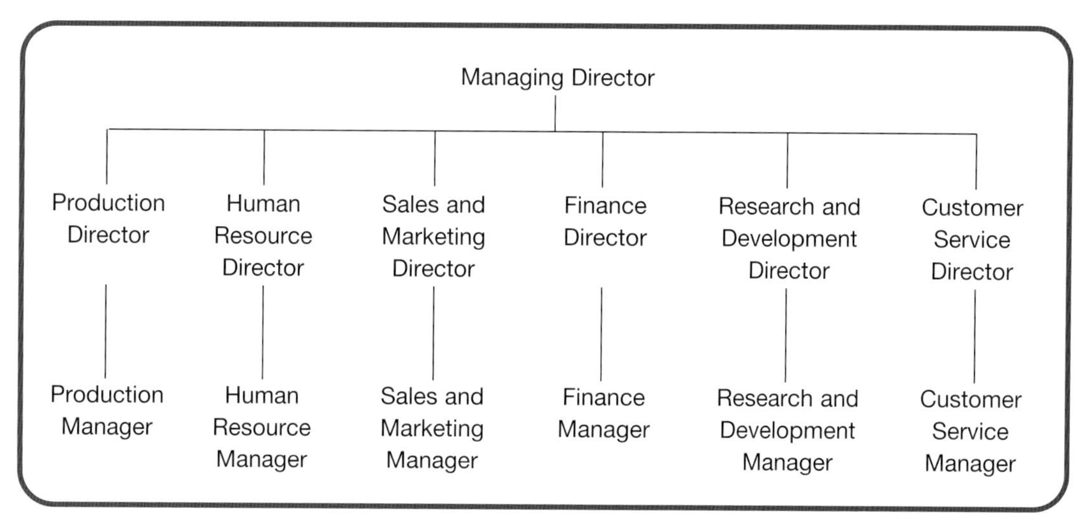

A typical management structure for a large production business

Below the managers will be other layers of staff such as assistant managers, supervisors and workers. As the layers go down, the number of staff in each layer increases, so the structure is known as a pyramid because of the shape of the organisation chart. If there are lots of layers in the pyramid, the structure is known as 'hierarchical'; if there are only a few it is known as 'flat'. A flat organisational structure often results in good communication between the top and the bottom of the organisation because it has to pass through fewer layers, leading to high motivation. In a hierarchical pyramid, people in each layer only interact with those immediately above or below their own layer.

The importance of administration

Administration involves the storing, processing, retrieving and spreading or disseminating information. The purpose of the information is to support the business functions. In a large business or organisation each functional manager will have administrative support to allow him or her to concentrate on management and decision making. Without the administrators, managers would not be able to devote their time to decision making, and this could affect the success of the business, for example in terms of market share or profits.

The type of tasks undertaken by administrative staff include things like preparing sales figures for a meeting so that decisions can be taken, for example to look for new products to sell or an item to be deleted from a catalogue.

Storing information is vital in an organisation and increasingly this is being done electronically. Administrative staff will be responsible for the safe storage of information and for keeping a backup in case electronic systems are damaged. Some information will need to be processed by administrative workers, for example invoices may need to be entered onto an accounting system so that the business has a record of cash coming in and going out. Administrative staff will also be expected to use databases or other information systems to retrieve information. They may be expected to use databases to search for customers who meet certain criteria, for example, customers who have purchased a car in the past 12 months.

Administration also involves the disseminating (passing on) of information to those who need it. In small organisations, although the need for different sorts of information may be the same, several (if not all) functional areas are overseen by one person.

Job roles

Within each large organisation there are a number of job roles, such as managers, supervisors and operatives.

Managers are generally responsible for the decision making in the organisation, and they pass on their instructions to the supervisors. The task of the supervisor is to ensure that the operatives or workers follow instructions and perform their tasks diligently. They may also give basic training to the workers.

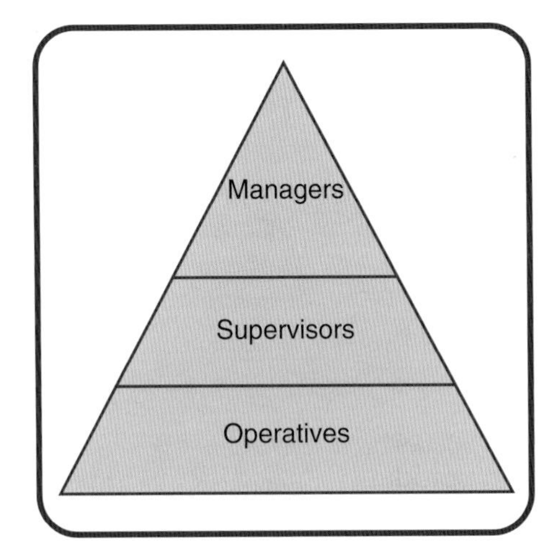

The different job roles form a pyramid

Let's go!

Activities

1 Investigate a business of your choice, it may be somewhere you have a part-time job or have done work experience. Describe the functional areas that exist in the organisation.

2 Choose a functional area that you may be interested in working in, for example finance or human resource management.

a) Investigate the range of careers available to someone specialising in this field.

b) Choose one of these career options to investigate further and find out what qualifications and experience people who do this job need to have.

3 Investigate the levels of hierarchy in the armed forces and produce a pyramid to show them. Colour each level differently.

Summary

- Administration is essential for the smooth running of businesses and organisations to ensure that they can compete with others in the same field.
- The primary function of administration is to support other areas by processing, storing, retrieving and passing on information to people who need it to run the business.
- Within larger businesses there are a variety of job roles in each functional area. The main functional areas may have a manager, a supervisor and operatives to fulfil these tasks. In small organisations the administration has to be done by fewer staff and sometimes just by the owner.

Key words

Marketing – providing a product or service that a customer wants at the right time and in the right place, at a profit.

Human resource management – employing and keeping the organisations' employees in the most efficient way.

Hierarchical pyramid – an organisational structure where there are few people at the top level and many more at the bottom level. Each person has clear responsibilities and roles.

Operatives – people at the lowest level in the hierarchical pyramid who are responsible for either making the product or delivering the service for the public.

Points for discussion

To what extent do you believe that the following statements are true?

1 'Organisations should not have a hierarchical structure because all workers are equally important to the business.'

2 'The NHS should concentrate on treating patients, not on administration.'

Give me five

Give five functional areas in a business.

Exam style questions

Jenny Begun is the managing director of a medium-sized business in the London area, which runs a small chain of coffee shops. All together the business has 56 staff working in eight shops. The shops sell a range of teas and coffees to both drink in and take away. There is also a flourishing sandwich delivery business based in the main store. Jenny employs a manager to help her with the finance side of the business. The finance manager is also responsible for the human resource management.

1 Explain what is meant by the term 'human resource management'. (3 marks)

2 State the functional areas which Jenny will be responsible for. (3 marks)

3 In each coffee shop, Jenny employs a supervisor. Explain what a supervisor is. (3 marks)

4 Jenny has decided that she needs to employ an administrative assistant to help her. Describe three tasks that the administrative assistant may be asked to do. (9 marks)

Chapter 4

Business management and planning

In this chapter you will learn:

- the difference between routine tasks and non-routine tasks
- how to identify appropriate decision makers
- the consequences of poor planning and prioritising
- the importance of planning for meetings.

Getting started

Who makes the decisions in your household? Does it depend on what the decision is? Some decisions are made regularly each day, week or year. For example, what to have for dinner is a decision that needs to be made each day, whereas where to go on holiday is a decision that is made only once or twice a year by most people. Who makes the final decision about where to go on holiday? Is it discussed? If it is, does someone do some research on the holiday before it is discussed? Other decisions only need to be made once, such as a decision to buy a computer or get a dog. Most people do not change their dog each year!

Some tasks are routine – it is hoped that brushing your teeth is a routine task, as you should be doing that twice a day! A non-routine task is something that you cannot predict will need to be done each day, week or month.

What you need to know

Routine and non-routine tasks

Routine tasks are those that are done regularly. There are some tasks that a business must do on a regular basis if it is to survive. Each area of a business will have its own routine tasks and those will vary according to the nature of the business. A shop will have different routine tasks from a manufacturing business. Some tasks will, however, be routine regardless of the nature of the business and many of these will be routine for legal or safety reasons, such as checking the safety of all electrical equipment regularly, perhaps annually. There will also be routine tasks associated with tax returns and payments to local government. Generally, routine tasks will be scheduled into the company diary each year so that nothing important is overlooked.

Non-routine tasks are by their nature unpredictable and can cause problems to businesses because of a lack of resources available to carry them out. If a non-routine task requires specialist staff, the business may need to appoint temporary staff or contract out the work to people outside the business. This can be expensive and the staff may not have the commitment to do as good a job as permanent employees. Examples of non-routine tasks could be those associated with setting up a new branch of the business, such as looking for new premises, recruiting new staff or building a factory extension.

Decision makers

Businesses are structured to enable decisions to be made. Most organisations have a few people at the top of the management structure and many more lower down. In a limited company there will be directors as the top line of management and below them will be managers and workers. Some businesses have few levels of management while others have many.

Passing down authority to make decisions is called delegation so, for example, a manager may delegate to a supervisor and a supervisor may delegate to a worker. If the power to make decisions is delegated to someone, they can always be overruled at a later date. If a business is centralised there will be very little in the way of delegation, but a decentralised organisation will have many people responsible for making decisions. One of the advantages of delegation is that it can motivate people because they feel more valued and important to the business. However, the disadvantages of decentralised structures are that decision making can be reversed and people can be unsure who is able to make a particular decision.

The consequences of poor planning

Poor planning and poor decision making can lead to much wastage of time and resources and ultimately to business failure. Planning needs to take place regarding all the resources of the business so that there are no shortages – for example, stock must be available continuously, and there must be enough staff to enable the business to be carried out. Imagine if a large supermarket near you totally ran out of milk or bread – customers would be unhappy and this would mean that the business would lose revenue and profit. If this happened regularly customers would cease to go to that supermarket. Similarly, if they were short staffed and there were very long queues at the checkout, customers would soon get fed up and shop elsewhere.

Planning for meetings

There are important considerations to be taken into account when planning a meeting, such as who needs to be invited to attend and what will be needed in terms of the meeting environment. It is important that the correct people are invited to the meeting and that they have a mandate (they are allowed) to make any decisions necessary. There is little point in meetings if they do not lead to decisions being made. It is also vital that meetings are small enough, wherever possible, to allow people to contribute to the discussion. If meetings are too large it makes it very hard for people to express their opinions. Business meetings are formal affairs with a chairperson and a secretary. All comments are made to the chairperson, who gives people permission to speak. People who wish to speak are expected to raise their hands and wait to be asked to speak, a bit like school or college really! There is also a secretary who takes down notes of what is discussed. These notes are called the minutes of the meeting.

The venue and equipment

Meeting rooms may need to be sound proofed if the matter under discussion is confidential. They also need to be lockable so that people attending can leave belongings such as laptops and confidential papers during breaks or lunchtime. Many people find it easier to work in a room with natural light and, of course, adequate ventilation and heating are needed if people are to concentrate for long periods of time. Many meeting rooms have a dry atmosphere and, because people are expected to be talking, water and other drinks should be provided.

Most meeting rooms are equipped with flip charts, marker pens, standard office supplies like staplers, hole punches, pens, paper, etc. and increasingly a data projector and screen. People attending the meeting are usually expected to provide their own laptops.

The agenda

In advance of a business meeting an 'agenda and notice of meeting' needs to be sent to those who are expected to attend. This sets out what is going to be discussed at the meeting and allows people to consider their views or gather information before any discussions take place. Agendas usually include some items that are regularly on the agenda (e.g. apologies for any absences) and others that are specific to that meeting. It is usual at a meeting to set the date and time of the next meeting.

Some organisations and committees have regular meetings weekly or monthly, and some have them annually. A limited company has a legal requirement to hold an annual general meeting (AGM) each year for the company shareholders.

Below is an example of an agenda. The items that usually appear on any agenda are printed in italics.

Agenda for the Business Communications Systems Question Paper Committee

16 February 2009

1 *Apologies for absence*

2 *Matters arising from the minutes of the last meeting*

3 Consideration of exam papers and mark schemes

4 Arrangements for the summer examinations

5 Collection of material

6 *Any other business*

7 *Date and time of next meeting*

The first item, apologies for absence, is a list of people who were invited to the meeting but were unable to attend. Their names are recorded so that it can be seen that the decisions taken at the meeting were done so without their input. The minutes (the notes taken) at the previous meeting are usually issued prior to the meeting so that people can read them and make notes of any inaccuracies. The second item on the agenda, *Matters arising from the minutes of the last meeting,* gives the opportunity for corrections to be made to the record of the previous meeting. Sometimes, only one item is up for discussion and at other meetings the list may be much longer. The last-but-one item is usually *Any other business,* which gives the people attending the meeting their chance to add items to the agenda and discuss any issues of concern. Lastly, it is usual to discuss the date and time of the next meeting so that people who are expected to attend the meeting are able to check their diaries and confirm whether they are able to attend.

Let's go!

Activities

1 List 20 routine tasks that you imagine need to take place in a hairdressing salon.

2 Imagine that your school or college has a committee organising your end-of-year prom. It has met once already to discuss venues and ticket prices but decisions still need to be made on these matters. The committee also needs to agree upon the disco that will be hired for the event. Use a word-processor to create a suitable agenda for the meeting.

3 Investigate the management structure of your school or college or a local business and draw a diagram to show it, using word-processing tools. Give examples of decisions taken by someone from each level of the organisation.

Summary

- Some tasks within a business are routine and others are non-routine. This does not relate to their importance. Some very important tasks are done regularly, such as examining the cash flow of the business, and others are done only once a year or even less frequently.
- Some tasks and decisions can be delegated to workers. If this happens often in the business, it is said to have a decentralised structure.
- A centralised structure, where only one or a few people make decisions, can be very efficient and decisions can be made quickly because nobody else is involved. However, workers can feel less valued and quickly become de-motivated.

Key words ?

Agenda – a list of items for discussion at a formal meeting, in the order in which they are to be discussed.

Delegation – the passing of authority to someone lower down the hierarchy.

Centralised organisation – an organisation where the decisions are made by one manager at the top of the organisation.

Decentralised organisation – an organisation where decisions are delegated to people lower down the management structure.

Minutes – the record of what happens at a meeting, taken by the meeting secretary.

Routine – a regular or fixed way of doing things.

Points for discussion

1 Do you think business meetings should still be held in a formal, structured way?

2 Has the internet meant that there is no need for meetings to physically take place in one room?

Give me five

Give five decisions that someone setting up their own business would need to make.

Exam style questions

Henry Lewin has set up a small business importing digital cameras. He stocks a wide range of different cameras, printing accessories, cables, batteries and memory cards. He has to import his cameras. He runs his business from a small shop in the High Street of Wellington. Henry has formed a limited company and has 15 shareholders made up of family and very close friends.

1 Suggest three decisions that Henry may have had to make before setting up his business. (3 marks)

2 Once the business was up and running Henry had many routine tasks to carry out. Explain, using a possible example from Henry's business, what is meant by the term 'routine task'. (2 marks)

3 Every year Henry has to hold an annual general meeting. Explain what is meant by the term 'agenda'. (3 marks)

4 State three items that would appear on the agenda for most meetings and explain why they are discussed. (6 marks)

5 Explain why it is important that Henry plans his stock of cameras for the business. (6 marks)

Chapter 5

Workplace organisation

In this chapter you will learn:

- that there are different kinds of working environment
- the advantages and disadvantages of different office layouts
- the impact of modern developments on working practices
- how ergonomics affects decisions about the workplace.

Getting started

Workplaces have changed considerably over the years. Organisations have different types of offices, for example, some workers share an office while others have their own workspace. The different types of layout are influenced by the needs of the organisation and the type of tasks that are done by the workers. Increasingly, environmental concerns are also influencing how the workplace is organised and run.

What you need to know

Open plan and cellular offices

Open plan offices are found in many businesses and organisations. These are often large rooms with many people working in them. They allow workers to have their own desks and basic equipment but also to share resources such as printers and filing cabinets. There may be screens between desks, allowing a degree of privacy, but these are usually movable to allow maximum flexibility. If teamwork is important in the organisation then an open plan layout will encourage this by making it easy for people to work together in their team. Even if teamwork is not essential for the tasks being done, having an open plan office can make workers more motivated because they have the opportunity to talk about work with their colleagues.

However, there are drawbacks to open plan offices.

- First, if the work is confidential it is hard in an open plan office to ensure the privacy that is needed. Office telephone calls and conversations can be overheard easily. In this case a small room would need to be set aside, where people could go when privacy was needed.
- Second, concentration can be affected. Not all people find it easy to work when they can hear other people's conversations, and it is easy to get chatting with someone working nearby.
- Third, although sharing printers and other hardware can be more cost effective, it can also result in time being wasted if more than one person needs to print at the same time.

Cellular offices are seen as the more traditional workplace organisation, with each worker having their own office. As the offices have to be individually built and furnished, as well as each office worker usually having their own equipment, this is often the more expensive option. Teamwork is harder as people work behind closed doors. Concentration on the task should be improved but it is harder to monitor individual workers.

Flexitime

An employee who works flexitime is allowed to vary their working schedule to fit in with their social or family requirements. Instead of working a 'normal' office day of 9 a.m. to 5 p.m., the employee is allowed to choose their own hours each day, provided that they complete the required total hours demanded by their employer for the week or month. Some employers insist that the hours add up to the correct amount each week, but others are more flexible and look at the monthly total. Most employers insist that employees are present at work for a core time, for example, from 10 a.m. until 2 p.m.

The advantages to the employee are that commuting need not be done at the busiest and most expensive time. Also, it may be possible for a parent to take their child to or collect them from school. This may lead to more motivated staff who take less time off work, which is beneficial to the employer.

In some businesses flexitime can be difficult to implement because, for example, customers expect to be able to contact employees during the normal working day.

Technology in the workplace

Video conferencing and teleconferencing

Technology is rapidly changing the workplace and bringing with it increased efficiency. Teleconferencing, at its simplest, is an audio conference where one or both parties use a speaker phone so that more than one person can be involved at each end of the conversation. Video conferencing is a development where computers are used to provide a video link between groups of people. Cameras send sound and pictures from one location to another so that a live meeting can take place. Both teleconferencing and video conferencing reduce the need for travel. Meetings can take place around the world with very little advance planning. Because people do not have to travel there is a tremendous saving of time and money.

Video conferencing and teleconferencing now share similar technology, so there is very little difference between the two. Many teleconferencing packages allow video to be transferred between locations. With a video link, facial expressions can be seen and items can be shown, making this more beneficial than teleconferencing without video.

In order to hold a video conference, there needs to be a high-specification computer at each location, connected to a phone line with the appropriate software. Each location also needs a video camera, a microphone and loudspeaker. The cost of all of this equipment is one of the drawbacks. Another drawback is that documents cannot be shared easily and original documents, such as contracts, cannot be signed by both parties.

Teleworking

Teleworking means working from home, using a computer and email facilities to communicate with the organisation for which the employee works. It means that the worker does not have to live near the offices of the organisation and can choose somewhere nearer their family or friends. It also saves the cost of commuting to work on a daily basis.

For the employee it means that family commitments can be fitted round the work as the working day can be arranged to suit them. This reduces stress for the employee and may benefit the employer as it could encourage qualified staff to return to work more quickly after a break to have a family. It may also reduce the amount of time an employee takes off work for family health reasons.

The drawbacks for the employer are that teamwork will be difficult to organise. Also, they must be able to trust that their employees are working the hours for which they are being paid.

The employee may find it hard to share ideas and therefore be less effective. They may work long hours and find it hard to achieve a good work–life balance because the telephone, the computer and email are always there.

Ergonomics

Ergonomics is the science of designing the workplace so that it is both comfortable and safe for the employees. This will be discussed in more detail in Chapter 7, where you will learn more about health and safety in the workplace.

Let's go!

Activities

1 Will Lawder is setting up a new fitness club and needs to design his office. He will be spending quite a lot of time at his desk, talking on the telephone and using his computer.

Use an online office supplier and look for appropriate equipment for his office. Choose the following and give reasons for your choice.

Piece of equipment	Reason for choice	Cost
Desk		
Chair		
Computer		
Printer		

2 The owner of a business, Mr Bhungard, has asked you to help him organise his workplace. The business sells software to businesses and employs 12 staff who work in four departments. Mr Bhungard also has an assistant, Mr Welsh. At the moment Mr Bhungard and Mr Welsh each have their own offices and there are four other offices, one for each of the following departments:

- Software Development
- Order Processing
- Deliveries
- After Sales Service.

You have been asked to redesign the business's office using an open plan layout. Use appropriate software to draw a plan of the new office. You will then have to present your plan to your class and justify the choices you have made.

Summary

- The workspace can be organised into open plan or cellular offices. The trend is towards open plan offices as these can make teamwork a lot easier and also motivate the workers more. However, they do have some drawbacks, for example, the lack of privacy when the work is confidential.
- Flexitime is also increasing in popularity. Most staff have to work core hours, but outside of these can choose their working hours, provided that they work the set number of hours each week or month.
- Video conferencing is a technological development that enables meetings to be held without expensive travel arrangements being made. Meetings can be held between people in different locations, provided that they have access to the appropriate technology.
- Teleworking allows people to work from home, fitting their work into their home lives and allowing greater flexibility. Workers are able to plan their own schedule and use computers and email to keep in touch with their employer.

Key words

Open plan office – a large room where several staff work at individual desks. The area may be subdivided with movable screens.

Cellular office – here each individual has their own private room in which to work.

Teleconferencing – the use of telephone technology to conduct a meeting between groups of people in different locations. This can be a sound link or a video link.

Video conferencing – the use of computer technology to create a video link between groups of people in different locations.

Teleworking – the use of computer and email facilities to enable workers to work from home.

Points for discussion

1. How is technology changing the way people work?
2. Is having open plan offices always the best solution? For what sort of businesses might it be less successful?

Give me five

Give five benefits of teleworking. State whether the benefit is to the employee or the employer.

Exam style questions

Phil Smith runs a recruitment business which finds people to work in offices in London. His staff work with companies that are looking for staff by advertising jobs for them. They also interview people who are looking for jobs and advise them if they have any suitable vacancies. He has 15 employees who work for him, six of whom are responsible for interviewing applicants for jobs. Each of these six employees has their own office. The remaining nine employees work in an open plan office, dealing with employers, finance and administration.

1 Explain what is meant by the term 'open plan office'. (2 marks)

2 Describe how having an open plan office may benefit Phil Smith's business. (6 marks)

3 Explain why you think Phil Smith has given the six employees who interview job applicants their own offices. (6 marks)

Chapter 6

The sustainable office

In this chapter you will learn:

- the importance of using resources economically
- the increasing importance of using resources in an environmentally friendly manner.

Getting started

These days, most families recycle some of the items that were previously thrown away and put into landfill sites. How many of the following have you or your family done?

- Taken clothes that you do not wear to a charity shop.
- Put paper out to be collected separately.
- Put glass out to be recycled.
- Bought some recycled paper products.

Local councils have been set targets for reducing domestic refuse and this has encouraged them to make it easier for families to recycle some of their rubbish.

Businesses, too, are looking for ways to demonstrate that they are environmentally aware.

What you need to know

What is an environmentally friendly office?

Environmentally friendly offices are not just about saving energy and recycling materials that are collected by the local authority. There are many other things that businesses can do, such as designing energy-efficient buildings, reducing pollution and reducing travel and transport distances.

An environmentally friendly office will be designed to have minimum impact on its environment. It may be constructed from materials that are sustainable, for example, if it is made out of timber then more trees are planted than were used in its construction. The offices themselves may be built on a site that had commercial buildings on it before – this is known as using a 'brown field site'. Insulation will be of at least the minimum standard so that the offices need little energy to heat them, and efficient boilers will be installed. When the offices are decorated, eco-friendly paint may be used to minimise the fumes that are given off. The business itself will seek to limit the pollution it causes in all it does.

Once up and running, there are many actions an office manager can take to reduce the impact the office has on the environment. For example, when purchasing ICT equipment, LCD monitors can be chosen as they use much less electricity and fewer materials in their manufacture than standard monitors. Devices can be purchased that switch off, after a period of time, any computers and other equipment that are left on standby. Energy-efficient lighting is another means of reducing the business's impact on the environment.

The paperless office has long been an aim for businesses. Paper is usually made from wood pulp and so limiting its use prevents forests being felled. Many companies include a request on their emails not to print them out unless really necessary. Many memos and business letters that would have been printed on paper and sent through the post are now created electronically and sent via email. Catalogues that would have been sent out to many people are often available on websites, which dramatically reduces the amount of expensive colour printing and waste. On many websites, businesses have a bank of frequently asked questions (FAQs), which reduces the need for people to write and ask the company for information. Where paper is used, many people are now ensuring that it is made largely or wholly from recycled paper.

Sourcing goods locally where possible is another way of reducing the impact the business has on the environment. Reducing the use of transport for staff or materials goes a long way to reducing the amount of carbon emissions released into the environment. This can be achieved by encouraging staff to share vehicles or cycle to the office. Food for canteens can be sourced locally and other products can be sourced from the UK rather than overseas.

Why businesses are interested in being environmentally friendly

Some business owners and employees have a genuine concern for the environment that is greater than their wish to make profits. They may feel that being environmentally friendly is all part of taking a long-term view of their business, rather than looking for a higher profit in the short term. These considerations form part of the ethics of the company that underpin its decision making. An ethical company can be said to be one where decisions are made on moral grounds to benefit society as a whole.

Another reason why some businesses are keen to adopt environmentally friendly solutions is that this can help them to reduce their spending on resources. We have seen that a paperless office, as well as reducing the amount of trees felled for paper, will also reduce the amount of money spent on printing. Equipment that uses less energy is cheaper to run and can save the business a great deal of money over its lifetime. Low-energy light bulbs use much less energy than standard light bulbs and need replacing much less frequently. In many instances, being green makes sound economic sense.

Being green makes great sense from a public relations point of view too. There are many logos that are recognised by the public and act as endorsements, thereby increasing sales. Marks and Spencer is an example of a business that proudly declares its 'Plan A' to help combat climate change. Their initiatives have included building eco factories which have reduced their carbon emissions by nearly 80 per cent, and using paper that comes from Forest Stewardship Council (FSC) mixed sources paper for its magazine. FSC mixed sources paper comes from well-managed forests and other controlled sources. By advertising these initiatives Marks and Spencer hope that they will gain a competitive advantage over businesses that do not show their commitment to the environment.

What are the disadvantages of making environmentally friendly decisions?

Environmental decisions may not be the cheapest ones, at least in the short term. If the costs of the business increase and the revenue does not do the same, then profits will fall. In difficult economic conditions businesses may just not be able to afford the greenest option. The owners of the business may also be only concerned about the return on their investment. A brown field site may well be more expensive to build on than a new site and for some businesses this will rule out the option.

If a business takes the bold step of using only its website for catalogues, some customers may suffer. Not everyone has access to the internet and it may have a bad effect on the reputation of the business if some of its customers' needs are ignored.

Let's go!

Activities

1 Produce a questionnaire for a local business to see to what extent they have taken up green initiatives and whether any factors are preventing this. Ask another student to comment on your questionnaire and amend as necessary. Present the results of your questionnaire using presentation software.

2 Imagine you are setting up a sustainable office for yourself and three others. Make a list of the equipment you would buy and explain how environmental issues have affected your choice.

Summary

- Decisions to act in an environmentally friendly way can be made on moral grounds, to save money or as a public relations exercise.
- There are many actions that a business can take to improve its environmental impact. These can start with the building and equipping of its offices, and then making changes to its working practices.
- Some owners are reluctant to take actions that will reduce short-term profits. Others may be concerned about losing customers if they change the way they conduct their business.

Key words

Recycling – the sorting of items into groups according to the material they are made of so that they can be reused. This reduces the amount of raw materials used and pollution caused.

Sustainability – a measure of whether something can continue into the long-term future.

Ethics – moral principles that determine decisions that are made.

Points for discussion

To what extent do you agree or disagree with these statements?

1 'Businesses should be made to act in a sustainable way.'

2 'Recycling is not worth the effort it takes.'

Give me five

Give five materials that can be recycled.

Exam style questions

Bridgewater Estates is an estate agency that sells property in the South East of the UK. They have six offices in large towns and are thinking of expanding into the South West. The company deals mainly with people selling or looking to buy houses and flats. They are keen to recycle wherever possible and use only timber from sustainable sources for their house 'for sale' boards.

1 Explain what is meant by the term 'sustainable'. (2 marks)

2 Suggest two materials that Bridgewater Estates could recycle. (2 marks)

3 Explain why Bridgewater Estates may wish to advertise the fact that they only use sustainably produced timber for their 'for sale' boards. (6 marks)

4 Describe one way that Bridgewater Estates could reduce the amount of paper they consume. (3 marks)

5 Explain, using two examples, how Bridgewater Estates could choose environmentally friendly equipment for their office. (6 marks)

Chapter 7

Health and safety at work

In this chapter you will learn:

- the importance of health and safety in the workplace
- the responsibilities of both employers and employees to act in a safe manner
- the way in which ICT users are affected by health and safety regulations
- how ergonomics affects decisions about the workplace.

Getting started

At its simplest, health and safety in the office starts with cleanliness. According to a report early in 2008 by the BBC, computer keyboards are the most likely source of infection. Research has suggested that on occasions there are more harmful bacteria on a computer keyboard than on a toilet seat. Common colds and even gastroenteritis can easily be picked up from a keyboard.

According to the Chartered Institute of Personnel and Development (CIPD) Annual Absence Survey carried out in 2008, workplace absence costs the average employer £666 per person each year. The major causes of employee absence were colds, stress, upset stomachs, anxiety and family commitments.

There are hazards wherever people work and offices are no exception. Employees need to do their best to keep their workplace safe. Tidiness is also important, as papers and equipment left around can be a hazard. Wires trailing over the floor and overloaded sockets are a danger to everybody. Employees must take care to avoid the risks of fire, know what to do in the event of a fire and keep fire doors closed, but not locked. If employees are required to lift goods or equipment they should be trained to lift properly. Training to lift is not just required in manual jobs – reams of paper are heavy and need to be handled with care.

Using computers can lead to a range of health problems and employers must be aware of the preventative measures they need to take to ensure the health and welfare of their employees.

What you need to know

The Health and Safety at Work Act

The Health and Safety at Work Act (1974) shares the responsibility for a safe workplace between the employees and the employers. The employee has a responsibility to report any concerns and to act in a safe manner at all times. The employer has a responsibility to make sure that the workplace is well maintained and that all equipment is kept in a safe condition. The employer also has a responsibility to provide adequate training for all their employees so that they know what they need to do to keep safe.

The Health and Safety Regulations (1992) cover working with visual display units (VDUs), in other words computers. In order to comply with the law, employers must provide the following for employees who work with computers:

- tiltable screens
- anti-glare screen filters
- adjustable chairs and foot supports
- sufficient lighting
- enough space to work comfortably
- training on how to use equipment correctly.

Employers must pay for regular eye tests for employees who need prescription glasses in order to use the computer. They must also make sure that employees have enough breaks away from their computer.

All of these actions are designed to prevent the possible health problems, such as stress, eye strain and injury to the back, neck or wrists, which employees who work with computers may be susceptible to.

Stress

There are many reasons why people who work with computers suffer from stress. Some employees worry that their job will be taken over by computers and that they will find it hard to get a new job. Others worry that they have not got the skills to use new software and that their old skills are not valued.

Using a computer can in itself be stressful, for example, email inboxes fill up very quickly. Because email and mobile phones make it easy for employees to remain in contact with their workplace, they can find it hard to separate work from home life.

Employees' output can be monitored using computers. The amount of time spent on various activities can be measured to see how they are performing, which places employees under a lot of stress.

Computer systems are becoming increasingly large and more complex. Files can be lost or corrupted due to human error or viruses.

Eye strain

Eye strain can cause headaches and blurred vision. It can also cause feelings of sickness, tiredness and itching eyes. Many computer users suffer from some of these symptoms at some time, so it is important that sensible precautions are taken to minimise the risks. The most obvious precaution is to take regular breaks of at least five minutes every hour. Other simple measures should be taken, such as making sure that the screen is cleaned regularly and adjusting the brightness and contrast of the monitor. Employees should also check that the monitor does not flicker and report any equipment that is not working correctly. Paying attention to the lighting, such as moving out of direct sunlight and providing a screen filter, can also reduce the risk to the employee.

Back or neck injuries

Sitting at a computer all day without taking sensible precautions can cause injury to an employee's back or neck. The key to preventing these problems is good posture, that is, sitting properly at the desk and not in an awkward or slouching position, and taking regular breaks. Employers should provide a fully adjustable chair with footrests so that both feet can be flat on a hard surface.

In order to prevent neck injuries, the employee should be able to tilt the screen so that their back and neck are not at an awkward angle.

Repetitive strain injury (RSI)

Repetitive strain injury can be caused by using a keyboard for long periods of time without a break. It can also be caused by poor posture at a computer, so the employee's arms are in an uncomfortable position. Some keyboards are badly designed and require too much pressure to input data. There is a range of symptoms that employees may suffer from, including wrist pain, swelling, stiffness, numbness, a burning sensation or continuous ache.

To prevent repetitive strain injury employees should be trained in the importance of adjusting their chair and using wrist rests. They should also be encouraged to take a break from using the computer every hour.

Ergonomics

Ergonomics is the design of safe and comfortable working environments. If thought is given to the design of workplaces, many health and safety problems can be avoided. In an office environment, care needs to be taken regarding the height of desks and how easy it is to reach equipment that is used often, such as telephones.

Let's go!

Activities

1 Visit the website www.rsi.org.uk and use the information in the links to create a leaflet for employees, giving them information about the dangers of RSI and steps they can take to avoid suffering from it, if they are computer users.

2 Use the internet to research health and safety for ICT users. Create a presentation on health and safety in a business, for new modern apprentices who will be using computers.

3 a) Create a booklet on health and safety in ICT rooms, to be given to new Year 7 students as part of their induction.

b) Create a second version of the booklet for their parents or carers.

c) In a word-processed note, explain how you have made your booklets suitable for their audience.

4 Create an A4 poster for display in an office, to advise employees what actions they should take to avoid getting eye strain. Add a suitable image and use bullet points to make the advice clearer. Use an appropriate font (not WordArt) and different font sizes. The title should be emphasised in three ways. Put a border around your poster and print a copy with your name in the header.

5 Copy the table below into a word-processed document. Complete the table by giving a reason why a business should provide each of the following:

	Reason for providing
Adjustable chairs	
Eye tests	
A short break every hour	
Tiltable screens	
Foot rests	
Suitable lighting or blinds	
Anti-glare filters for the screen	
Foot rests	

Summary

- Ensuring that the workplace is well designed is the responsibility of the employer, but reporting any problems that arise is the responsibility of the employee. The employer also has a responsibility to give proper training to all their employees. Eye strain, back or neck injuries and repetitive strain injury are common complaints found in computer users, but stress is also an important cause of staff absence.
- It can be seen that a poorly designed workplace can lead to a range of health problems in employees. The choice of suitable equipment, such as adjustable chairs, is a first step that needs to be taken to ensure that the workplace is safe.
- As well as it being a legal requirement that the workplace is safe, it also makes sound business sense. Employees who are off sick cost the employer money in terms of lack of productivity – if an employee is not there they are not doing their job. Either somebody else has to be paid to do their job or the work just does not get done. Also, good employees are unlikely to remain with an employer who they feel does not look after their health. If they leave, the employer has the cost of recruiting and training new employees.

Give me five

Give five ways in which an employer could try and prevent his employees suffering from eye strain.

Key words

Ergonomics – the science concerned with designing comfortable and safe machines and furniture to avoid injury to the user.

Repetitive strain injury or RSI – this is damage to parts of the body, in the case of computer users often the hands or arms, caused by repeating the same movements many times.

VDU – the initials stand for ‘visual display unit’, but the term is used now for any display screen which is usually part of a computer and is used to show text, numbers or graphics.

Exam style questions

Wigland Bank is a national bank with branches throughout the United Kingdom. Most branches have staff who are employed to key information into the computers and who sit mainly at their desks during the working day. The Welchurch branch of the Wigland Bank employs six clerks to key in information.

1 Which of the following does the Wigland Bank *not* have to provide for its clerks?

a) foot rests

b) enough room to work

c) a laptop

d) anti-glare filters (1 mark)

2 Describe three ways in which the bank can try and prevent its employees from suffering back injuries. (6 marks)

3 Explain what is meant by the term 'ergonomics'. (2 marks)

4 Explain why businesses such as the Wigland Bank would want to improve their health and safety record. (9 marks)

Extension activity

On the internet, look up www.hse.gov.uk/pubns/indg36.pdf. This is the guidance the Health and Safety Executive (HSE) gives on working with VDUs. The HSE gives clear guidelines as to what employers need to do to meet the requirements of the Health and Safety (Display Screen Equipment) Regulations 1992. It also gives many practical tips on working with VDUs. The leaflet attempts to answer questions that are asked about health issues and gives a summary of the law concerning working with VDUs. It also explains how employers and VDU users can obtain further advice should they need it.

Read through the leaflet and discuss in groups the following points:

a) To what extent is the leaflet trying to allay people's fears about working with VDUs?

b) Is the guidance for employers of people who use ICT any different from that for any office worker?

c) Are the practical tips for employees who work with VDUs any different from that for any office worker?

d) Is there too much emphasis on health and safety? What would you say to an employer who said he could not afford to implement the advice given?

Chapter 8

ICT data systems in business

In this chapter you will learn:

- that there are a wide range of primary and secondary sources of data
- that information collected needs to be accurate and relevant to be of any use to a business
- how data can be best inputted and stored on a computer
- about the most commonly used output devices.

Getting started

Blackwood Garage sells second-hand cars from its site on a retail park in Whitchurch. It employs 12 staff and has been trading since 1994. Dave Wilson works at Blackwood Garage as one of their six salespeople. He is responsible for approaching potential customers to see what sort of car they are looking for and trying to sell them one of the many that he has available. A clerk inputs, onto a database, details of all the cars that are for sale when they arrive at the garage, with a picture and their selling price. When a customer arrives, Dave takes them to the computer and searches the database for suitable cars. Before he can do this he has to ask the customer lots of questions to see what sort of car they are looking for. The output from the database will be a list of suitable cars for the customer. If Dave is successful in finding a vehicle for the customer, Dave then has to input details about the sale onto the computer when the purchase is made. The computer also stores details about who has sold the car, as the salespeople are paid commission on every car they sell.

What you need to know

Primary and secondary sources of data

Primary data is data that has been collected for a specific purpose, by asking people directly for the information that is needed. The information can be collected on a questionnaire or in an interview. For example, a dairy might employ a market research company to stand in a high street and interview people about their preferences for different types of cheese or butter. The interviewer, who could be from the dairy or a market research company, records the data (probably on a questionnaire) and sends it to the person who requested the data.

When designing a questionnaire a great deal of thought has to go into the phrasing of the questions so that the results can be analysed. Usually closed questions (those where a choice of answers is given, from which one has to be chosen) make it easier to analyse data. If, for example, you were trying to find out which sandwiches were the more popular in a school, and you did not give a choice of answers for people to choose from, you could get a very long list with many similar sandwiches but a not very conclusive result.

If Question 1a was asked (see below) there could be almost as many answers as there were people asked, which would mean that either the researcher had to link some answers together or the data would not be helpful. Question 1b shows closed questions, where all the possible options are listed. There can be no other responses to the question. This would be easier to analyse than Question 1a, regardless of the number of people questioned. Question 1b would also make it easier to put the results in a graph so that they could be seen very easily.

Secondary data is data that has been collected previously and is already published. Often this sort of data is available using the internet, by finding the results of previous research. Secondary data can also be found in books, magazines and newspapers.

It is possible to buy published market research reports. In our example the business could buy a market research report into trends in popularity of different sandwich fillings, but the results may not be helpful to the person needing the information. In the example we have been looking at the researcher was trying to find out about the preferences in school, but these may not be the same as preferences in the general population. Perhaps people do not eat eggs at school because they are concerned about chicken welfare, but would do so if they were at home and knew that they were made using free range eggs.

Another issue that a business must take into consideration when choosing to use secondary data is how old the research is. Tastes change, for example you probably eat different food from your grandparents. For some products technology moves on quickly, for example research on how people listen to music would need to take into account MP4 players and the iPhone. If you use research that was done before these were launched then the popularity of MP3 players could be overstated.

It can also be important that the research is conducted in the appropriate geographical location,

Question 1a

Which is your favourite sandwich?

egg

egg mayo

cheese

cheddar cheese and pickle

cheese and sweet pickle

egg and cress

tuna

egg and watercress

cheddar cheese

Question 1b

Which is your favourite sandwich?

Egg ☐

Cheese ☐

Ham ☐

Tuna ☐

Chicken ☐

Other ☐

None ☐

which may be the right country or even the region or town. People in the North East of England may have different tastes in sandwiches from those in South Wales, and for some bizarre reason the most popular sandwich in Redruth might be peanut butter with strawberry jam!

Although using secondary data can be a lot cheaper than commissioning primary research, a lot of consideration has to be given as to whether it will provide accurate enough results for the business to make decisions on. A decision taken using the wrong data could lead to a loss of business and less profit or even to a business going bankrupt.

Input devices

Once it is collected, data needs to be put into a computer to be stored and analysed. To do this, an input device of some sort is needed. The most common forms of input device are keyboards, mice, scanners, voice recognition devices and digital cameras. The type of device used will depend on the nature of the information that needs inputting, for example, a picture may be scanned onto a computer if it already exists on paper, or it may be taken with a digital camera and connected directly to a computer. Most forms of input device are connected to the computer by a USB cable. When purchasing input devices, the main considerations are cost and usage. It is also important to take into account health and safety considerations. Keyboards that are used to input a lot of text should be designed to reduce the incidence of repetitive strain injury. There are also specialist keyboards, for example ones with large coloured keys for people with visual impairments.

When purchasing digital cameras it is important that they are fit for the purpose they are bought for. Some businesses will need cameras that are capable of high-quality pictures with a high resolution (which means the pictures are made up of a large number of dots), and they must be prepared to pay for the higher quality. Digital cameras enable the user to download photographs directly to a computer and send them over the internet immediately. The images can also be edited, for example they can be cropped or the size can be altered.

Storage devices

Data, once input into a system, needs to be stored on the computer. To do this a storage device of some sort is needed. The most common forms of storage device are hard disks or drives, CDs, DVDs and USB memory sticks.

Computers are being built with increasingly large hard disk drives. The size of the hard disk on many home computers today is greater than many commercial computers had in the past. It is also possible to buy removable hard drives to increase the size of the memory on a computer or to back up data if necessary.

CDs are used to hold a variety of reference material such as text, pictures and archives of photographs. DVDs, on the other hand, are more commonly used to store multimedia presentations and video footage.

USB memory sticks are probably the most portable medium available and are used by many people to transfer data from home to work, school or college. As with much computer equipment, the cost of these has come down considerably and the size of the devices available has increased. Memory sticks are, however, quite vulnerable to damage and need to be backed up regularly.

Output devices

Data that is stored will at some point need to be taken off the computer in order to use it. To do this an output device of some sort is needed. The most common forms of output device are monitors, printers and projectors. Monitors (computer screens) are available in a range of sizes, and the choice of monitor will depend on the type of data being viewed. It is essential that health and safety issues are taken into consideration, for example they should have a low flicker rate and should be fully adjustable. TFT screens (a type of liquid crystal display or LCD) have lower environmental impact than traditional monitors and they also take up less room.

Printers also need to be chosen with care because the price of the machine itself and the printing cost per sheet can vary widely. In some organisations the speed of printing, the size of paper that can be used and the ability to print in duplex (double-sided) are also important considerations. Most printers now print in colour and black and white.

Many organisations now use data projectors to deliver presentations to customers or for training within the organisation. The projectors can be static (usually fixed to the ceiling) or movable, depending on the needs of the organisation.

Let's go!

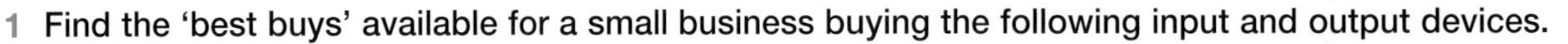

Activities

1 Find the 'best buys' available for a small business buying the following input and output devices.

Piece of equipment	Item chosen	Reason for choice	Cost
Keyboard			
Monitor			
Digital camera			
Printer			

Add three other items to the list and complete the table.

2 Imagine that you are going to open a coffee bar in your home town.

a) Create a questionnaire to gather information about what you should put on the menu. Ask two people to complete your questionnaire so that you can check that it works.

b) When you are satisfied that your questionnaire will give you useful information, ask 20 people to complete it and analyse the results. Use charts where appropriate.

c) Search on the internet to see if there is any secondary data which would help you make a decision about the menu.

d) Explain your findings.

3 The owner of a small clothes shop has asked you to research what computer system she should have. Make some suggestions about what she could use the computer for in her business and suggest suitable components the system should include.

Summary

- There is a wide range of data available to businesses in the form of secondary data or available for the asking using field research.
- The most important criteria of any information that a business collects are that it is up to date and relevant to that business or organisation.
- Once collected, the information needs to be carefully and appropriately input onto the computer and then stored until it is needed.
- At some point the data will need to be used, and to do this it will be taken off the computer via an output device such as a printer.
- When purchasing hardware, consideration needs to be given to what it will be used for, the price, value for money and efficiency.

Key words

Primary research – obtaining first-hand data that is needed by the business.

Secondary research – information obtained from sources that already exist, which has been collected for a different purpose.

Input device – a means of putting data into a computer.

Output device – a means of getting data out of a computer.

Storage device – a means of keeping data until it is needed.

Points for discussion

How far do you agree or disagree with the following statements?

1 'Modern businesses do not need a printer – all their communication can be done electronically.'

2 'Digital cameras have been superseded by the latest generation of mobile phones.'

3 'Market research is best left to the professionals.'

Give me five

Give five input devices.

Exam style questions

Sally Begum is thinking of setting up a small business, in the south of England, making house signs. She intends to employ three other people, two to make the signs and one person to help her sell them. She intends to do all the advertising and management herself. To make the signs Sally will use a computer-controlled engraving machine. Sally also wants to use a computer for customer records, wages, sales income and costs. At the end of the week Sally wants to work out how much profit she has made.

1 Which one of the following is an input device?

   USB memory stick   hard drive   printer   keyboard   (1 mark)

2 List three input devices that Sally would find useful for her computer and give an example of what she might use them for. (9 marks)

3 Sally has to choose between the following three printers. Describe the advantages and disadvantages of each printer and explain which you think would be best for her business.

   Printer 1 is a compact photo printer which can produce high quality photos at home for the digital camera enthusiast. The maximum print size is 10×15 cm. Cost £98.

   Printer 2 is a business inkjet printer which can print high-quality black-and-white documents at up to 37 A4 pages per minute. It has a capacity of 120 sheets and low power consumption. Cost £50.

   Printer 3 is a professional multi-function printer which can print in full colour at sizes up to A3. It works as a scanner and a fax machine, and can be connected to a network so that users can share it. Cost £250. (12 marks)

4 Describe one piece of primary research that Sally should carry out and one piece of secondary research that she should use before she sets up in business. (6 marks)

Chapter 9

Security of data

In this chapter you will learn:

- the importance of the security of data
- the main methods of protecting data from unauthorised access
- what the Data Protection Act covers
- the eight principles of the Data Protection Act.

Getting started

Housemaker's Store sells a range of household goods such as paint, wallpaper, garden furniture, basic kitchen equipment and household furnishings. It employs 6 full-time staff and 12 part-time staff and has been trading since 1969. Eddy Smith works at Housemaker's and is responsible for the management of staff, maintaining staff records on the computer and doing the payroll. In his job he is responsible for a great deal of personal and sensitive data. This includes employees' names, addresses and banking details, which he needs in order to be able to pay their wages. It also includes sensitive personal information such as copies of medical notes which staff give him when they are off sick, trade union membership information, and racial or ethnic origin information which he collects to make sure that he gives equal opportunities to all. He even has information about the religious affiliations of his staff in case there is an accident at work. With all this information in his hands it is vital that Eddy keeps the information secure and acts within the law.

What you need to know

The Data Protection Act

The Data Protection Act was set up in 1998 to provide rules that people or organisations which store data about living people must follow. The main purpose of the Act is to protect the privacy of the individual, so that private information cannot be given or sold to businesses without the consent of that individual. The Act also gives the individual the right, in almost all cases, to look at the data and check that it is correct. If it is incorrect they can insist that changes are made, and if the company was negligent in the way it collected the information and it caused harm, the individual can claim damages. All organisations that hold data about people must register their use and will be fined if they do not do so.

The Act applies to all data. Most information is stored on computer these days, but the Act also applies to any data stored on paper. An Information Commissioner is responsible for enforcing the rules, and any organisation that intends to store data must apply to him for permission. The person who stores the information is known as a Data Controller and he must act in accordance with the 'eight principles of data protection'. The Data Subject is the person about whom the data is being collected.

The eight principles of the Data Protection Act are:

1. Data must be obtained and kept within the law. The Data Controller must register with the Data Commissioner and must ask the Data Subject for permission for data to be used.

2. The Data Controller must only use the data for the purpose he asked permission for.

3. The data must be relevant and not excessive; the Data Controller must not collect more information than is necessary for his purposes.

4. The data must be accurate and kept up to date.

5. The data should not be kept for longer than necessary.

6. The Data Subject must be allowed to look at the data and it must be kept in accordance with his rights.

7. The data must be kept securely so that only people who are allowed to access it are able to do so.

8. Data can only be used within the European Union unless another country has similar data protection laws to the EU's.

The Information Commissioner's Office is the UK's independent authority which has been set up to promote access to official information and to protect personal information. The website (www.ico.gov.uk) gives detailed advice to both Data Subjects and Controllers.

Loyalty cards

Supermarkets and other retailers are potentially able to store a lot of information about their customers from information gained at the tills. If they have the names and addresses of people and details of what they purchase, they can see patterns building up over time and target information and advertisements very accurately. This can save them a lot of money by not sending coloured brochures to people who do not need particular products. If, for example, a supermarket can see that a person has bought nappies for six months, they can assume that there is a baby in the household and then target information about baby food to the shopper. This can be done legally if the person has consented to the data being collected, and one of the easiest ways for a retailer to get this consent is to get their customers to join a loyalty scheme.

The Tesco Clubcard Charter states that they use their Clubcard members' details to send offers and information that they think will interest them. They explain that they specifically target vouchers so that they are appropriate to the member, for instance, they do not send vouchers for meat to people who state that they are vegetarian. They also explain that they will not send any offers or information if the member has said they would rather not receive them, but point out that this means they may be missing out on some advantages of being a Clubcard member. In addition, they say that they will only contact people for research if they have agreed to it. They promise to stop mailing if they are requested to do so and they say that they comply fully with the Data Protection Act.

Storing data securely

Using passwords

In the workplace, passwords can be used to access computers to authenticate the user and allow them onto the system. Only if a person types in the correct password will they be allowed access. There are usually guidelines as to what constitutes a secure password; in general it should contain at least eight characters and should include numbers, lower and uppercase letters and punctuation. Using this wide range of characters lowers the risk of the password being copied by someone who is watching while it is being entered. The more secure the data needs to be kept, the more care should be taken with the choice of the password. An example of a secure password is 4iSh-f0r/lit8.

Passwords can be also be used to access folders and files once the user is in the system. This should make the files more secure. Having to enter three different passwords to reach a confidential database will considerably slow someone down and give time for someone to be seen and questioned. Passwords can be set to both open and edit a document, so it is possible to allow appropriate people access to a file to read it but not to change it. This means that data will not be altered without permission.

A network manager can give different permissions to different users, so he or she can set up the network software so that each user can only access documents that they need to see. These permissions are known as 'access privileges'.

Remember that you should never write down a username or password or allow anyone else to use your login.

Firewalls

A firewall is a software function that allows or denies access to people who are attempting to access a system, based on a set of rules. The purpose of the firewall is to prevent or delay access to the internal network of the computer (in the same way that a fire door in a building prevents fire spreading). The software checks data and IP (internet provider) addresses and can prevent access by viruses, malware (software designed to infiltrate or damage a computer system) and the wrong sort of downloads and uploads.

Screen savers

A screen saver is a type of computer program that was originally designed to prevent damage to computer monitors by blanking the screen or filling it with moving images to prevent phosphor burn-in (where a faint image is left permanently on the screen). On their own screen savers do not make data secure, but they can do if they require a password to regain access to the computer. Screen savers may also stop someone from accidentally seeing a file that is open on a computer. These days screen savers are used more for entertainment than for security purposes.

Encryption

Encryption means putting data into a secret code. When sensitive personal data is stored in a database it can be encrypted to protect it against theft. To encrypt data you need to buy specialist software that uses an algorithm, which is a set of rules to put it into code and a key that will decrypt it back to its original state. All characters, including spaces and punctuation marks, are encrypted so it is impossible to tell how many letters there are in a word. For example, Mrs Wort could be encrypted to 2/f3s 9w.

Virus protection

A computer virus is a type of software program that copies itself onto system files or data on a computer and damages them. As well as viruses, malware, spyware and adware need to be prevented from coming into the system. All computer systems should have a form of up-to-date antivirus protection to prevent corruption or loss of data. Antivirus protection is a software program that is used to identify viruses or other forms of harmful software and then remove them. You should also take care when opening email attachments, as these are one of the most common sources of viruses and malware.

Let's go!

Activities

1 List the organisations you think have data about you. Swap lists with another person in your group. Did you miss out any organisations?

2 Go to a local supermarket and pick up a brochure about their loyalty scheme. List the information you need to complete to join a supermarket loyalty scheme.

3 Below is a shopping list. Study the list of products and describe in as much detail as you can what you think you know about the person whose list it is.

4 Create a table with two columns. In the first column list the information you think your school or college has about you. In the second column suggest how your school or college might use the information. For example:

Information held	Possible use
Name of parents	To know who to address in letters and phone calls
Phone number of parent	

Summary

- Security of data needs to be a priority for all organisations. Both personal and sensitive information must only be accessible to those who have a right to see it.
- The Data Protection Act makes it illegal to store information without the permission of the Data Subject and it has to be available for them to check its accuracy. Data must only be used for the purpose that the organisation has stated and must not be passed to anyone without the consent of the Data Subject.
- There are a number of ways that data can be kept securely on a computer system. One of the most important ways to prevent access to systems, folders or files is through the use of secure logins and passwords.
- Firewalls, encryption and virus protection software are all ways of securing the data or system from external threats.

Key words

Data Controller – a person who collects or keeps information about people.

Data Subject – a person who has data stored about themselves by other people or organisations.

The Data Protection Act – a law designed to protect people who have personal data stored about them.

Encryption – coding sensitive data or files, using specially designed software, before they are sent over a network.

Firewalls – software designed to allow or deny access to people who are attempting to access a system, based on a set of rules.

Virus – software that has been created to damage a computer system.

Points for discussion

To what extent do you agree or disagree with these statements?

1 'Loyalty cards enable businesses to collect too much sensitive information about their shoppers.'

2 'Banks should be allowed to share information about their customers with other businesses to protect them from getting bad debts.'

3 'Doctors should be able to inform employers about the health of their employees to protect the public.'

Give me five

Give five ways that data can be protected.

Exam style questions

Whichford Garden Centre is a small garden centre on the outskirts of Birmingham. There are lots of other garden centres within ten miles of the business, so to try to encourage customers to return Whichford is thinking of starting a loyalty scheme. To join the scheme they are going to ask customers to fill in a form giving their name, age, marital status, address and size of garden. They are thinking of asking other questions such as size of family and ages of children, as well as general information about other interests. They are going to ask loyalty scheme members if they are happy to be contacted with special offers and other advertising material.

You have been asked to advise the owner of Whichford Garden Centre on the best way of setting up the loyalty scheme.

1 Explain, using an example, what is meant by the term 'personal data'. (4 marks)

2 Describe how Whichford Garden Centre can use passwords to make sure that only authorised staff can view the loyalty scheme members' information. (9 marks)

3 Explain why having a screen saver on a computer may not help make the data more secure. (4 marks)

4 Explain why Whichford Garden Centre should put antivirus protection on all its computers. (4 marks)

5 Explain what Whichford Garden Centre will need to do to comply with the Data Protection Act. (9 marks)

Extension activity

Many hair salons keep records of their clients on a database and use their computer system for booking appointments. Information that is often stored includes names, addresses, telephone numbers, dates of appointments, details of colours applied to hair and other 'treatments' given.

a) Explain in detail what a salon owner needs to do to comply with the Data Protection Act.

b) Create a strategy to ensure that all data at a salon is kept secure.

c) Explain how the salon could benefit by using mail merge facilities to contact their clients.

SECTION 2

HUMAN RESOURCES

Chapter 10

Recruiting staff: advertising and internal recruitment

In this chapter you will learn:

- about the methods used to advertise for staff
- the purpose of a job description and person specification
- the advantages and disadvantages of using internal and external recruitment.

Getting started

Many of you will have started to think about getting a part-time job or may already have one. How do you find out about jobs in your area? Some of you may hear from a friend that a job is going, others will look out for an advertisement.

How will an employer make a choice if more than one of you applies for the job? How can he or she be sure they have the best person for the job? These are all things you need to know about recruitment and selection.

What you need to know

The first decisions

When a business wants to employ a new member of staff, the first consideration is what exactly they want the person to do. The human resource manager or owner of the business will make a list of the key tasks that the person will need to carry out, and this forms part of a document called a 'job description'. They will also list the responsibilities the person will have and the location of the job.

Look at the job description on the next page – it contains all a candidate would need to know about the job before they decided to apply or not for it. A job description is usually sent out to candidates for a job along with an application form.

A job description for cabin crew

Air cabin crew are responsible for the safety of passengers and are specially trained to deal with emergencies.

Air cabin crew are also employed to ensure passengers are comfortable and that the flying experience is an enjoyable one.

Cabin crew attend to passengers throughout the flight and serve food and drinks.

Tasks typically include:

- Attending a pre-flight briefing, during which air cabin crew members are assigned their working positions for the upcoming flight.
- Carrying out pre-flight duties, including checking the safety equipment, ensuring the aircraft is clean and tidy, ensuring that all meals and stock are on board.
- Welcoming passengers on board and directing them to their seats.
- Informing the passengers of the aircraft safety procedures.
- Serving meals and refreshments to passengers.
- Selling duty-free goods.
- Giving first aid to passengers where necessary.
- Completing a routine flight report.

Another key document that has to be produced before the job is advertised is a 'person specification'. This describes the sort of person that would be ideal for the job. It includes details of the qualifications the successful candidate would be expected to have, as well as the experience needed and what personal qualities they should have.

You might find the following included on a person specification for a member of the air cabin crew in the job specification:

- Some knowledge of languages (modern European or modern non-European), or some nursing, paramedical or business experience. Candidates who have the ability to converse in a modern language are often highly desirable.
- Most airlines require four or five GCSEs (A–C) or equivalent, including English.
- A good standard of health and fitness is important, with some airlines requiring candidates to swim a minimum of 25 metres unaided.
- Airlines often set a minimum height of 5′2″ for safety reasons, and ask that height be in proportion to weight.
- Applicants must have clear speech, good hearing and eyesight, although glasses and contact lenses are allowed. A medical examination may also be required.
- A Criminal Records Bureau (CRB) check is necessary due to increased security measures at airports.
- All airlines demand that candidates have a valid passport permitting unrestricted travel worldwide.
- Candidates will also need to show evidence of good communication skills, the ability to be part of a team and confidence in dealing with a range of people. The ability to remain calm under pressure and in emergency situations is also essential.

Once these key documents (job description and person specification) have been produced, the owner or human resource manager will need to decide whether to advertise the post internally or externally.

Advertising jobs

Internal advertisements are placed inside the business, for example on internal notice boards or on the intranet. Internal advertisements can be cheap to produce as they can be as simple as a flyer on a notice board or a mention in a meeting – no expensive media advertising is needed. Another advantage of advertising a job internally is that the managers already know the applicants and are therefore less likely to choose the wrong person. Also, advertising internally can motivate employees as they can see promotion as a reward for loyal or good service. The major disadvantage is that the job advertisement will have a restricted audience and therefore the business may not get the very best employee for the job.

External advertising uses advertisements that are seen by people outside the business. Examples of external advertisements include advertising in brochures, job centres, newspapers, magazines and on websites. Some of the media used to advertise externally, such as magazines, may look glossy and can be very expensive. There can also be a long delay between writing the advertisement and its publication, which can delay the appointment of the new employee.

If the human resource manager decides to advertise externally, the next decision is what type of media to use. The main things to consider are where the sort of people that are required are likely to look for a job, and how much the business can afford to spend on advertising it. One of the cheapest methods of advertising jobs is in job centres, but these are not often visited by people who are already working. Newspapers are a much-used way of advertising for staff and so, increasingly, is the internet. All of these methods are relatively inexpensive for small to medium-sized businesses. Some technical jobs are advertised in specialist magazines or with specialist job agencies, which are often more expensive options.

When designing the advertisement, the human resource manager of a large business will have to decide whether applicants will complete an application form or to send in a curriculum vitae (CV). Using an application form makes it easier to compare applicants because they all use the same headings for their information. However, it can delay things a little as applicants have to complete it rather than just sending a CV they have already produced. Some small businesses may just require people to write a letter or phone up and bring copies of their certificates and references. Applicants will use the information that they are given by the employers in the person specification and job description to help them create their letter of application or complete parts of an application form.

Advertisements need to contain key information as shown in this example.

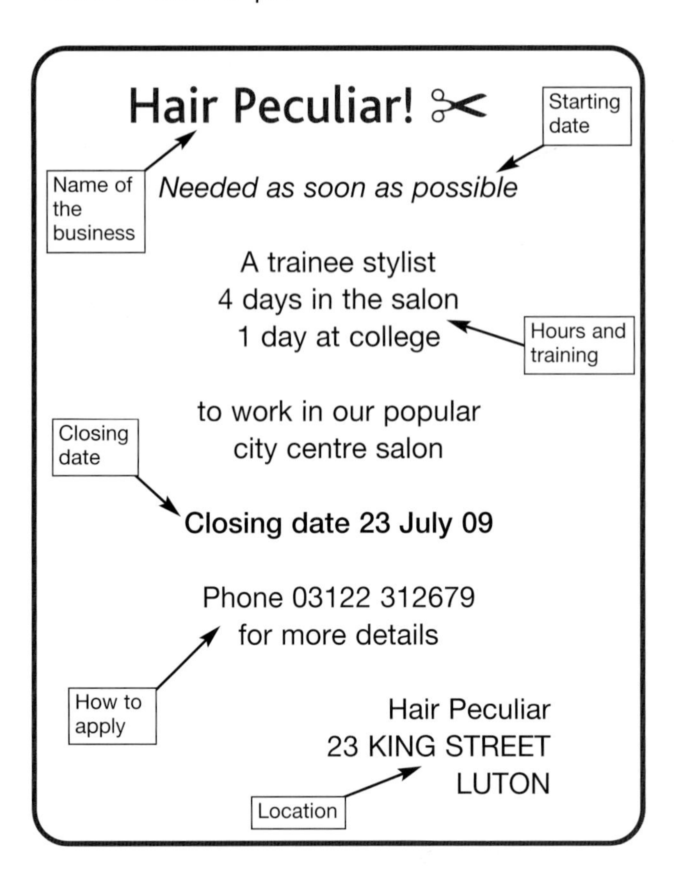

Some advertisements will specify salary or training opportunities and others may list non-financial perks such as the use of a company car or free haircuts!

Once applications have been received the decision maker needs to compare the information from the applicants against the person specification. Only those applicants that have the necessary knowledge, skills and experience listed on the person specification will be considered.

Let's go!

Activities

1 Look at two job advertisements from a local newspaper and make a list of the key information that is common to both of the advertisements.

2 Using a desktop publishing package, create an advertisement on behalf of Air Europe for a member of their cabin crew based at Manchester Airport. Request that applicants send their CV to you at Air Europe, Three Towers, Manchester M7 3UG by 23rd May. Full training will be given and the salary is £24,500 per year.

   Find out the cost of placing the advertisement in your local newspaper.

3 Look at the careers or jobs website at any business in which you have an interest, for example you could look at www.innocentdrinks.co.uk/careers/.

   a) What do you notice is the difference between jobs that are advertised there and the newspaper advertisements that you looked at earlier?

   b) Explain why you think your business has chosen to advertise on the internet rather than in a newspaper.

Summary

- Businesses can choose between advertising internally or externally.
- Internal advertisements can appear on notice boards or on a staff-only area within the website.
- External advertisements will attract many more applicants if they are placed in newspapers or magazines or on websites, but they can be expensive to produce.
- Businesses often produce a job description listing the key responsibilities and tasks involved in the job, and a person specification stating what knowledge, skills and experiences are needed in the job.

Key words

Recruitment – the whole process of obtaining a new employee for a business. It includes identifying the need for the employee through to the selection of the most suitable applicant.

Job description – a detailed statement of the tasks and responsibilities of a job.

Person specification – a statement listing the characteristics, qualifications and experience required of a person to do a job satisfactorily.

Human resource manager – a manager responsible for the people within a business, including their recruitment and training.

Points for discussion

1 To what extent do you agree that all jobs should only be advertised internally so that people already working for a business have the chance for promotion, rather than employing outsiders?

Give me five

Give five places a business could advertise the job of new finance manager.

Exam style questions

Helly Designs Ltd is a company that has been running for six years creating websites for small businesses. The managing director Chris Helly set up the business in London and it now has an office in Birmingham. Revenue has been increasing for the past three years and Chris has decided to recruit two more website designers for the Birmingham office. At the Birmingham site the business currently employs 12 website designers and a further 3 clerical staff.

1 Explain, using an example, what is meant by the term 'internal recruitment'. (3 marks)

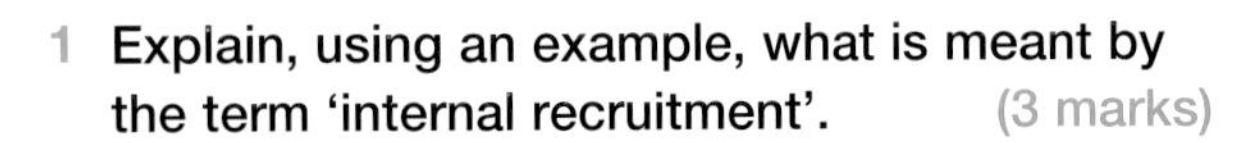

2 Chris wishes to place the advertisement in a monthly computer magazine. Explain the advantages and disadvantages of this action. (9 marks)

3 Suggest three items (skills or experience) that should appear on the person specification for a website designer. (6 marks)

4 Explain why Chris would send a job description to people who are interested in the post. (6 marks)

Chapter 11

Recruiting staff: selection and appointment

In this chapter you will learn:

- what happens once a job has been advertised
- the processes involved in the selection of staff
- about the different types of contracts of employment.

Getting started

Once an advertisement for a job has been placed, the process selecting staff begins. Imagine that your friend Sara has seen an advertisement for a part-time job working in the local library. She likes the idea of the pay and is interested in the job. What happens next? Most advertisements ask applicants to contact a named person for more details and to get an application form; some ask applicants to send a curriculum vitae (CV). Once the application form or CV has been sent, there is a wait before applicants hear whether they have been selected to have an interview or have been unsuccessful. What has been going on during this time? If you are successful and are going for an interview, what is it like? And then what happens?

What you need to know

Job applications

Before a business can advertise a job vacancy, someone has to make the decision about how applicants should apply for the job. The most common ways are to ask applicants to fill in an application form, send a CV with a covering letter, fill in an online application form or just write a letter.

Application forms

Many businesses and organisations have an application form either printed or supplied online, which they expect all applicants to complete. The information that is asked for usually includes contact details, education history from secondary school, employment history, skills, training received, personal interests and references. Alongside the application form the applicant often writes a supporting letter explaining why they would like the job and what skills they would bring to it. The advantages from the employer's point of view of asking people to complete an application form is that they can be compared easily if there are a lot of applicants. If they are handwritten it is also easy to see which applicants have taken a lot of care over them. The employer can also ensure that all applicants provide the same information and can easily see if a section has been left blank, for example if they have had no training.

Letters

A letter of application may be requested alongside either an application form or a CV and is an opportunity for the applicant to write in detail about their strengths. The letter can contain reasons why they think they would be a benefit to the business and why they particularly want that job. From an employer's point of view, the letter is very useful because it really differentiates between those who are prepared to put in a lot of effort to get a specific job and those who are doing multiple applications using a standard letter. No employer wants to think that he is just one of hundreds being approached. Literacy skills can also be judged through the letter, although it is of course possible that the applicant had the letter written for him. However, even that shows that the candidate is at least keen!

Primhill House
Cowmans Green
Newchurch
Shropshire
SY13 23H

24th January 2009

Dear Sirs,

I am interested in applying for the job of Legal Secretary in your firm of solicitors...

CVs

The curriculum vitae or CV is a brief story of the applicant's life. The CV given below shows the main headings that are often used. There is quite a variation in style but usually agreement that ideally it should fit on one page of A4.

Charlotte Goodchild
25 Dog Lane
Whitchurch
Shropshire
SY13 3AL

Mobile [illegible] cgd@good.wc.uk

Personal Statement

I have just completed my A levels in ICT, Business Studies and French and am awaiting my results. I am predicted grades B in ICT, C in Business and E in French. As well as being academically able in ICT I am also good at networking and programming using Visual Basic.

Education

Kindly School
GCSE 2006. 8 GCSE passes including grade A in English and Mathematics and a grade B in ICT.

Work Experience

Tourist Information Office, Shrewsbury, where I assisted customers from all over the world.

Interests

I have represented my school in running and in football.

I assisted last year with the Prom where I was responsible for organising the tickets and programmes.

I help with the local Scouts.

Referees

I am happy to supply these on request.

Short listing

Once the closing date has passed, one of the managers will look at the application forms, letters and/or CVs and compare them with the 'person specification'. The applicants that do not meet the minimum criteria, have submitted untidy applications or have not followed the instructions on how to apply will usually be rejected and the rest will be placed on a 'long list'. The long-listed applications will be looked at in more detail and the most suitable candidates, usually no more than five, will be placed on a 'short list' to come for interview. Those on the long list who did not make the interview will probably not receive a letter of rejection until someone has accepted the job, just in case there is a need to reconsider.

Interviewing

In large businesses or organisations, setting up an interview for those candidates on the short list is part of the job of the Human Resource Management (HRM) Department. The HRM Department will set up an interviewing panel, which usually consists of the human resources manager, a line manager and another person, although in small businesses it may be just the owner.

Having set up the panel the HRM Department will then need to organise the venue for the interviews and any testing that needs to be done. Interviews take place in a variety of locations depending on the seniority of the post and where applicants are coming from. Because applicants often receive travel expenses, some organisations that recruit all over the UK will choose a central venue. The venue may need to be prepared, for example if applicants have to show a presentation about an aspect of their experience or about a problem affecting the business.

At the interview the applicants will be put at their ease and then asked a series of pre-prepared questions. The responses may be taped or noted down. Also, the applicants will be assessed on their personal characteristics, such as their body language, care with appearance, tone of voice and ability to get on with people. The applicants will also have an opportunity to ask questions of their own, so that they can see if they would fit in with the company and enjoy working there.

At the interview, or shortly after, the applicants may be given a range of skills and personality tests which attempt to objectively judge their suitability. There are many examples of tests, some of which may be useful and others less so. Just because a test appears to be objective as opposed to subjective, unlike a conversation, does not mean that the test is necessarily accurate. Some applicants are given tests in numeracy, literacy and ICT irrespective of whether they have a GCSE in those subjects.

Although interviews are useful alongside application forms and CVs, it is quite difficult to assess people's performance in them. They can lead to the best person for the job not being appointed, particularly if the interviewer is not specifically trained in interviewing.

After the interview it is usual for references to be taken up. The applicant is usually asked to name two referees, which normally include the current employer or, in the case of a school leaver, the head teacher. If these are not named it is likely they will be contacted anyway as it is assumed that the applicant has not given them for a good reason! The referees will be asked about the applicant's performance, time keeping and honesty as well as specific questions relevant to the job they have applied for.

Quite rarely, the business will not appoint anyone they have short listed and the job will be re-advertised at a later date.

Appointing the successful applicant

Once the most promising candidate has been offered the job, there is a short period of time before the other interviewed candidates are told they have not been successful. This is in case the successful applicant decides to decline the job and the business needs to offer the job to another person who was on the short list. Once the successful applicant has verbally accepted the job the other applicants will be told that they have not been successful on this occasion. Some may be told that their application would be welcome in the future if the business thinks that they have potential to succeed with them.

After the interview the successful applicant will be sent a formal job offer, often with a contract of employment. If the contract is not sent with the letter it must be given to the employee within 13 weeks of starting the job. The contract of employment will contain information about the starting date, pay and hours of work as well as holiday and pension entitlement, sickness benefits, place of work, period of notice required to end employment, disciplinary procedure and trade union agreements.

Let's go!

Activities

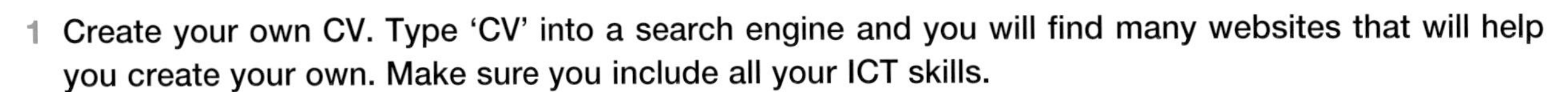

1 Create your own CV. Type 'CV' into a search engine and you will find many websites that will help you create your own. Make sure you include all your ICT skills.

2 Read the information in the advertisement below and create an application form for the theatre to use in its application pack.

> **Small Local Theatre Publicity Department**
>
> Central London location
>
> Enthusiastic Assistant required to create brochures, flyers and manage the finances of the theatre.
>
> Pay £22k+
>
> Good knowledge of Excel and Photoshop
>
> Sense of humour and love of theatre is essential
>
> *Email theatreo@googlemail.com for an application pack*

3 Write a letter of application for the job advertised above and complete a copy of the application form you have created.

4 In a word-processing application, create a table with 2 columns and 11 rows. In the first column make a list of ten questions you think you could be asked at interview if you applied for the job. In the second column add the answers you think the theatre would be looking for.

5 Choose two businesses that advertise job vacancies on their website. Compare the way they advertise their vacancies and what they want potential applicants to do in order to apply. Also compare how easy it is to apply for the jobs. Does the application process vary according to the different type of job? Which business do you think has the better method?

Summary

- Once a job has been advertised, applicants are expected to send for further information and either write a letter of application or send in a CV or completed application form.
- The business will read through the application forms and form a long list of the more suitable applicants.
- From the long list another list will be created of applicants suitable to interview; this is known as a short list.
- The final stages of the selection process are interviewing candidates and taking up references from a previous employer or school.

Key words

Curriculum vitae – a detailed account of a person's education and work background.

Application form – a form with questions to answer and boxes to complete to apply for a job.

Long list – applicants who have been selected for further consideration.

Short list – a small number of applicants (usually about five) who are selected from the long list to attend an interview.

Points for discussion

To what extent do you agree or disagree with these statements?

1 'Interviews are a waste of time – anyone can blag their way through one.'

2 'It's fine to make up your CV – you won't get caught out.'

Give me five

Give five headings on a CV.

Exam style questions

Holchurch Leisure Centre

Swimming Attendant

Needed full time, starting in June 2***

You need to be an enthusiastic swimmer and have or be prepared to study for a life saving qualification. You need to have a warm, friendly personality and be reliable.

Application forms can be collected from the baths or by sending an email to bathos@gmail.com

Closing date 27th May 2***

This advert appeared in a newspaper, and Holchurch Leisure Centre received the following applications:

- Mary Shells, aged 23 has worked at another swimming pool for three years and has her Level 3 life saving qualifications. She is a popular member of a hockey club in the area and has completed several swimathons for charity.
- Felix Shore, aged 17 is a member of the local football club and enjoys all sports. He has not got a life saving qualification but would be prepared to learn.
- Elba Bolas, aged 45 has recently become a member of the local fitness club and is keen on most sports. She has a degree in Business Administration and has recently moved into the area. She is a non-swimmer.
- Jagdish Patel, aged 19 is a non-swimmer but would like to learn. He has excellent academic qualifications and lists his hobbies as reading and playing chess.
- Sunita Kaur, aged 22 is a keen county swimmer, has a life saving qualification and is a member of a sports clubs. She is a reliable member of the Amateur Dramatics Society and is currently working in a school. She needs to give three months' notice and could not start a new job before August.

1 Explain, using an example, what is meant by the term 'short listing'. (3 marks)

2 Read the details about the applicants above and explain who should be put onto a short list. (8 marks)

3 Suggest two questions that should be asked of the candidates at interview. (4 marks)

4 Describe what will probably happen after the interview has taken place, before the contract of employment is sent out. (12 marks)

Chapter 12

Training

In this chapter you will learn:

- how a business can develop and train its staff both in-house and externally
- what induction training is and why it is important
- how to choose the most appropriate method of training for a particular purpose
- the benefits to the individual and the business of training staff.

Getting started

TESCO Training & Development

Onwards and upwards ...

As part of Every Little Helps, our commitment to our people is that we will give them the opportunity to get on so that they are able to get the training they need to do their job and to develop their careers at Tesco.

We want Tesco to be a great place to work for all our staff. That's why we want everyone here to feel free to follow the career path that's right for them.

There are a number of ways we support our people to achieve this, be it through an Options Development Programme, offering an Apprenticeship or encouraging the studying for a qualification while at work.

So we've trained ourselves to be obsessed ... about training.

Get with the programme

At any one time we've got 7,000 members of staff on development programmes specifically designed to help them gain the experience and skills they need to move on to the next Tesco challenge.

You never need fear getting stuck in a rut with us – each year, some 10,000 of our staff prove that by changing jobs within the company.

In fact, there's a training scheme for every major career stage at Tesco which is often flexible and tailored to your personal needs – which is one of the reasons why 80% of our management roles are filled by existing team members.

Think back to your very first day at secondary school – there was so much to learn, new teachers' names, where the toilets were, where to get food at lunchtime, what you had to bring to school each day and generally what was expected of you. It is really not very different when you start work.

The sort of training you have on your first day is called induction training and is given to all new employees. Training does not stop there, however, it often goes on throughout an employees' career with a business, and can take place either on or off the employer's premises. Employees need training to operate new machinery, to do different tasks or make new products. Although training costs the business money it is of benefit to both the business and the employee.

ICT is a continually changing environment, so people working in this area have to retrain or up date their skills regularly. Buying in technical help when new software is developed or hardware needs to be upgraded or replaced is very expensive. Many people have to find their own training and they can do this through magazines, the internet and online help facilities.

What you need to know

Methods of training

In-house or on-the-job training takes place at the workplace where the job is being done. It usually means working with an existing, experienced worker who shows the new employee how the job is done and then watches as the new employee tries to do the tasks. On-the-job training has the advantage of getting new employees working straight away, while they are at their keenest. It also helps motivate the experienced worker chosen to do the training, as they feel more confident and valuable to the business. However, sometimes there are too many distractions in the workplace, which may mean that the new employee finds it hard to concentrate so they make mistakes.

Off-the-job training takes place away from the job, for example in a college or in a training centre if the business is large enough to finance this. For ICT the training is often particularly expensive because the trainers themselves need constantly to up date their skills. Training may be on day release, where the employee is let out from work for one day a week to attend the course, or it may be done in a block of time. In many cases the training leads to a qualification such as an NVQ IT Practitioners Level 2.

One of the advantages of sending an employee on a training course is that it makes them feel valued by the business which is investing in their future. Also, the courses are taught by specialists who have themselves been trained in how to train, so may be better at explaining the new skills than an untrained person would be. However, the training on a course will be broader than on-the-job training and may not help directly in the workplace, so the employee may think that much of what they are learning is irrelevant. While employees are away from their jobs a backlog of work may build up, which will be hard to catch up with.

Choosing the most appropriate type of training

Before choosing how the training should take place, the manager responsible needs to consider:

- what the training is
- the safety of the employees
- the cost
- the time the training will take
- possible disruption to customers or other employees.

Some types of training need to be undertaken physically because the skill cannot be learned from watching others or reading about it. For example, you do not become faster or more accurate at word processing by watching someone input text on a computer – you actually need to practise the skill.

There is some training that ideally needs to take place in the workplace. For example, a new receptionist at a hotel needs to be trained on the hotel's booking system. If this is not possible for safety reasons, then simulations or DVDs can be used. For example, rather than taking employees on a tour of a dangerous workplace like a nuclear power station, they could take a simulated tour using a computer. However, these may not be as effective and where it is possible most employees will learn more by being physically shown around the buildings.

Training courses that take place in a purpose-built training centre or hotel can be expensive. The business needs to balance the cost of the training course with the benefits in terms of quality of training or increased motivation. Travel costs are increasingly being taken into account when making decisions about training courses – the cost in terms of both fuel and the time taken to get to the venue.

In places such as leisure centres or shops, some training may need to be away from the actual workplace to avoid too much disruption to the service. Customers may not feel that they are getting a good professional service if a new employee is asking lots of questions or making lots of mistakes while they are being served.

Induction training

Induction training is where a business introduces new employees to the workplace so that they learn what is expected of them and what to do in emergencies. The training usually takes no more than a day, but a lot of information is given to the new workers about the business and what it does. There may also be tours of the premises and DVDs to watch about the business's products or services, along with health and safety information. The new employee will be introduced to their fellow workers and other key people they will be working with. In some organisations the employee's training needs will be assessed, for example, they may not have used software that they will need to use in their new job.

Induction training can be an effective way of telling employees about the aims and objectives of the business. It can also be a chance to develop teams if several new employees start at the same time. The purpose of induction training is to increase the efficiency of the business so that when the employees start work they are more knowledgeable and able to fit in confidently with their fellow workers.

The benefits of training

Training is a way of motivating staff – a highly motivated staff will perform better and be more efficient. Both the trainer and the trainee can benefit from increased motivation: the trainer increases his self-esteem and the trainee feels that he is having his skills developed. Training is seen as an investment in the workforce. It also has the possible benefit to the employee of leading to promotion. Increasingly, as technology develops and certain types of job disappear, it is important that employees are retrained to help avoid the threat of redundancy.

These days, people are more aware of dangers in the workplace than they were in the past, and training can help prevent accidents as well as show that the business is complying with the demands of the law. Accidents, in addition to harming employees, can be very expensive for businesses and may result in poor public relations, so any attempt to make them less likely is welcome.

Much training is devoted to increasing the efficiency of employees. If employees are well trained, they should be able to do their jobs faster and better, which will result in higher output and less waste. Trained workers will be able to do a greater variety of tasks too, which should enable the business to respond better to change. If employees are able to do a variety of tasks they are described as multi-skilled.

Businesses need to train their employees so that they can benefit from the latest technology. By upgrading the skills of their workforce employers can introduce new technology, confident that their employees can both use and maintain the systems. For example, a business upgrading to a new release of software for handling the accounts needs to be confident that the employees can use the software fully and that it will run on their computer network.

Let's go!

Activities

1 Type 'Carphone Warehouse training' into a search engine and read about its training and development programme.

a) Why does Carphone Warehouse think training is important for all its employees?

b) What benefits does Carphone Warehouse get from training its workforce?

c) Which new employees are expected to attend induction training?

d) What training takes place next?

2 Think of a career which you are interested in, such as banking, sports management or health care. You may get some ideas for possible jobs from www.connexions-direct.com/jobs4u. Find one specific job and research what training you will need before you can work in the job, and the training you might get once you have started the job. Produce a written report of your findings.

Summary

- All workers need training at some point in their working lives, usually beginning with induction training before they actually start work.
- Training can take place on the job or off the job, but before decisions about this can be made the costs and effectiveness need to be considered.
- There is a cost to the business in providing the training, but the business gains by having safe, knowledgeable employees who are motivated and are more likely to stay with the company.

Key words

On-the-job training – a method of training whereby employees learn how to do the job as they are doing it. They are usually supervised closely while they learn 'the ropes'.

Off-the-job training – training that takes place away from the workplace so that the trainee can learn and make mistakes without impacting on the customer.

Induction – training for new staff that serves as an introduction to the company and its objectives, as well as the premises and where their job fits in.

Points for discussion

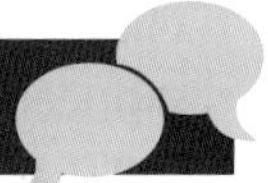

1 What do you think should be part of an induction programme for new teachers to your school or college?

2 'After you have completed an induction programme you should not *have* to do training – it should be optional for staff.' Do you agree with this view?

Give me five

Give five benefits of training to either employees or the employer. State who benefits.

Exam style questions

The following information about training for new managers is from the Pizza Hut website:

As a new Manager, your training begins with a 16-week induction programme which will give you all the technical skills and information you'll need for the road ahead. And you won't stop learning until the day you leave the company (which if you're anything like the majority of our people, won't be for some time in the distant futuro).

From the word 'go' you'll be assigned to a training restaurant and an experienced Restaurant General Manager. He or she will act as your coach and mentor as you complete a series of training modules and apply your new-found expertise 'on-the-job'. You'll attend one of our dedicated management training centres, where you'll take part in various workshops on subjects ranging from business management to leadership.

While there are no formal exams, you'll be expected to complete a range of assessments during the training programme to gauge your progress. As well as benefiting from ongoing reviews with your line manager, you'll also get the chance to share your ambitions with us by putting together a personal development plan.

Source: www.careersatpizzahut.co.uk/html/trainingandDev.htm

1 Explain what is meant by the term 'induction training'. (2 marks)

2 Describe what you would expect to find on the induction training programme for a new manager. (8 marks)

3 Explain why you think Pizza Hut also uses management training centres. (4 marks)

4 Explain why you think it is important for Pizza Hut to invest a large amount of money into training its new managers. (8 marks)

Extension activity

Look at the information that Sainsbury provide about their IT jobs at www.extrabyte.co.uk.

Read the profiles of current employees. Discuss the sort of training you think they will have received.

Chapter 13

Rewarding staff

In this chapter you will learn:

- the main methods by which businesses remunerate employees
- other types of reward given to employees.

Getting started

On its website, Pizza Hut states:

'We've a strong culture of rewarding our people and acknowledging their achievements. This is reflected in many ways, from competitive salaries, benefits and bonus opportunities to an annual awards ceremony which celebrates successes. Put simply, we actively look to recognise and reward those who excel in their day-to-day roles.'

Clearly these claims by Pizza Hut are designed to encourage people to want to work for them. Rewarding employees is important in both recruiting and keeping staff.

What you need to know

The main ways of remunerating employees are by:

- time rates or flat rates
- overtime
- payment by results (piece rate or commission)
- bonuses.

Time rates, flat rates and overtime

People paid according to the time they work are usually paid on a flat rate. This means they are paid a fixed amount per hour for however many hours they are contracted to work. For example, if an employee is paid £5.80 per hour and is supposed to work a 36-hour week, they will be paid 36 × £5.80 = £208.80 per week basic pay.

If they work any extra hours they are paid overtime, which is a higher rate paid to employees who work extra hours. The employee who earned £5.80 per hour may get overtime at 'time and a half' or at 'double pay'.

If he gets 'time and a half' then he will earn one and a half times £5.80 per additional hour: £5.80 × 1.5 = £8.70 per additional hour.

Or at 'double pay', twice the basic pay, he gets: £5.80 × 2 = £11.60 per additional hour.

If the employee works a total of 40 hours in one week he will earn his basic pay and 4 times the agreed rate of overtime. At double pay he would therefore earn: 4 × £11.90 = £47.60 plus his basic pay of £208.80, giving a total wage that week of £256.40.

Asking employees to work extra hours is costly for the business but it is much quicker and more flexible than taking on an extra member of staff who would need to be recruited and trained.

Payment by results

In manufacturing industry it is usual to pay employees by piece rate, which means they are paid a rate per finished item that is made. The benefits to the employee are that if he works harder and faster, he is able to increase his wage. To ensure that quality remains acceptable employers build in quality checks and insist that a certain standard is reached before payment is allowed.

In the retail industry payment by result often takes the form of commission, which means the sales staff are paid a small percentage of the value of each sale they make. In some instances sales staff are only paid by commission, with no basic pay, which results in no pay if no sales are made. The commission can be calculated per day, per week or per month.

If an employee works at a commission of 5 per cent of each sale made, and sells £6000 worth of goods in a week, they would be paid £300 on commission only, with no basic pay.

The idea of commission is to make the sales staff try harder to increase the sales for the business, which will increase its revenue and thus make the business more profitable.

Bonuses

Bonuses are a form of payment by results, but may be dependent on the performance of all the staff within the business, not just the individual. Bonuses may be paid if a production target is reached or an advertising campaign has been particularly successful. A bonus is where an employee is given an additional reward of extra pay or possibly shares in the business. The reward may be given at a special time of year, such as Christmas. In some industries employees expect to be paid a bonus each year, so it just becomes part of the salary package. There is much controversy over the payment of bonuses, with some people believing that the sums involved in certain sectors of business are getting out of hand.

In a news report from BBC on Sunday 18 January 2004 it was stated that a City trader had been given a record bonus of £30 million. The fortunate trader, Driss Ben-Brahim, worked for the US investment bank Goldman Sachs. He is believed to have received his bonus, which was paid in cash, shares and share options, for having generated millions of pounds in profits for the bank in 2003. Mr Ben-Brahim, it was reported in the *Sunday Times*, made the profits by developing a complicated trading strategy. The bonus put him in the top 25 earners in the UK, along with JK Rowling.

More recently, in 2008 the BBC reported that most of the 350,000 workers in London's financial services industry receive a form of annual bonus, with thousands receiving more than £1m and a small number reportedly being awarded as much as £10m.

Other forms of reward

Fringe benefits are perks or benefits that are not a direct part of the salary package but which are often advertised with the job. Generally, the higher up the organisation an employee is, the greater the fringe benefits offered, as can be seen from comparing the rewards package offered to team members at Pizza Hut with that of managers. Although fringe benefits can cost a company a great deal, their main purpose is to attract good applicants and to keep them motivated once employed. The costs of the total package of wages and fringe benefits have to be weighed against keeping the wages of a business under control.

Pizza Hut
Rewards and benefits

Team members

As a team member, you'll not only be offered a competitive salary, but also:

- 4 weeks' paid holiday
- 4 weeks' sick pay
- An employee discount card, offering great savings
- Loyalty awards to recognise length of service
- Share plans enabling you to save towards becoming an owner in Yum! Brand Inc.
- Flexible shift patterns to juggle studies or family commitments
- 100% of tips – something which our competitors have only just come into line with.

Not least, you find we offer a commitment to your training and development that's second to none, and plenty of scope to develop your career.

Managers

Join us in a managerial role, and you can look forward to a highly competitive salary which is reviewed annually. We also offer bonuses of up to 50% salary for Restaurant General Managers and 25% for Deputy Managers.

Additionally, you can look forward to a range of valuable benefits including:

- A 'Life Plan' pension scheme offered in association with Zurich, including company contributions
- 28 days' holiday (including Bank Holidays)
- Private healthcare for Restaurant General Managers in association with BUPA
- Company sick pay
- A Childcare Voucher Scheme offered in association with Allsave
- Share scheme enabling you to save towards becoming an owner in Yum! Brand Inc.
- Loyalty awards to recognise length of service
- An employee discount card offering savings across both our Equity and Franchisee businesses
- A wide range of third party discounts varying from RAC Roadside Recovery and Thomas Cook Holidays to fun days out at venues such as Alton Towers and Legoland
- Personnel Support Programme providing confidential, professional help and support
- Incentive programmes such as the Refer a Friend and Site Finder Award Incentive

Please note: if you are part-time, your salary and benefits will be pro-rated accordingly.

Source: www.careersatpizzahut.co.uk/html/rewardsandBenefits.htm

Let's go!

Activities

1. Look at the jobs online at www.jobcentreplus.gov.uk. Find a job advertisement that states an hourly rate of pay. Calculate the weekly pay for someone working full time in the job. If the hours are not given, assume that they are working 36 hours.
2. Look in the local and national newspaper job sections and create a page of nine job advertisements showing different remuneration packages. Try and find advertisements that show hourly pay, piece rate, bonus, overtime, commission, different fringe benefits and annual salary. Label your job advertisements A to I and copy and complete the table below.

Type of reward	Advertisement
Hourly pay	
Piece rate	
Bonus	
Overtime	
Commission	
Fringe benefit: pension	
Fringe benefit: health care	
Fringe benefit: discount	
Fringe benefit: paid holiday	
Annual salary	

Summary

- Employees are usually paid either according to the number of hours they work or how much work they do.
- Manual workers are usually paid per hour – this is known as a wage. Salaries are usually paid monthly to non-manual workers.
- Salaries are usually stated on advertisements or contracts as an annual figure.
- Commission is often paid to sales staff as it motivates them to perform better.
- Usually only hourly paid workers are paid overtime. This is where they work more than their set hours and receive a higher rate of pay per hour than their normal rate.
- Other means of motivating employees include giving bonuses for good work and offering a range of fringe benefits. There are many different types of fringe benefits, but private health care, discounts on holidays and the company's products are particularly popular.
- The overall package that a business provides needs to be good enough to attract good applicants for the jobs and also to keep them motivated. However, there is a limit to the amount a business can spend on pay and it must be kept under control.

Key words

Hourly pay – a fixed wage rate per hour for a set number of hours.

Piece rate – when workers are paid for each finished item they make.

Bonus – a special amount given as an additional reward over and above a salary or wage.

Overtime – a higher rate of pay given for extra hours over those agreed as a normal week. These hours are often paid at 'time and a half' or at 'double pay'.

Commission – a system of paying employees a percentage of the value of the goods they sell. Usually paid alongside an hourly rate, but some staff can be paid commission only.

Fringe benefit – a form of remuneration used to motivate staff. The perks or fringe benefits may have a monetary value but they are not added to the financial package to be spent as the employee wishes.

Points for discussion

1. Are bonuses that are greater than the average annual salary obscene or deserved by a few?
2. Should teachers be paid by results?
3. Would you take a job that paid commission only? Are successful sales figures something that the employee can always control?

Give me five

Give five jobs that are usually advertised with the annual salary not an hourly or weekly wage rate.

Exam style questions

Gateway Airlines

Cabin crew wanted flying from Heathrow and Gatwick. Basic salary £12,100.

Contract type: Permanent

Our full-time employees receive seven free flights a year to a wide range of global destinations. Beyond a whole world of travel opportunities, we also offer an excellent benefits package including:

Pension

Private medical schemes

Life assurance

Excellent discounts on additional flights and with lots of other companies

Dental plans

Health screening

Read the employment details above and answer the following questions.

1 Explain what is meant by the term ‘fringe benefits’. (2 marks)

2 Gateway Airlines is considering paying commission to cabin crew on the sales of alcohol they make to economy class passengers. Describe the advantages and disadvantages of this action. (9 marks)

3 Explain why Gateway Airlines provides fringe benefits to its staff. (6 marks)

4 At each airport, Gateway employs cleaning staff to prepare the plane for the next flight. Suggest a pay system that would be appropriate for the cleaners and explain why you have made your suggestion. (4 marks)

Extension activity

Investigate the current rates of the national minimum wage in the UK. When the national minimum wage was introduced there was resistance from a number of businesses. Produce a report on what the effects of having a minimum wage have been on businesses in this country.

Chapter 14

Employment rights and responsibilities

In this chapter you will learn:

- that all workers should be given a written contract of employment within two weeks of starting work
- that contracts of employment can be for temporary, part-time or permanent work
- that legislation affects the employment rights, equal opportunities and responsibilities of all employees.

Getting started

What do you need to know before you start work? One of the most important pieces of information you will need is the start date – the first day you are supposed to show up for work. You will also need to know the hours of work so that you know when to turn up and how long your working days are going to be. It is likely that you will also want to know, before you start work, how much you are going to earn and how much holiday you are entitled to. All of this basic but essential information forms part of your 'contract of employment', which you are legally required to have.

What you need to know

Contract of employment

A contract of employment is a legal requirement because of the Employment Rights Act, 1996. It is an agreement between an employer and an employee and is made as soon as the employee accepts the job offer. Both sides are then bound by its terms until it is properly ended. The rights and duties of the employee and those of the employer are called the 'terms' of the contract. Usually the contract is written down, but if it is not then the employee has to have a written statement of the main terms within two months of starting work. A contract can be ended by either the employee or the employer, by giving notice or by mutual agreement.

The written statement of employment particulars sets out some of the main terms of the contract. The statement must include: pay, hours of work, holiday entitlement, sick pay arrangements, notice periods and information about disciplinary and grievance procedures.

Equal opportunities in the workplace

Domino's Pizza

Domino's Pizza state that they are committed to the development of policies to promote equality of opportunity in employment. They state that their aim is to ensure that no job applicant or employee receives less favourable treatment on the grounds of sex, marital status, race, colour, creed, ethnic origin, sexual orientation, religious beliefs, age or disability.

Equal opportunities laws are concerned with giving all individuals identical rights regardless of their gender, race, age or physical characteristics. Protests made by women sewing machinists at the Ford Motor Company Plant in Dagenham led directly to the passing of the Equal Pay Act. However, there has been slow progress in closing the gender gap. In 1975 women were paid on average 30 per cent less than men for full-time work. Today those in full-time work have seen an improvement, but women in part-time work are paid significantly less than men.

The Equal Pay Act, 1970 states that a man and a woman in the same organisation should be paid the same if they do the same or broadly similar work. To make a claim the woman has to prove that the job she is doing is the same or of similar value to that of the man. In 2007 the BBC reported a case where a group of dinner ladies in St Helens won a pay dispute – the House of Lords ruled in favour of the women who were seeking similar pay to road sweepers.

The Sex Discrimination Act, 1975 was introduced to try and prevent any sex discrimination in the workplace on wider issues than pay, covering selection procedures, employment terms, fringe benefits, selection for redundancy and training and development opportunities. The Act is designed to protect potential employees from both direct discrimination, for example only advertising a job as suitable for males, and indirect discrimination such as traditionally only employing females.

The Race Relations Act, 1976 made it illegal to treat people unfairly on the grounds of colour, nationality or ethnic or national origins. It covers every part of employment including recruitment, terms and conditions of employment, training, promotion and redundancy and dismissal. There are very few instances where race can be specified, but it is legal for a television company to specify that a black actor is needed for a programme or film.

The law identifies four main kinds of discrimination:

- direct discrimination – deliberate discrimination (e.g. where a particular job is only open to people of a specific race)
- indirect discrimination – this may be where working practices disadvantage members of any group (e.g. insisting that women wear skirts)
- harassment – accepting behaviour that offends someone or creates an unpleasant atmosphere (e.g. allowing the telling of racist jokes)
- victimisation – if someone has complained about racial discrimination they must not be treated less favourably.

The Disability Discrimination Act, 1995

This Act states that organisations that employ more than 20 people should employ disabled people as 3 per cent of the workforce.

The Disability Discrimination Act, 1975 and its amendment in 2005 covers things like application forms, interview arrangements, proficiency tests, job offers and work-related benefits such as access to recreation or refreshment facilities. Under the Act, the employer has a duty to make 'reasonable adjustments' to ensure that the disabled employee is not at any disadvantage due to employment arrangements or physical features of the workplace. The sort of adjustment that the employer could be asked to make, in consultation with the employee, includes providing modified equipment, training or retraining if they cannot continue with their current job, and allowing time off for medical treatment.

Let's go!

Activities

1 Use a word-processing package to create a contract of employment for yourself working at Homily Leisure Centre as an Assistant Sports Leader. You have been given a permanent job and will be working 36 hours a week for £7.20 per hour. You will start work today and you will be paid monthly. You are entitled to four weeks' holiday and paid sick leave a year and need to give two weeks' notice if you wish to terminate your contract. Both you and the Leisure Centre Manager will need to sign and date the contract.

2 Imagine you work on a local newspaper as an Agony Aunt. Use the Directgov website to find information to answer the following problem letters.

Dear Charlie,

My employer has treated me less favourably than others because I use a wheel chair to get around and I cannot eat lunch with my fellow workers. How should I go about solving this problem?

Evie

Dear Charlie,

I have lived over here for several years now but still have my Irish accent. Recently some people have been making racist jokes about the Irish in front of my boss but he takes no notice. Do I have to put up with this?

Patrick

Dear Charlie,

There are lots of redundancies about to happen at my workplace. Because I am nearly 50 I am sure that I will be one of the first to go. Is that fair or legal just because of my age?

Ted

Summary

- When a business employs a new employee it must provide a written statement of the terms and conditions of employment. However, a contract exists even before it is written down.
- When employing people a business must obey laws that provide equal opportunities to all its employees. Although these laws may increase the costs of employing staff, they also ensure that the business gets the best person for the job. The benefits to the business and society as a whole usually outweigh any additional costs.

Key words

Equal opportunities – equal treatment and respect for all, regardless of gender, race, age or physical characteristics.

Discrimination – is the prejudicial treatment of people, based on certain characteristics.

Contract of employment – an agreement between the employee and employer concerning the employee's terms and conditions of employment.

Points for discussion

1 'Small businesses should not be forced to employ people who have a physical handicap; they create the wrong image.' What arguments would you present to someone who held this view?

2 'It makes sound commercial success to have a diverse workforce.' Why?

Give me five

Give five laws that businesses must comply with when employing people.

Exam style questions

Jenny Smith has bought a large old shop in Hokey town centre which she hopes to convert into a coffee bar. The shop needs some renovation as the décor is very old fashioned and there are several steps up to the toilets at the rear of the shop. Hokey has a mixed-race population and Jenny is keen to appoint staff who will be the best for the job. Jenny has done some market research and found that the coffee bar will appeal to customers from across the age range of 14–70.

After interviewing 12 people Jenny decides to appoint three full-time and six part-time employees.

1 When recruiting a new employee it is illegal to not employ someone because of their:

   a) experience

   b) qualifications

   c) age

   d) references. (1 mark)

2 Explain why Jenny should remove the steps up to the toilets when she has the renovation work done on the building. (4 marks)

3 Explain how following equal opportunities laws will help Jenny employ the best people for the vacancies. (6 marks)

4 Once the new employees start working for Jenny they will need to be given a contract of employment. List five items other than names and addresses that should be included in the document. (5 marks)

Extension activity

Boots

Diversity

Women at work

It probably won't surprise you to hear that women make up a large proportion of our workforce, and our customers too. So it follows that we make sure we're a great place to work for women. In fact, we've a long tradition of it, becoming one of the first companies to employ welfare workers in 1911, responsible specifically for the welfare of our female workers. More recently, we've embraced flexible working practices such as job sharing, term time working and career breaks, which are an essential for most working mums (and dads).

Cultural diversity

We believe there's little point in putting our pharmacies at the heart of local communities if our own workforce doesn't reflect the whole of the UK's population. And to fully understand all of our customers, it helps if our own Boots community is equally diverse. This is why our diversity policy relates to gender, race, religion, belief, age, disability, sexual orientation, family status and nationality. If they share our values, then everyone's welcome.

Source: www.bootsjobs.com

a) Choose three well-known businesses and research their equal opportunities policies. Can you find any news stories which suggest that they have not lived up to their intentions?

b) Explain what is meant by the following terms that are sometimes included in a contract of employment:

probationary period

garden leave

collective agreements

grievance procedure

intellectual property.

SECTION 3

COMMUNICATION

Chapter 15

Methods of communication

In this chapter you will learn:

- the purpose of communication
- about the communication systems that are used by businesses
- how to choose the most appropriate communication medium
- about the barriers that can prevent effective communication taking place.

Getting started

How do you communicate? Many of you will use social networking sites and mobile phones to stay in contact with your friends, but would not dream of trying to communicate with your mum or teacher in this way. Without really thinking about it you select an appropriate communication medium for the audience, taking into account the content of the message. You are probably also aware of some of the barriers to communication, for example on a busy high street it can be hard to talk to someone using a mobile phone because of the background noise or because the signal is unreliable.

Communication is vital to businesses both within the business itself and to people outside the business, such as suppliers and customers. Effective communication is essential to help a business achieve its objectives.

What you need to know

What is communication?

Communication within any business is extremely important. The purpose of communication is to acquire information or to disseminate it, in other words to obtain information from someone else or to give them the information that they ask for or need.

For communication to take place there needs to be a sender and one or more receiver, a message and a medium. A communication could be from a manager (sender) to a worker (receiver) to tell them to come into work early the next day (message) via an email (medium of communication).

Communication is divided into internal (within a business) and external (to and from those outside the business). Internal communication could be communication within teams of workers within the same level, such as manager to manager. This type of communication is described as horizontal. It could also be between a manager and a worker, as in the example above. This is described as vertical communication. External communication could be between businesses or between a representative of the business and another stakeholder such as a shareholder or customer. For communication to be effective it needs to be appropriate to the audience as well as accurate and clear. Businesses also need to be aware of the image and tone that is being conveyed by their communications.

Formal communications are those that take place through official channels, such as manager to worker. Informal communication is when information is passed on in a way that is not an official channel of communication, for example gossip or a leak of information.

Another way of classifying communication is to divide it into that which is confidential and should only be seen by those who need to know, and non-confidential which can be seen by anyone. Usually, financial information is classified as confidential and, if the method of communication is a letter, it will be marked as 'only to be opened by the addressee'.

Communication can also be classified as urgent or non-urgent. This will affect the method of communication used – speaking with someone face to face, or over a telephone, or via instant messaging are all ways of communicating quickly with another person if the matter is urgent.

The benefits of effective communication

If communication is effective, workers will be well informed about the goals of the company and therefore motivated to help achieve them. For example, if an employee works in customer service and is well informed about future developments, they will be able to answer customer queries. If employees in a business do not know much about the workplace or what is happening they can easily create a poor image by not seeming interested. A poor image is very hard to overcome, so businesses need to take steps to ensure that they do not get into that position. Good communication helps all workers work towards achieving the company's objectives.

Choosing the methods of communication

The main groups of communication are categorised as oral, visual, written and graphical or pictorial. A person who needs to communicate with others will choose one of these methods, according to the content of the message and the person or groups of people who will be receiving it. Sometimes more than one method of communication will be used at any one time, the most usual combination being graphical information combined with written information in presentations or on signs.

Oral communication

Oral communication can take place via face-to-face meetings, telephones or teleconferencing. These methods are ideal where there is no need for a record to be kept of what is said, and they are also immediate in terms of the ability of the people involved to respond to what is being said. Because there is usually little in the way of a record of what is said, this sort of communication is not ideal for complicated messages or messages where detail is required.

Visual communication

Visual communication is a term used to describe video conferencing and electronic notice boards, both of which are made possible by the use of technology. Video conferencing is a way of holding a virtual meeting by making use of digital cameras and computers. It has the advantage of allowing the senders and receivers to see facial expressions and share documents, although there may be no record made of what is being said. It also has the advantage of not needing people to be all at the same location, which can save substantial amounts of money (travel expenses) and time (travel time). The main disadvantage of video conferencing is the cost in terms of purchasing the equipment needed and setting up the system.

Electronic notice boards are increasingly used in reception areas of a business to create an image of a highly successful organisation to outsiders visiting the business. If placed around a business they can be used to provide employees with up-to-date information. With electronic notice boards communication is all one way, from sender to receiver. Messages need to be relatively short so that they can be read before the screen scrolls to another page. With these notice boards there is obviously a set-up cost that needs to be taken into consideration.

Written communication

Written communication can take a wide range of forms from the electronic to the paper based. Increasingly, email messages are being used for both internal and external communication. Email can be, but is not always, instantaneous, and is very low in cost or free once set up. It is possible for emails to be marked as high priority and to be copied to other people, both openly and without the recipients seeing who else the message has been sent to. To log into email systems a password is usually required, but no email system can be guaranteed 100 per cent secure.

Internal written communication can be in the form of memos, which are paper-based messages, sometimes hand written. No addresses are included as the document is an internal one, so they are quick and easy to produce. Because the system is an internal one they are also quick to deliver. The only costs are the paper and printing if done on a word processor.

Other forms of written communication include financial documents, reports, letters and advertisements. These methods of communication produce a hard copy of the message that can be kept indefinitely if necessary, and are excellent for complex information that needs to be reread or studied closely. All of these forms of written communication can be used for internal or external communication. A new employee may receive a formal letter of appointment or there may be an internal advertisement for a new job. Suppliers may be written to with the details of a new contract and a job advertisement may be placed externally in a newspaper.

Graphical communication

Graphical communication can be in the form of production drawings, images, graphs or charts which are usually accompanied by some form of written or electronic communication. The purpose of most forms of graphical communication is to make a complex message more easily understood. Graphs or charts are usually used to make it easier to understand the relationships between numerical data.

Barriers to communication

Barriers to communication can be physical, but there can also be other reasons why a message is not received. These barriers can prevent effective communication taking place. Barriers can be specific to certain methods of communication, for example external noise, such as a party going on in the background, can make effective oral communications impossible. Poor network coverage can be a barrier to oral communications made using a mobile phone.

Other barriers to communication include the use of jargon and making the message too complex for the person receiving it. If the message is too complex then it may be ignored or misunderstood.

Let's go!

Activities

1 a) Produce a questionnaire for a local business to investigate how technology has changed the way people communicate both internally and externally. You should ask about their use of video conferencing, emails, etc.

b) When you have produced a copy of the questionnaire, discuss it with another student and amend your questionnaire as appropriate.

2 You work for a business in Reading which also has a branch in Hull. It has been suggested that rather than attempt to hold meetings at one or other of the sites, you should be using video conferencing. Research the costs of setting up a video conferencing solution, assuming that there is no other equipment you could use for this purpose.

Summary

- Communication between people within a business, between businesses and between a business and its customers is at the heart of any business.
- There are four methods of communication: oral, visual, written and graphical.
- Choosing the correct method and medium depends on knowing what the message is and knowing the skills and attitudes of the recipient.
- If barriers to communication exist it can damage the reputation and the profits of the business.

Key words

Vertical communication – the passing of information up and down the hierarchy of management, for example from office manager to clerk.

Horizontal communication – the passing of information between people in the same hierarchy of management.

Recipient – the person receiving the message.

Teleconference – a 'meeting' that takes place using telecommunication technology to enable people in more than one location to speak to each other.

Video conference – a 'meeting' that takes place simultaneously at more than one location using ICT to enable people to see and speak to each other.

Points for discussion

To what extent do you agree with the following statements?

1 'There is no need to have expensive conferences in exotic locations any more. Conferences should take place without anyone leaving the workplace.'

2 'You need to see a person's face in order to communicate effectively.'

Give me five

Give five different media that can be used for external communication.

Exam style questions

Tatlers is a modern department store with branches throughout the UK. They sell cosmetics, perfumes, men's and women's clothes, furniture, household furnishings, kitchen equipment, toys, electrical and sports goods. They have a reputation for excellent customer relations and their objective for the coming year is to expand. Each store has its own management structure reporting to a head office in London.

1 Communication within each store is best described as:

interval external internal pictorial (1 mark)

2 Explain why it is important for Tatlers to communicate appropriately with their customers. (6 marks)

3 Give two examples of written communication. (2 marks)

4 Describe two barriers to communication that might occur when mobile phones are used. (6 marks)

5 Explain what would be needed in order for Tatlers to conduct a meeting between all their managers without them travelling. (5 marks)

Chapter 16

The internet and e-commerce (1)

In this chapter you will learn:

- what the internet is
- how businesses use the internet
- how the internet helps businesses to achieve their aims.

Getting started

Many people use the internet to access shops' websites and choose goods from web-based catalogues. Once they have selected what they want to buy, they enter their credit or debit card details to pay for the goods; there is often a small delivery charge added. The goods are then despatched using a parcel delivery firm or courier. E-commerce is a part of life for many people, especially those who go out to work and are short of time. It is convenient for busy people, and it helps others, such as people with mobility problems or very small children, to be less dependant on others.

What you need to know

The internet

The internet is a worldwide network of computers that are connected together. To be able to access the internet you need a computer connected to a modem, which connects to an internet service provider with a username and password. To see the text, images, videos and to be able to interact with web pages you need a web browser.

- The most common web browsers are:
- Firefox
- Internet Explorer
- Safari
- Netscape.

All pages on the internet have a special web filename which is individual to that page; this is known as a Unique Resource Locator (URL). The URL is made up of a domain name and a filename. In front of this is usually http://, which stands for Hypertext Transfer Protocol and is the system used to download the files to a computer from the web server.

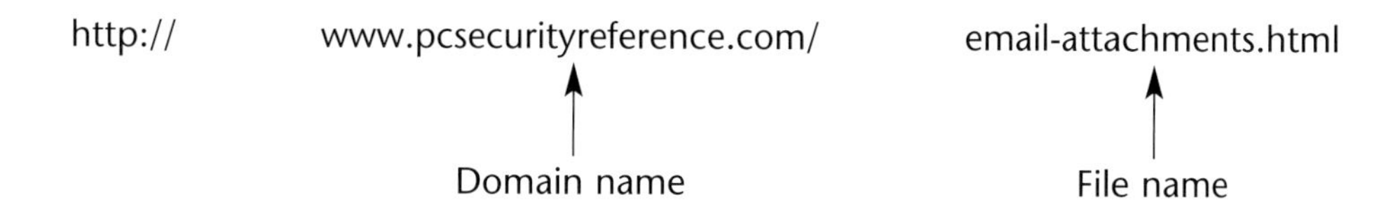

A domain name is made up of:

www.	bbc.	co.uk
a site on the world wide web	a name for the website	a company in the uk

Domain names can have various different endings which signify different things.

Ending	Meaning
.co or .com	a commercial company; com usually means it is an international business
.gov.uk	produced by the British Government
.ac.uk	a university or college in the uk
.org	a charity or non-commercial organisation
.pl	a site registered in Poland
.au	a site registered in Australia
.info	a site that provides information
.sch	a site belonging to a school

How businesses use the internet

Businesses are really not very different from individuals in the way they use the internet. They can use the internet in a variety of ways.

Research

The internet is a good way for businesses to access information about their customers and their needs and wants. They can look up market research done by other businesses or organisations, although they may have to pay to do so. They can find out about the local area in which they hope to trade by looking at websites such as www.upmystreet.com.

Other research they can do is to look at their competitors' websites and find out what goods or services they provide, and the prices they charge. The internet enables businesses to stay up to date with what is going on in their industry and with new products that are available. They can also find out about conferences that are going on which may help them with running their business.

Another way the internet helps businesses is that it helps them keep up to date with laws that affect their business. When changes occur, the internet makes it quick and easy for the business to find out what the changes are and to obtain advice on how to implement them.

All of this information is useful both to businesses that are just setting up and to established businesses, but it is only useful if the information is up to date and obtained from a reliable source.

Communication

Businesses can use the internet to communicate with customers and suppliers, or internally, in a variety of ways:

- email
- social networking sites such as Facebook and Bebo
- chatrooms
- blogs.

Email is a method of sending a message from one computer to another without having to print anything. Pictures and photographs can be sent either in the email or as an attachment.

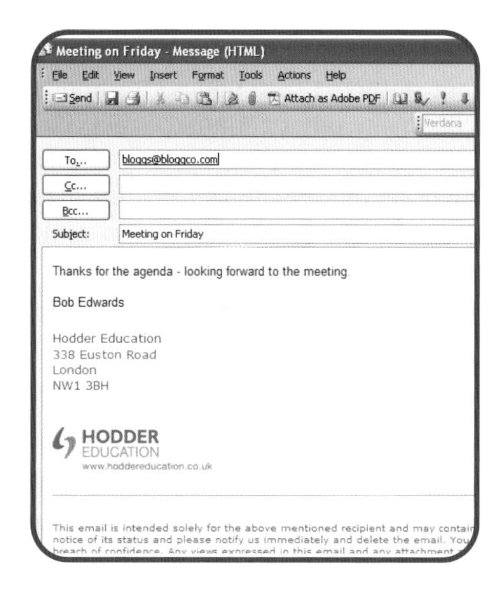

Businesses can create enormous mailing lists of customers and send a copy of an email to all the people on the list. There are no postage costs and the message is usually received very quickly. Email can also be used to send information to employees or suppliers and to keep in touch with employees when they are away from an office. Emails can now be accessed on many mobile phones, making it even more simple to keep in contact. However, as with any other form of communication, errors can occasionally occur and messages may not be received. Some people also receive hundreds of emails a day and cannot or do not read them as many may be unwanted. Email software can be set up to recognise spam (unwanted mail) so that it does not go to their inbox. Care must also be taken, when sending emails, to ensure that the email addresses are correct.

Businesses can also use social networking sites by setting up groups. For example, a Smarties Appreciation Society could be set up, or a group set up for fans of Laughing Cow Cheese. The business can then post information on the group site that they want their customers to know, for example new product launches or special offers. Businesses can also use blogs and chat rooms in a similar way.

Obtaining supplies

Businesses can look at a range of suppliers on the internet – whatever they need it is pretty certain that they can find it on the internet. The internet makes it easy to compare prices and designs of goods. Some websites allow items to be looked at in a 3D design so that people can 'walk round' them, giving even clearer ideas as to an item's suitability. This speeds up the whole process as the business does not have to wait for catalogues to be sent out. Good-quality photographs can easily be uploaded onto a website, again making the choice of goods easier.

E-commerce

Online shopping

In e-commerce the 'e' is short for electronic, which means that the sale and purchase of goods is carried out using an electronic system, usually the internet. Some e-commerce is entirely electronic and no actual physical goods are handled, for example reading an e-book bought from Amazon.

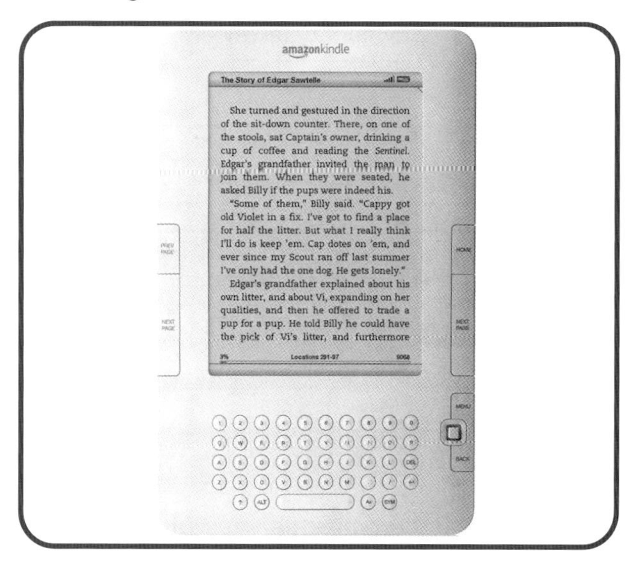

E-commerce has led to many new businesses setting up without purpose-built premises, for example, the many small businesses that only trade on eBay. More established large businesses, such as Amazon, are able to trade without having actual retail premises.

To sell goods using e-commerce a business needs first to have an internet connection on a computer. It then needs to register a domain name, such as 'waterstones.com', and have a website built at this domain name to contain the web shop. The web shop will contain information and pictures about all the products and services for sale. Alongside this the business will need to buy a secure payment program that will process credit and debit card payments. Most e-commerce businesses then have an automated process for sending confirmation of the order to the customer's email address. The final step in the transaction is to physically send the order to the customer if it is a product, or to electronically transfer the information or service that has been paid for.

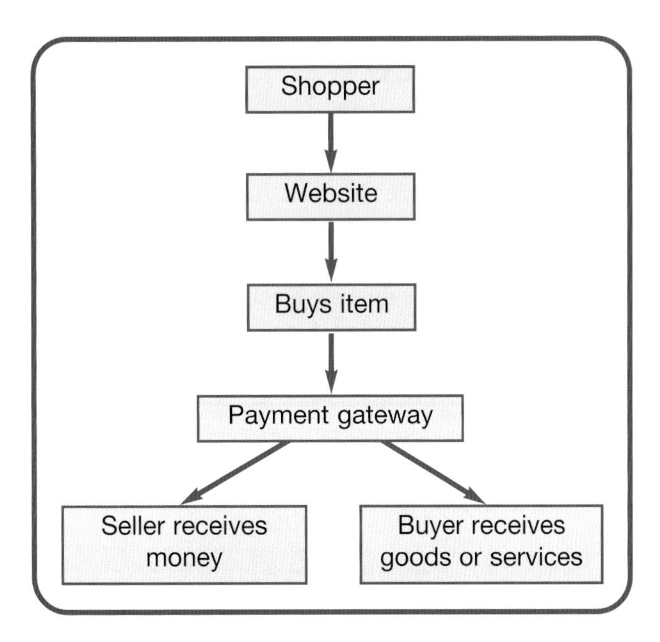

Online booking

E-commerce is not restricted to shopping for goods, however. There are many other commercial activities that can be done online, such as booking a train ticket, a cinema ticket or a package holiday. The internet allows the customer to check availability and price before booking the ticket or seat, by linking to a remote database.

Online auctions

Businesses do not have to advertise the goods at a set price – they can choose to sell them through an online auction. The most well-known online auction is that run by eBay. As with any other e-commerce site, the customer usually needs to pay for the goods with a credit or debit card. When selling through an online auction, the seller can either set a 'buy it now' price or can set a minimum amount that they are prepared to sell for. The online auction site usually charges a fixed fee for each item sold and extra for including pictures.

Businesses can, of course, choose to purchase goods that they need as well as selling.

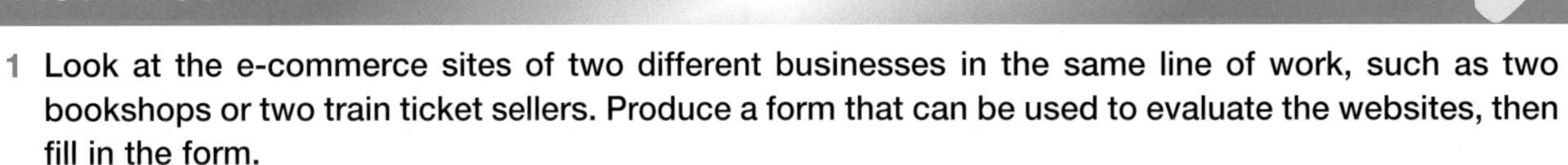

1. Look at the e-commerce sites of two different businesses in the same line of work, such as two bookshops or two train ticket sellers. Produce a form that can be used to evaluate the websites, then fill in the form.
2. Look at the website store.manutd.com. Describe the process a new customer needs to go through in order to purchase an item. Illustrate your work with screen shots.
3. Design a questionnaire aimed at parents to find out if they use e-commerce to purchase goods specifically for their children. Try to find out about the types of purchase and the frequency. Give your questionnaire to ten adults and produce a word-processed document showing your findings. You should try and use graphs to illustrate some of the questions.
4. Domain names end with codes such as .gov, .com, .co, etc. List as many different types of website as can you find. Find an example of a website for each and state briefly what the website is for.

Summary

- Businesses can use the internet in a variety of ways:
  - The internet can be used for researching new products, customer requirements, or competitors.
  - It can be used as a tool to communicate both internally and externally. Examples of this are using email, social networking sites, chat rooms and blogs.
  - The internet can be used to find the raw materials that the business needs at a competitive price.
  - A business can develop its own website and use it to advertise or sell their products or services. For example, Tesco sells its groceries online and Odeon Cinemas sell tickets for films.

Key words

Internet – a huge network of computers, world wide, which are connected together and exchange information using common software.

E-commerce – a system that allows customers to access a business's website to obtain goods or services.

Modem – a piece of hardware that converts data from a computer into a form that can be sent down a telephone line to connect it to the internet.

Internet service provider (IPS) – a company that allows you to connect to its network to gain access to the internet.

Web browser – a program which allows people to use the World Wide Web (www).

Email – messages and documents that are sent and read electronically, without the need for a printed copy.

Blog – a diary-style website where individuals or businesses can add comments about a particular topic.

Social networking site – a site which allows people to communicate with each other via messages.

Chat room – a website which allows real-time messaging between individuals or groups of people.

Spam – unwanted emails.

URL (Unique Resource Locator) – a special file name which is different for every page on the internet.

Points for discussion

1. Whitchurch Little Theatre Group would like to start a website. What information should it contain?
2. How important is it that websites have a sensible name? Do you know of any that don't?

Give me five

Give five ways that a coffee bar could use the internet.

Exam style questions

Karl Price runs a coffee shop called Coffee Active, close to the library in the centre of Tinford, employing five staff. The coffee shop is open between 8 a.m. and 6 p.m., six days a week and sells a range of coffees, teas and other drinks alongside paninis, sandwiches and cakes. In the shop he also displays paintings and other craft work from local people, which he sells on their behalf.

1 The domain name for the website for Coffee Active is most likely to end in:

a) .com

b) .gov.uk

c) .co.uk

d) .fr (1 mark)

2 Describe two ways in which Karl could use the website to inform people about his business. (6 marks)

3 Explain how Karl could use the internet to research about his customers. (6 marks)

4 Explain why it is important for Karl to have access to the internet. (6 marks)

Chapter 17

The internet and e-commerce (2)

In this chapter you will learn:

- how businesses are using the internet more
- how the internet helps businesses be more competitive
- the advantages and disadvantages of using the internet for research
- the advantages and disadvantages of having a website
- the advantages and disadvantages of using email.

Getting started

In the previous chapter we looked at the numerous ways in which businesses can use the internet. In this chapter we are going to look at the advantages to businesses of using the internet, and also some of the disadvantages. The internet offers some amazing advantages for businesses as well as individual users, but it is not without its problems. Using the internet, businesses can find out almost limitless information from all over the world. They can also communicate easily with other internet users all over the world. The internet allows the almost immediate transfer of documents from one computer to another.

The downside to the internet is that it is now so vast that it is impossible to police, so there is both incorrect information and offensive material (in the form of text or images) on the web that can be accessed by anyone. Because there is so much material on the internet, businesses cannot always be sure that information is true unless it has come from a site that can be trusted. In addition, viruses can get into a computer from the internet. These can damage a computer by deleting files or changing them. Anyone that accesses the internet needs to ensure that they have up-to-date virus protection.

What you need to know

Trends in the UK

According to the Office for National Statistics (ONS) report published in November 2008, internet sales rose by 30 per cent in 2007. The total figure for 2007 is quoted as being £136 billion, an increase of more than 30 per cent on the figure of £152.2 billion in 2006. Other key findings in the report were that internet sales represented nearly 8 per cent of the total value of non-financial sector businesses, and that just over 70 per cent of businesses had a website.

Using the internet for research

Advantages

- Using the internet for secondary market research is a quicker way for a business to get information about what the market wants and needs than commissioning or undertaking the research themselves.
- It is likely that any commercially available research will have questioned a larger sample of people than any research the business could do itself.

- If the information is available electronically it is easier for the business to edit it and to place it in its own documents.
- It is easier to obtain information about competitors than to take the time to visit them individually, not to mention the saving in fuel cost.

Disadvantages

- It can be expensive to buy the market research findings that a business needs, as seen in the holiday centres example opposite.
- When taking research from the internet it is important that the business satisfies itself that the research is up to date and accurate. It is not enough just to check that the research was published recently, the business should look to see when the actual research was done. Ideally the research should have been done by an organisation that is well known and trusted.
- The business should only use research that has been conducted in a similar locality. There is no point in looking at research conducted in London if the business is located in rural Wales.

Holiday Centres – UK

By: *Mintel International Group Ltd.*

Holiday centres are collectively investing millions of pounds upgrading accommodation, facilities and restaurants and are reaping the rewards. Butlins reported a boom in bookings over the August holiday peak season, expecting some 150,000 guests across more …

Search inside this report: Cost $3000

Having a website

Advantages

- Having a website, or being featured on a website, can give a business a global presence which it would otherwise not be able to afford. Instead of just being seen in a small town, the business can be 'reached' across the world.
- Some businesses, for example a publishing company, do not need to be located anywhere near their customers, so having a website means that they can realistically serve a very wide area.

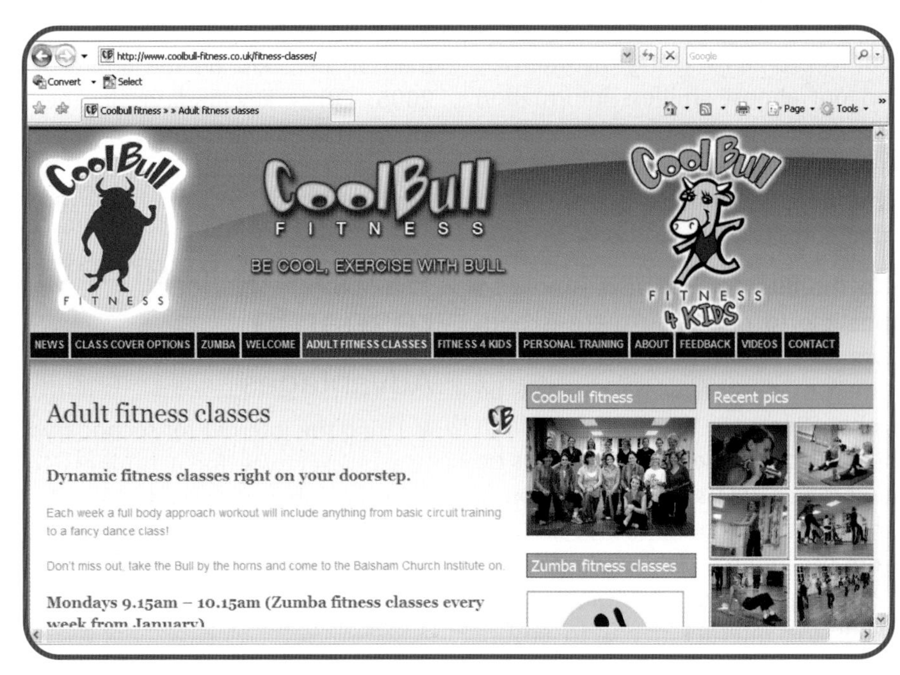

Cool Bull Fitness: an example of a small business website

- Having a website and making it into an e-commerce site, that is a website that you can actually buy from, means that the business is open 24 hours a day, 7 days a week. This can dramatically increase the amount of revenue a business earns.
- A website will appear in full colour and may have many links and hyperlinks to different pages. The cost of producing the material as brochures and other forms of advertising would be very high.

Disadvantages

- Most websites are designed by commercial businesses, and the cost can be high depending on the complexity and size of the site.
- A fully functioning e-commerce site depends on powerful databases to run the stock-control systems and booking systems. These take a lot of time to develop.
- Secure systems are needed to allow customers to pay for goods and services, so that other people cannot access their information and buy goods fraudulently. A secure server is indicated as a padlock icon at the bottom of the internet window.
- If a business is trading globally it must have the stock available to service the demand, otherwise customers will become frustrated and it will give the business a bad name. Maintaining high levels of stock is, however, expensive because the business has to pay for the goods that it has stored unless they are sold very quickly.
- Not all customers wish to use a website and if that becomes the norm for that business the non-technically minded customers may go elsewhere.

Using the internet for communication via email

Advantages

- Unlike post, emails usually arrive very quickly after they are sent, provided that the recipients refresh their email page regularly.
- Businesses can communicate easily with their customers regardless of where they live. There are no individual costs for sending emails once you have paid for the use of the internet. There is no increase in cost if a lot of emails are sent or if they are lengthy.
- It is quicker to write an email than a business letter because it does not require a formal layout. Many features of a business letter are unnecessary, such as the date or the full postal address of the sender and the person receiving the email. It is also easy to add a signature which can be applied to all emails.

- Most email systems automatically attach a copy of the original email received alongside the reply, so it is easier to follow the drift of a correspondence.
- Email is one piece in the jigsaw of the paperless office. Sending emails rather than posting letters means that there is no need to buy stamps, paper or envelopes. This not only saves the business money but is also environmentally sound as it does not use up resources.
- Businesses can email people in different time zones, such as from the UK to America, because they can be read and replied to at the convenience of the recipient rather than telephoning at an inconvenient time.
- The features of email make it attractive to use, such as the ability to add multiple attachments of pictures and documents which can be downloaded and saved on the recipient's computer. It is possible to set up a distribution list which means that group emails, that is emails to a number of people at once, can be sent quickly in one action. It is possible to copy (cc) or to blind copy (bcc) the email to individuals. Blind copying means that the recipient of the bcc is secret from the other recipients of the email.

- Encryption can be used for confidential emails. This is where the message sent over the internet is put into a form of secret code by the computer. This makes the email system very secure.

Disadvantages

- The email system relies on everyone having the equipment needed to send and receive emails and checking their inbox regularly. Non-technologically minded people may resist the change and may find that they are not receiving information that they need if they cannot or will not use email. The equipment is also expensive in comparison with the cost of pen and paper.
- Emails can easily be sent to the wrong person and this can cause problems due to lack of confidentiality.
- Many email users receive too many emails in their inbox each day; some of it is junk mail, which results in many unread emails. This can cause people a lot of stress as well as risking important emails being swamped by the rest.
- It is possible for email systems to be hacked into and therefore it should not really be used for confidential material.
- If the person receiving the email needs a document that is not saved on a computer it needs to be scanned in first, which can take longer than using a fax machine.

Let's go!

Activities

1. a) Set up a distribution list of six people in your class and then send a group email to them with the definitions of the key words from any chapter, mixed up for them to sort. Ask them to email you the correct response.

   b) Print out the reply, showing the answers and your original message.

2. Create a document with screen shots for younger students, showing them how to create a suitable email signature.
3. Create a document with screen shots to show how to set up and use a distribution list.
4. a) Create a questionnaire for local businesses to see whether they have or intend to have a website. If they do then try and find out how long they have had one, why it was developed and how it is changing their business.

   b) Think of five other questions you could ask them and collate the results. What are your conclusions?

5. Produce a guide booklet for Year 7 pupils on how to use the school email system.

Summary

- Businesses are increasingly using the internet to enable them to operate more efficiently and to help them make more profit.
- The main ways in which they use the internet are for research, promotion and selling and for communications.
- Although there are downsides to the use of the internet, these can be managed and overall the advantages outweigh any disadvantages.
- Research done using the internet is considerably cheaper than primary research done by the business and, provided that it is up to date, can be useful. It does need to be supplemented by thorough research of that distinct market if the business is just in one area.
- An attractive website, provided that it is maintained regularly, can help a business advertise and sell goods.
- A website is available all day every day, unlike many small businesses, so having one can greatly increase the amount of revenue the business receives.
- Communication via email is almost instantaneous, provided that the recipient checks their email. It saves on costs too, both for the business and environmentally as there is no need for printing or posting paper-based messages.

Key words

Virus – a program that can be transferred from one computer to another, damaging the computer system.

Recipient – the person who is receiving the email that has been sent.

Distribution list – a list of email addresses and names of people that can be emailed as a group.

Encryption – when data is put into a secret code so that it can only be read by the sender and someone authorised to receive the email.

Attachment – a document which is stored as a file on a computer and sent alongside an email, such as a photograph, image or report.

Points for discussion

1. 'Business letters are unnecessary, expensive to produce and there is no need to send any.' Discuss.
2. Is there any need for a business to conduct its own market research now that all businesses have access to the internet?
3. 'All businesses need a website to survive in this century.' How far do you agree with this statement?

Give me five

Give five advantages to a business manager of using email to communicate with his customers.

Exam style questions

Hesturnton Sports Shop is a small business in the centre of the market town of Hesturnton. The town has a population of 8000 people and has a small secondary school nearby. There are also local hockey, football, cricket and rugby teams. The shop has been open for 22 years and has slowly increased in size. The owner, Jim Brown, is very interested in finding out how using technology can help his business, and whether there would be any major disadvantages.

1 A document sent alongside an email message is called:

   a recipient   a template   an attachment
   a browser (1 mark)

2 A business consultant has warned Jim that having a website can be costly for his business. Give two reasons why this statement may be true and explain them. (6 marks)

3 Explain the likely advantages to Hesturnton Sports Shop of having a website. (9 marks)

4 Explain whether you think Jim should go ahead and have a website for the Hesturnton Sports Shop. (6 marks)

5 Jim likes to email his suppliers with his orders for stock. Give two reasons why email may well be the best method of doing this and explain your answer. (6 marks)

6 Jim did decide to have a website for the shop and, a year later, he is sure that having the website has helped him to expand his business and make more profit. Describe how this may have happened. (9 marks)

SECTION 4

ICT IN BUSINESS

Chapter 18

Selection and use of software

In this chapter you will learn:

- how to select and use appropriate software for different business situations
- the importance of accessing stored information
- how to analyse information
- what is qualitative data – numerical and graphical data
- what is quantitative data – internal and external sources
- the characteristics of different software
- the use of local and wide area networks.

Getting started

You will have been given a variety of information about many different subjects over the years you have been at school. There will have been many occasions when you will have been told how to display the information, such as in graphs and charts in maths and in tables in science subjects. In the working environment, your employer will expect you to know which method of displaying data (information) will be most suitable for the task in hand. Do you display the work in a chart? Or in a report? Or in a PowerPoint presentation? Or even as a database or spreadsheet? The method you choose will depend on various factors, including the audience you are preparing the information for. It is therefore important that the method chosen is the correct one.

Different businesses will require different software for their day-to-day tasks. The user will need to decide what they want to produce before selecting the software. Do you ever think about whether the software you are going to use for different tasks in lessons is appropriate?

What you need to know

Software applications are constantly developing and changing, with new ones being introduced and existing ones being improved. Think about Windows XP and how this has now evolved to become Windows Vista. Have you ever used Windows Vista? Is there much difference between it and Windows XP?

The software that different businesses use will depend on the tasks that need to be carried out. It is important that users consider the type of data that is being used.

Qualitative data

Qualitative data is text-based data. It can range from letters to information leaflets. Appropriate software for presenting this sort of data includes Word or Publisher. Each software package enables the user easily to type, edit and save documents such as letters. Word is particularly useful for letters, as a standard letter can be saved and amended according to the user.

Think about letters that you have received from school. Have you ever wondered how each letter is addressed to pupils individually? Imagine Sainsbury's were trying to send promotional letters to all their Nectar card customers – it would take ages to type out each letter individually! Word has a tool that allows information from a spreadsheet or database to be 'mail merged'. This means that key information, such as names and addresses, can be linked to letters without having to type out the information separately for each letter.

Quantitative data

Quantitative data is numerical- and graphical-based data. Examples could include sales figures, showing information about the past and the present in a graphical format so that it can be compared easily.

Think about how your school could plot your attendance over the school year. It can give you the information by working out the percentages for each term or, to make it easier, it could display the information in a graph.

Organisations often have weekly meetings at which figures are discussed. Michael Sant works for Aston Martin and his role is to review the stock. As there are lots of parts needed to make an Aston Martin, Michael has to keep track of wastage each month. In a meeting, Michael will use data, but will also use a visual aid in the form of a graph to support his presentation.

Spreadsheet and database software are two packages that would help schools and Aston Martin to display numerical and graphical information in an effective way.

Characteristics of word processing software

Many word processing programs now have features similar to those of desktop publishing software. They can be used to create a variety of business documents, from business cards to leaflets. In both kinds of software you can use a wide variety of fonts, colours and formatting techniques such as italics and bold. It is also easy to import diagrams and pictures into documents. Generally, text can be created in a number of columns and printed either landscape or portrait. It is easy to create tables in the software, and page numbers can be generated automatically.

Characteristics of presentation software

Presentation software is used only for creating presentations in the form of a slide show. It is frequently used with a projector and shown to a number of people, and because of this it is important that there are not too many words on each slide.

Slides can be multimedia and include sound and video. They can be printed as handouts with more than one slide per page and space for the audience to make their notes. A presenter giving a slide show will usually prepare notes for himself or herself using the same software. Within the slide show, transitions can be set between the slides so that they move independently and animations can be created for text or pictures to enter and leave the slide. Backgrounds can be created; these should be consistent and used with care so as not to detract from the presentation.

Characteristics of spreadsheets

Spreadsheets can be formatted in the same way as in word processed documents, using colour and different fonts with formats such as bold, italic and underline. Cells can be shaded in colour or greyscale to enhance their appearance. Spreadsheets can be used to create charts or graphs.

Characteristics of databases

Databases can be used to store information and then to create reports on specific queries. When you set up a database you specify the fields that are needed to store the data, and the type of data to be used in each field. For example, in a database about pet dogs you may have a field for weight in kilograms: the data type will be numerical. Data is stored in a table but can be entered via a form.

A relational database contains a number of tables with at least one common field. The common field links the tables and enables queries to be made that combine information from all the linked tables.

Factors that influence software choice

There are several general points to consider when selecting the most appropriate software.

- The type of information is an important factor, but consideration must also be given to where the data comes from. Internal data can include sales figures, customer details and staff information. It is information that the organisation is able to gather easily from its own records. External data can be found from government statistics, journals and competitors' information. It is information that the organisation can use, which has been collected for another organisation.
- If the user wants to produce an information sheet, leaflet or letter, and the information is mainly text based, the most appropriate software is likely to be a word-processing package, such as Word. Word will also allow the user to insert tables and graphics, such as a company logo to make the document look more professional.
- If the user wants to include a mixture of images and text to produce a promotional leaflet, then desktop publishing software such as Publisher would be ideal. The user could also use a page template to help lay out their work appropriately.
- If the user wants to do calculations and include graphs, then spreadsheet software such as Excel would be most appropriate. The user will also be able to merge information from the spreadsheet into a letter.
- If the user wants to hold information about staff or customers, then database software such as Access would be most appropriate. This software would also allow the user to produce reports based on the data.

All software packages allow the user to edit, save and delete their documents as necessary.

Local and wide area networks

A local area network (LAN) is a network, either connected by wires or wireless, which is usually contained within a single physical boundary. It links computers to each other or to a server, enabling computer users to share files and resources such as printers and back-up systems. In your school or college, computers are probably connected by a LAN so that you can see your files whichever computer you are working on.

Wide area networks (WAN) are networks that cross physical boundaries; a WAN may cover a wide geographical area such as a town or may even cross countries. It enables sites to be linked together; for example, your school or college may be linked to other schools in your Local Education Authority by a WAN.

Let's go!

Activities

1 Think about your doctor's surgery.
   a) What software would it use to keep your personal details?
   b) What software would it use to keep a record of all the appointments for each day?
2 Think about your school.
   a) How does your school keep you informed of important dates?
   b) What software do you think it would use to do this?
   c) How could your English teacher display the results of a test?
   d) Which would be better for displaying the results – a table of figures or a graph?
3 Think about a fast food restaurant.
   a) How could the restaurant keep track of the number of bread buns that go to waste each week?
   b) What software would allow the restaurant to calculate the weekly waste?
   c) Apart from the displaying the waste in a table, how else could spreadsheet software display the results?

Summary

- Using the most appropriate software will not only enable the user to complete their job effectively, it can also affect how customers perceive the company.
- Handwritten documents can be tatty and unprofessional, whereas a neatly typed document is much neater and more professional.
- Consideration should be given to the type of data that will be included within the document. Calculations cannot be carried out and graphs created using word-processing software, and tables containing hundreds of customer details would not be stored using a graphics package. You would need spreadsheet and database software respectively for these tasks.

Key words

Quantitative data – numerical and graphical information.

Qualitative data – text-based information.

Internal source of information – information taken from inside the business, such as sales.

External source of information – information collected by another source; often includes statistics such as demographics.

Relational database – a database that contains multiple tables which are linked by common fields.

Give me five

Give five ways you could format a word-processed document.

Exam style questions

1. Give an example of quantitative data. (1 mark)
2. Identify two internal sources of information that a business could use to create a graph. (2 marks)
3. Explain why spreadsheet software would be used to record monthly sales, rather than database software. (6 marks)
4. Describe what software features you would use to create a presentation about sixth-form courses for an audience of parents. (9 marks)

Chapter 19

Word processing

In this chapter you will learn:

- how to create a business letter
- how to display an advertisement
- how to produce a flyer.

Getting started

Letters are still used throughout the world as a means of communication between one company and another. However, there has been a decline in the number of letters that companies send to each other and this will probably continue into the future, as more and more people turn to faster and more efficient methods of communicating.

However, people will still need to advertise their company, product or service, so effective advertisements will still need to be created. Flyers will still be produced to inform people about events, such as courses being run at a local college, or about the particular products or service offered by a company.

What you need to know

Letters

A letter can be seen as your 'ambassador', representing you to the recipient, so it is important that it is good and makes the correct impression. A well-written, well-presented letter with no mistakes will certainly create a much better impression than one that is full of errors or poorly presented.

It is important that your letter is accurate and clear, so the reader is not confused and can easily understand what you have written. There are some basic rules that will help you to achieve this:

- Avoid using slang words or phrases that someone else might not understand.
- Avoid using abbreviations, for example using 'don't' instead of 'do not'.
- Try and write in a more formal style.

Layout of letters

Most companies will have their own preferred style of layout, known as their 'house style'. Many will also have a template that can be used for all letters, which makes it much easier to follow their house style.

The most common layout for a business letter is described as 'open punctuated and fully blocked'. This means that every single line begins at the left-hand margin (rather than indenting the first line of each paragraph). Punctuation is only used in the body or message of the letter, as show in the example below.

Check your work carefully

Sometimes you will have to rewrite your letter several times, so it is much easier and quicker if you can word process it. Make sure that you spell-check your work very carefully as silly errors will stand out to the person reading the letter. Spell-checkers are good, but you will need to be very careful when using them. Remember that some spell-checkers are American, so words are spelt differently – you can change the

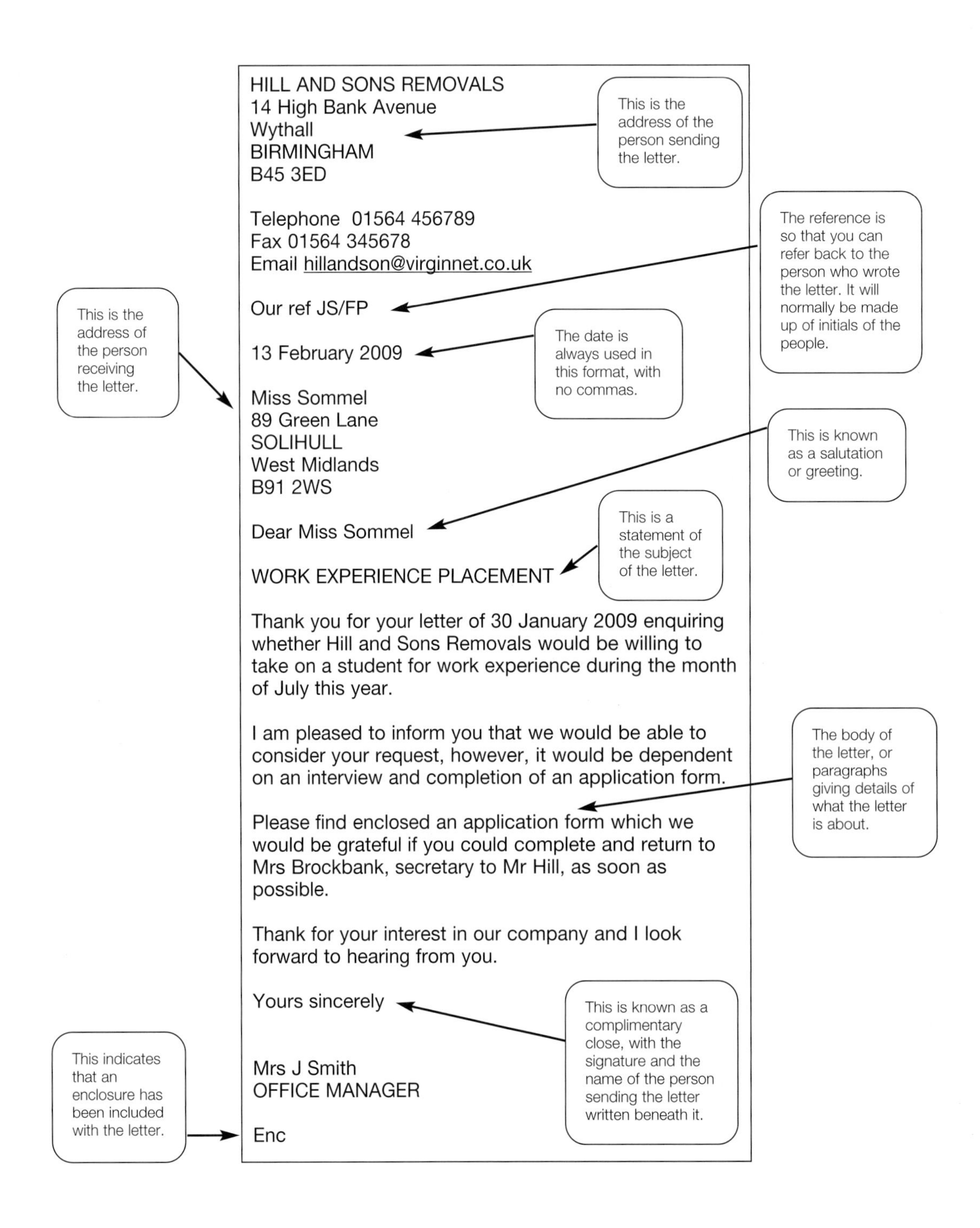

HILL AND SONS REMOVALS
14 High Bank Avenue
Wythall
BIRMINGHAM
B45 3ED

Telephone 01564 456789
Fax 01564 345678
Email hillandson@virginnet.co.uk

Our ref JS/FP

13 February 2009

Miss Sommel
89 Green Lane
SOLIHULL
West Midlands
B91 2WS

Dear Miss Sommel

WORK EXPERIENCE PLACEMENT

Thank you for your letter of 30 January 2009 enquiring whether Hill and Sons Removals would be willing to take on a student for work experience during the month of July this year.

I am pleased to inform you that we would be able to consider your request, however, it would be dependent on an interview and completion of an application form.

Please find enclosed an application form which we would be grateful if you could complete and return to Mrs Brockbank, secretary to Mr Hill, as soon as possible.

Thank for your interest in our company and I look forward to hearing from you.

Yours sincerely

Mrs J Smith
OFFICE MANAGER

Enc

'language' setting in some software so that it uses UK rather than US English. Also, a spell-checker will only highlight words that are not in its dictionary – it will miss words that are spelt correctly but used wrongly, for example if 'there' is used instead of 'their' or 'form' instead of 'from'.

Make sure that your tone and manner are appropriate for the letter you are writing. It helps if you leave an important letter for a short time and then go back and reread it to see if it makes sense and reads the way you would like it to. It might also be useful to ask someone else to check it for you.

Ensure that you are consistent throughout the letter. If you are writing in the first person, using 'I', then continue throughout and do not change to 'we' halfway through as this may confuse the reader.

Advertisements

Advertisements are used in a variety of situations, from providing information about an organisation's services or products to persuading a customer to buy a product. Organisations from small independent retailers to large multinationals will use advertisements.

There are advantages and disadvantages to using advertisements, and care needs to be taken when preparing them. There are many different types of advertisement, including those in magazines, on billboards and on television.

Advertisements may appear to be simple to design, but great care needs to be taken to ensure that the information is correct. There are many arguments for and against advertising, but all advertisements must comply with certain regulations. They can be very powerful and so must not mislead or exploit consumers in any way. There are codes of practice and laws designed to protect the consumer.

The Advertising Standards Authority (ASA) is responsible for monitoring all advertising in the United Kingdom. It makes sure that advertisers obey the rules of the British Code of Advertising, Sales Promotion and Direct Marketing. This is a voluntary agreement which stresses that advertisements and promotions must be legal, decent, honest and truthful and must not cause widespread offence. It covers all newspapers, magazines, cinema adverts, leaflets, brochures and posters, but not radio and television advertising.

There are a number of different software programs that can be used to create paper-based advertisements. Most small-business owners are now able to design and create their own promotional material instead of having someone else do it for them. This can be time saving and cost effective. Most small companies will use either a word-processing program or a desktop publishing program, although a DTP program is really more suitable. Some companies be even more adventurous and use a drawing package. In general, people are now more computer literate and can use drawing programs without much training or prior knowledge.

Advantages	Disadvantages
Information is clear.	There is no feedback from the audience on the impact.
They are an interesting and engaging way of informing audiences.	Is the message understood and received?
They can be animated as films or videos, which may make more of an impression.	The audience is limited to those who actually see them.

Creating an advertisement

Jackie, Sian and Megan run a small chain of hairdressers called Just for You. Megan has gained qualifications in ICT at school and is very keen to use her skills and knowledge to help the company and save money. She knows that the advertisements can be produced quickly and can then be edited and updated quite cheaply on a regular basis for all the salons in the chain.

Follow the instructions below to create a basic advertisement for Just for You hairdressers.

1 Open the program Microsoft Publisher.

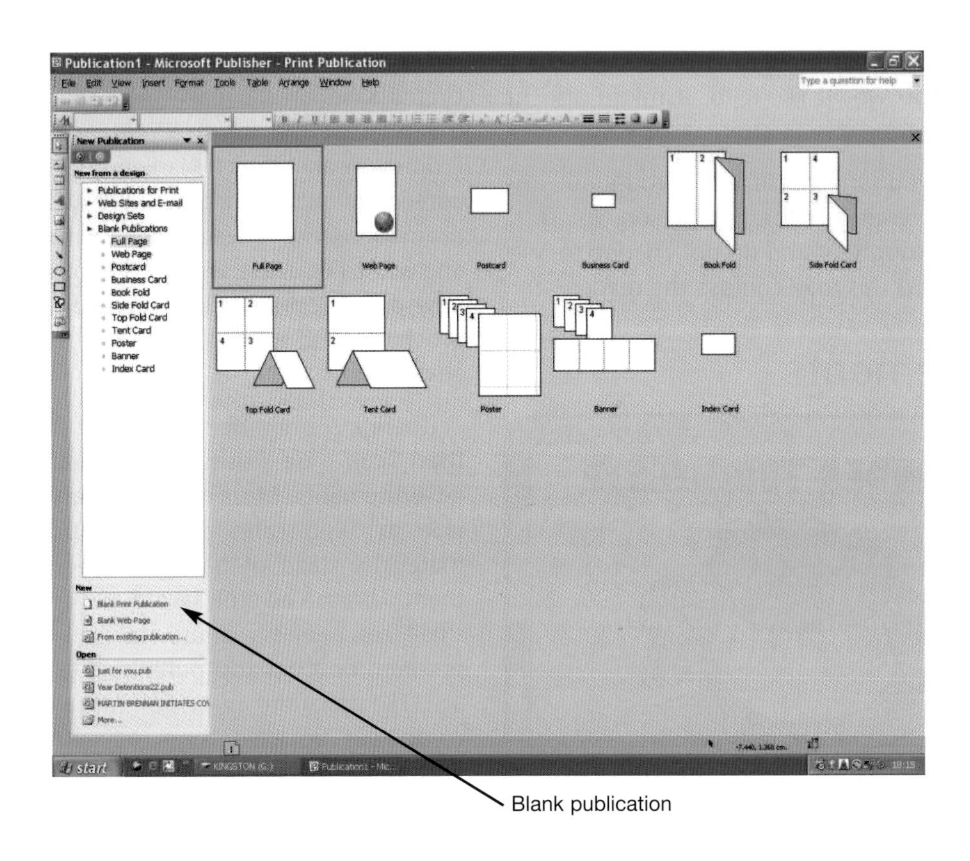

2 Select a blank publication. There are many different ways you can present your work – study the examples shown above.

3 Select a 'Full Page' and click on 'Blank Print Publication'.

4 You can use WordArt to make the heading more appealing for people to read. Using the tool bar at the top of the program, you can then add different styles and fonts and move the work around the page.

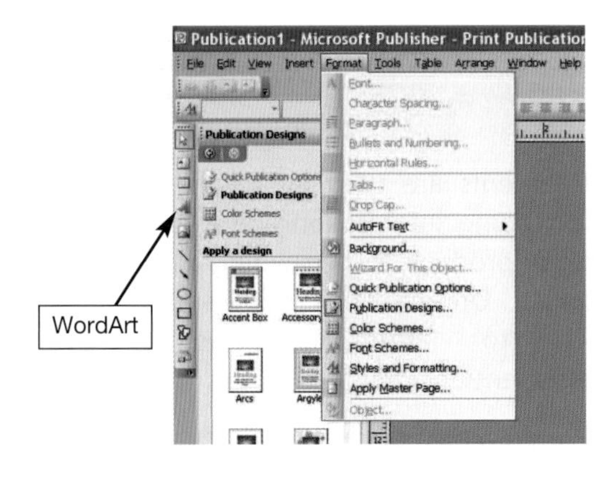

5 Click on 'Format' and use the drop-down menu.

6 You may now wish to add pictures to your advertisement by clicking either on the clipart tool in the menu at the side of the screen, or getting a picture from the internet and adding this to your work. An easy way of doing this is to use the computer's copy and paste facility. Remember to save special fonts or pictures that you want to use, especially if copying them from the internet.

7 You then build up your advertisement by adding text boxes or pictures. The more practice you have using the program the more features you can add to your document.

Remember to avoid going outside the blue box, and always check your work before printing. You will need to check for spelling errors as well as layout. Going to 'Print Preview' will give you an idea of what the advertisement will look like when printed on A4.

Flyers

Flyers are similar to advertisements – the only difference is the way you will lay your work out. If using Publisher then you might decide to choose the 'Book Fold' option.

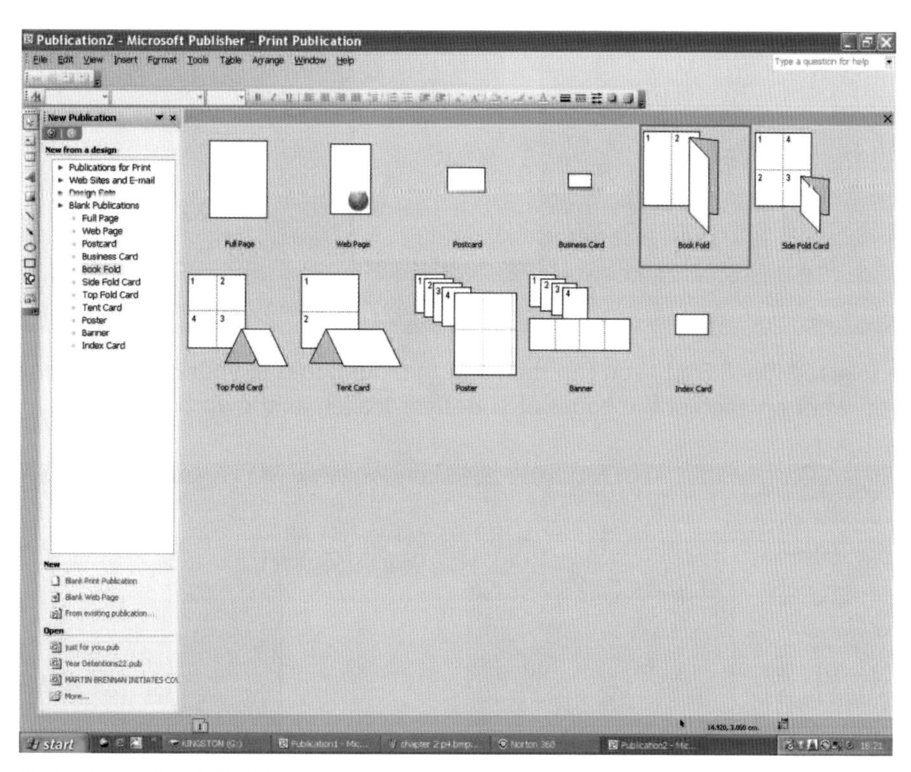

Selecting 'Book Fold'

This will allow you to work on the different sides of the flyer or leaflet, and when you have finished you will know where to fold the document.

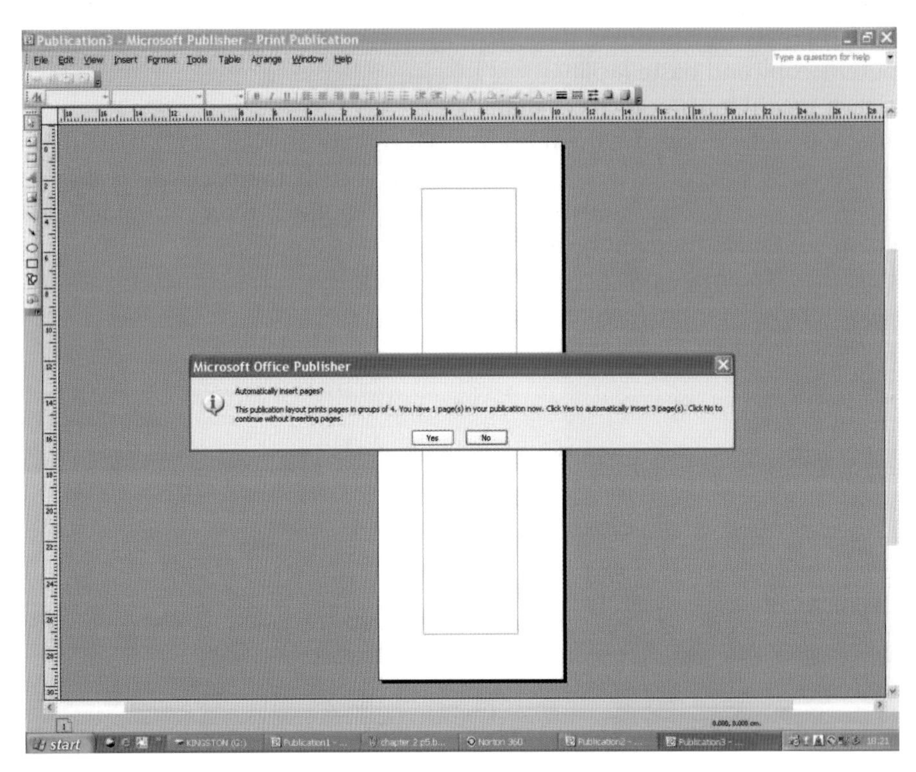

Once you have selected 'Book Fold', you can then add the four pages to your document and begin to display the information you want on each of the pages of your flyer/leaflet, as shown below.

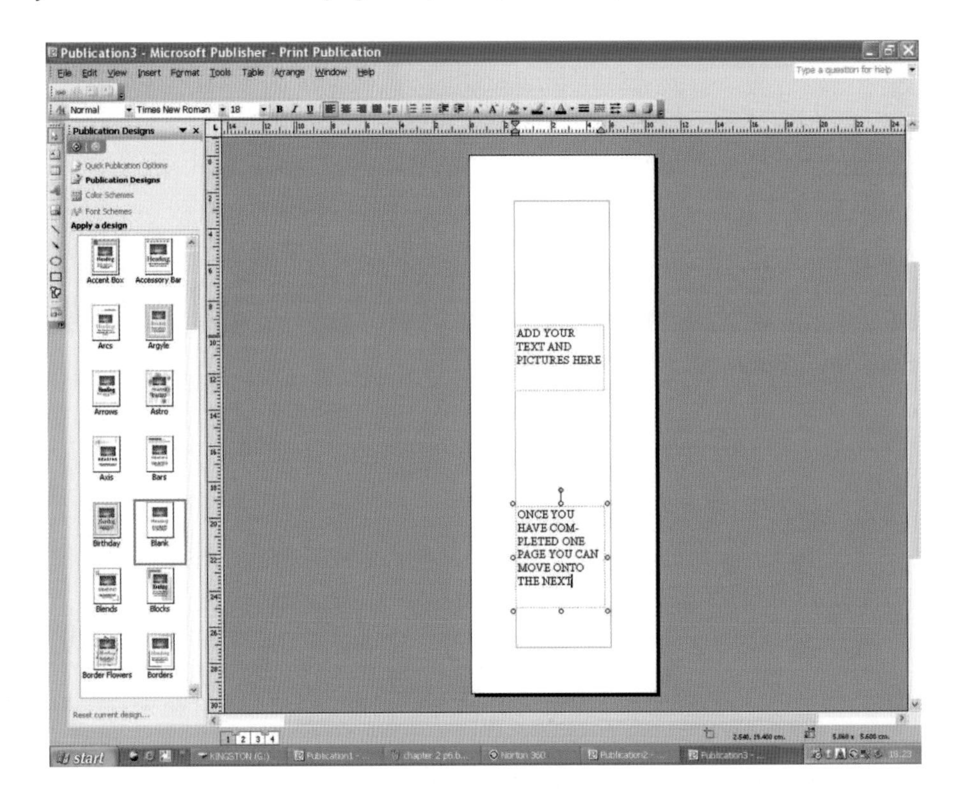

You can see below how to add information to the other pages. Remember that you can still use the other functions that Publisher offers, such as WordArt, adding pictures from clipart or even getting pictures from the internet.

There are many different ways to display your work and they can be as complicated or as colourful as you wish. The design is really up to you and how you want your work to look.

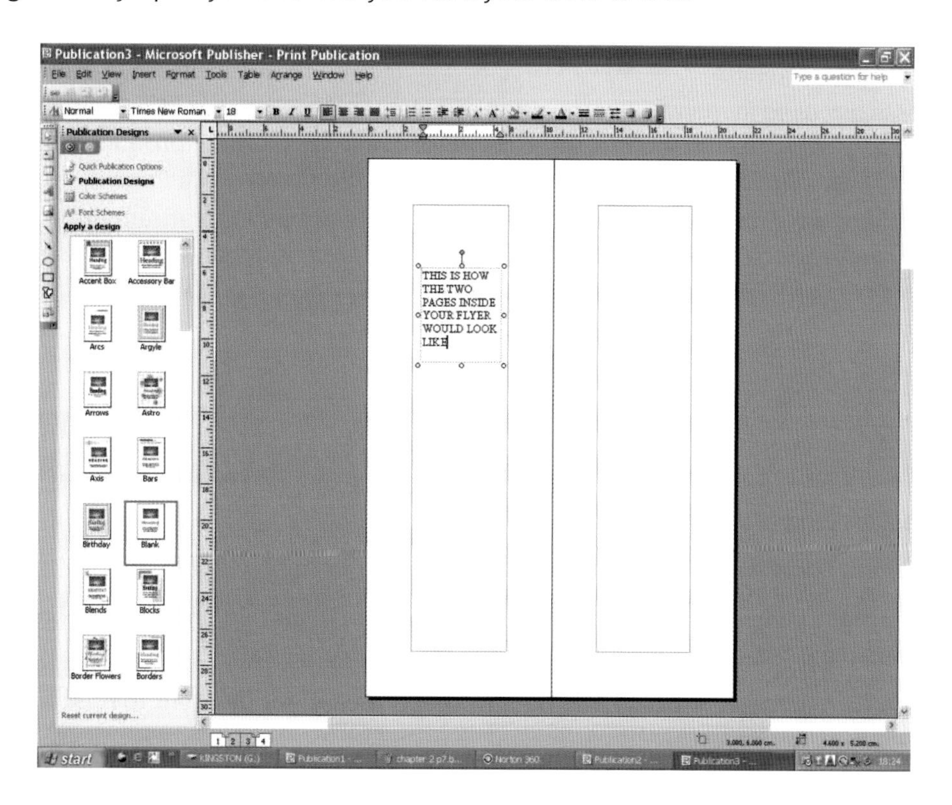

Let's go!

Activities

1 In pairs, try to collect examples of the following:

a) a letter

b) a newsletter

c) a flyer

d) different advertisements.

Look at the different examples you have collected and decide among yourselves which one has the most appealing layout. Suggest how the others could be improved.

2 Design your own logo to add to your letters as part of your letter heading. You might have several ideas which you could share with your friends, asking for their opinion on which is more suitable.

3 Find a job advertisement and write a letter of application for the position. In groups or pairs, discuss whether you have covered everything that is needed to meet the requirements of the advertisement.

4 Design a chart to help with letter writing. It could be set as a list of Do's and Don'ts. You may need to refer to other reference books to help you, or ask friends and family for their suggestions.

Summary

- Letters are still used in many businesses today, although the number being sent is on the decline.
- When you have written a letter, it is important that you check your work carefully to ensure that what you have written is exactly what you mean. Try to avoid any possibility of confusing the reader.
- These days, letters are used mostly in situations where copies are required, for example a copy may be required for legal reasons.
- Advertisements are used in many different situations, from advertising on eBay to sell something that belongs to you, to advertising jobs in a local paper or publicising a new product that has just come on the market. Their aim is to attract the attention of the target market.
- Flyers and leaflets are similar to advertisements in that they are used to attract attention and market something. However, they usually contain slightly more information than an advertisement.

Key words

Letter – a formal method of communication.

Flyer – a type of advertisement sent out by companies in the form of a leaflet.

Newsletter – a report that gives information which is of interest to certain groups of people, for example the members of a club.

Template – used as a framework which can be saved and reused for different things.

Give me five

1. Look at the following websites to help with writing letters and letter layout.
   www.learnenglish.org.uk
   www.writeexpress.com/sample-business-letters.html
2. Prepare a letter of application for when you leave school or are applying for a part-time job. This will save you time later and if something comes up you will have a letter already prepared.
3. Look at a selection of advertisements and analyse the information given on each one. You could use the ones on the display board outside your local newsagents. Write down the main headings in each advertisement.
4. Using a local paper, cut out the advertisements. Compare these with the advertisements you looked at in question 3. Is there more or less information in them? Explain any differences.
5. In a folder, keep a selection of letters, advertisements, flyers and leaflets and make a note of their good points and bad points. Keep this for future reference.

Exam style questions

You work for your local estate agents, Kelly Homes, Wythall Parade, 28 Hollywood Lane, Wythall, Birmingham B47 5QA. Telephone number 01564 561233, Fax 01564 561234, email kellyhomes@aol.com. You have been asked by the manager to carry out the following tasks while he is out of the office today.

1 Design a flyer that you could send out to the local community informing them that Kelly Homes is about to start letting houses and flats. You will need to include pictures of houses and flats for rent, details who applicants need to contact at Kelly Homes (Mr Turner, Lettings Manager), and at least two other details you think are appropriate. (15 marks)

2 Mr R Jones of 2 Middle Lane, Alcester AC23 2CV has phoned to enquire about selling his house through Kelly Homes. Design a letter head for Kelly Homes and prepare a letter to Mr Jones, thanking him for his telephone call. Inform him that you are sending a form with the letter, which he will need to complete and return as soon as possible. (15 marks)

3 Your next task is to display details of the house that has just come on the market. Include the following details:

- a picture of the house
- the address: 25 Bunbury Road, Wythall, Birmingham B56 3ER
- viewing through agent only
- 5 deluxe bedrooms
- 2 en suite bathrooms
- 1 family bathroom
- double garage
- lounge
- dining room
- gardens well maintained front and back
- see website for further details
- price offers over £410,000

(15 marks)

Chapter 20

Spreadsheets

In this chapter you will learn:

- how to create a spreadsheet for a business purpose
- how to format a spreadsheet
- how to manipulate data.

Getting started

How often have you seen people trying to work out which mobile phone company has the best tariff? With so many different providers and options, the amount of information often results in confusion. This is a similar situation to one organisations face, in that they have to keep track of lots of information, such as the number of hours each employee has worked each week, and then use this to make calculations. For example, they have to work out the total pay for all of their employees and subtract the tax that must be paid. This is a lengthy process and can be complicated if it is done manually.

What you need to know

The use of spreadsheet software such as Excel can ease the task of calculating the wages for staff. The range of functions available in Excel includes validation, conditional formatting, using formulas and even creating graphs.

Creating a spreadsheet

Many organisations use spreadsheets to record information, especially staff information, such as details about their wages. Hannah Thai owns The Flower Exchange florist shop and employs five people. She has found that calculating the wages by hand is time consuming and she often makes mistakes. She invests in a laptop and teaches herself to use Excel to create a spreadsheet to record and calculate staff wages.

Hannah uses the headings from the handwritten table that she uses to record the weekly wages. It is important to use appropriate headings so that it is clear what information each column contains and it is easy to refer to.

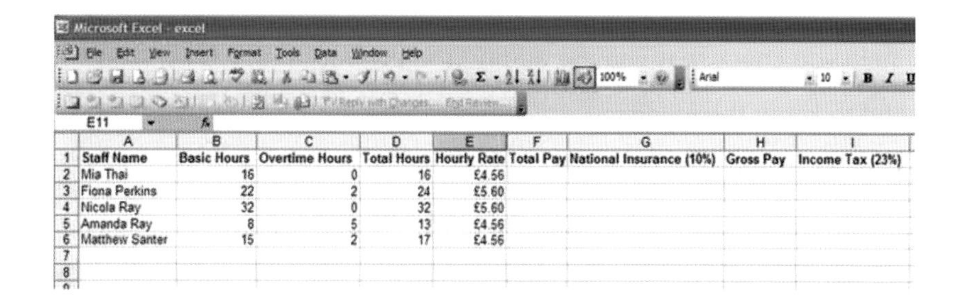

	A	B	C	D	E	F	G	H	I
1	Staff Name	Basic Hours	Overtime Hours	Total Hours	Hourly Rate	Total Pay	National Insurance (10%)	Gross Pay	Income Tax (23%)
2	Mia Thai	16	0	16	£4.56				
3	Fiona Perkins	22	2	24	£5.60				
4	Nicola Ray	32	0	32	£5.60				
5	Amanda Ray	8	5	13	£4.56				
6	Matthew Santer	15	2	17	£4.56				

As you can see, Hannah has entered the name of each employee. The next step is to fill in the basic hours, overtime hours and hourly rate for each employee.

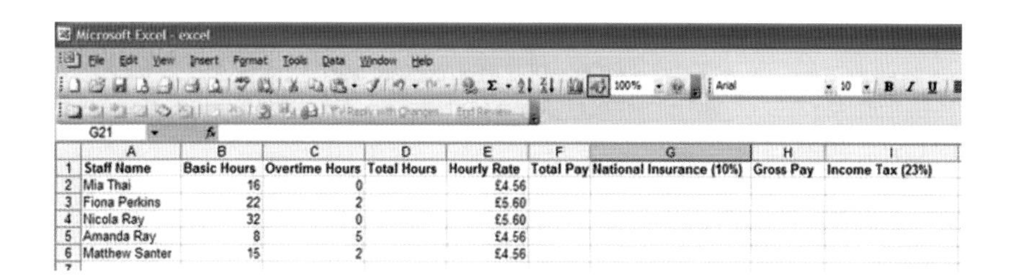

	A	B	C	D	E	F	G	H	I
1	Staff Name	Basic Hours	Overtime Hours	Total Hours	Hourly Rate	Total Pay	National Insurance (10%)	Gross Pay	Income Tax (23%)
2	Mia Thai	16	0		£4.56				
3	Fiona Perkins	22	2		£5.60				
4	Nicola Ray	32	0		£5.60				
5	Amanda Ray	8	5		£4.56				
6	Matthew Santer	15	2		£4.56				

Next, Hannah has to calculate the total hours and total pay. To do this she would use the formula function. This allows Hannah to calculate the total hours and total pay without using a calculator.

The following functions will be useful when you use formulas:

- A formula will always start with = .
- To add two or more cells type in =sum(cell reference:cell reference).

Instead of using figures, Excel formulas use the cell reference to do calculations. Think about the game 'battleships', or reading the co-ordinates of a map. A letter and a number are usually used to indicate a point on the grid. For example B4 is the cell that is in row 4, column B which, in the example below, is 32.

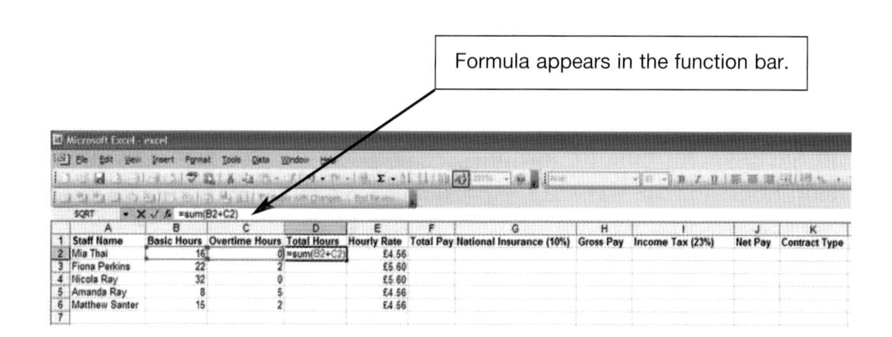

	A	B	C	D	E	F	G	H	I	J	K
1	Staff Name	Basic Hours	Overtime Hours	Total Hours	Hourly Rate	Total Pay	National Insurance (10%)	Gross Pay	Income Tax (23%)	Net Pay	Contract Type
2	Mia Thai	16	0	=sum(B2+C2)	£4.56						
3	Fiona Perkins	22	2		£5.60						
4	Nicola Ray	32	0		£5.60						
5	Amanda Ray	8	5		£4.56						
6	Matthew Santer	15	2		£4.56						

Can you see how the formula appears in the function bar? The cells that you are adding together are also highlighted. This will help you check that you are adding the correct numbers.

You may find it useful to know the following signs that can be used:

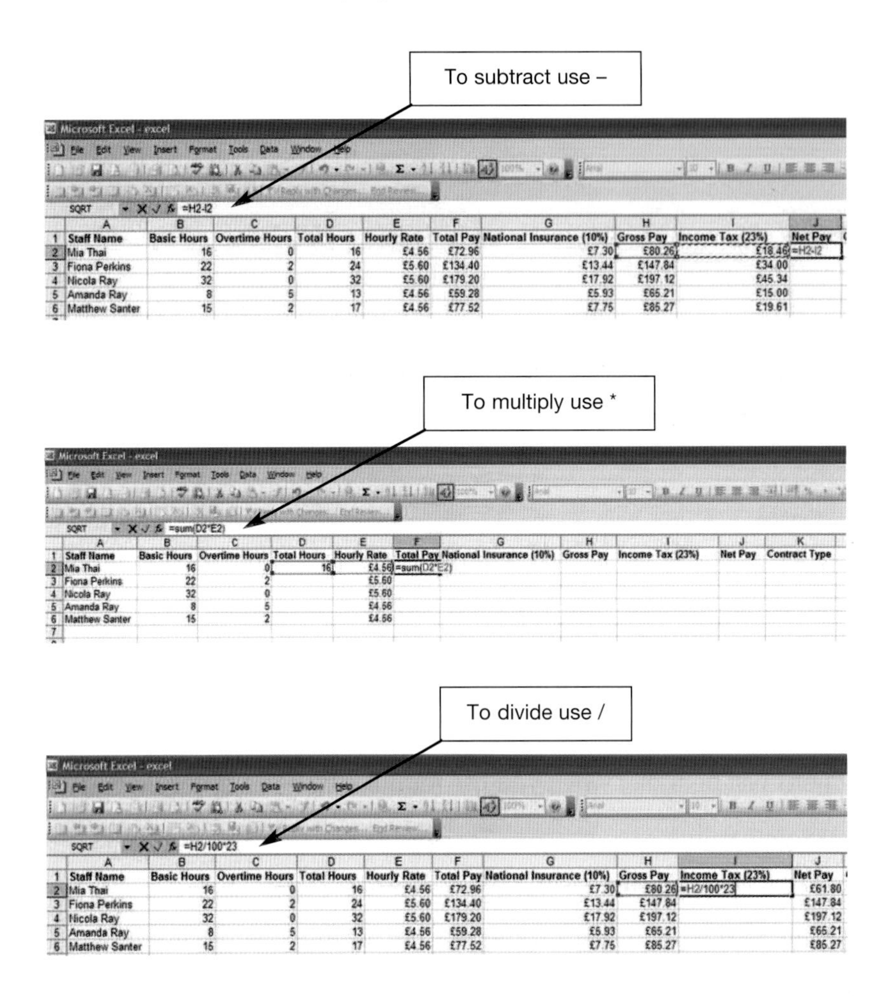

Hannah has used a combination of division and multiplication to find the percentage that needs to be subtracted for tax. (Please note these are not the actual formulas used when calculating tax payments).

Hannah has used an AVERAGE formula to find out the average total working hours for the week.

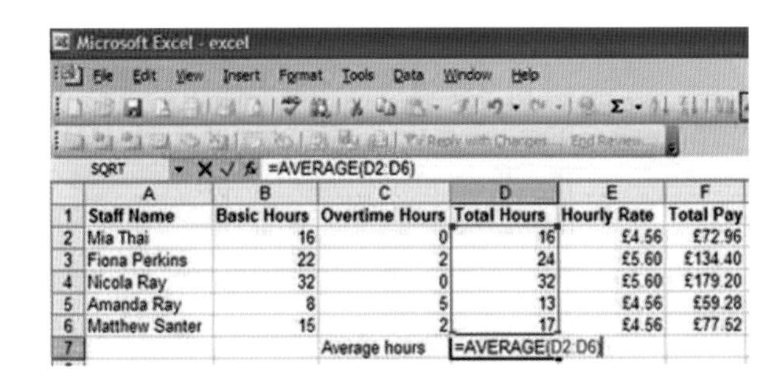

The answer appears once she has pressed enter.

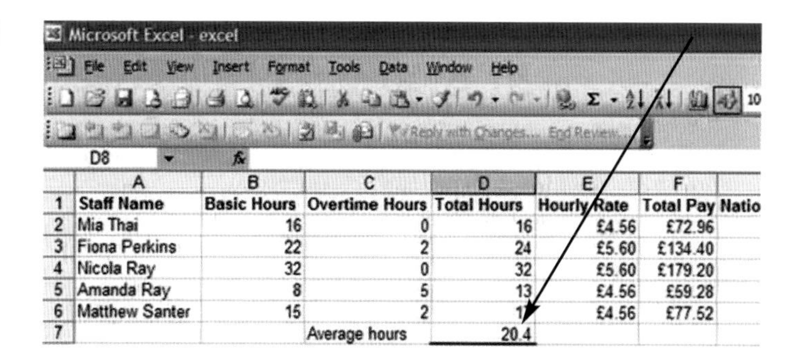

D8

	A	B	C	D	E	F	
1	Staff Name	Basic Hours	Overtime Hours	Total Hours	Hourly Rate	Total Pay	Natio
2	Mia Thai	16	0	16	£4.56	£72.96	
3	Fiona Perkins	22	2	24	£5.60	£134.40	
4	Nicola Ray	32	0	32	£5.60	£179.20	
5	Amanda Ray	8	5	13	£4.56	£59.28	
6	Matthew Santer	15	2	17	£4.56	£77.52	
7			Average hours	20.4			

Hannah can also use the IF function, which is like a 'true' or 'false' question. For Hannah's purposes she wants to check which staff members are full time and which are part time. She does this by using the basic hours. As you can see, Hannah has typed =IF in the function bar, and then the number of the cell that she wants to be used.

Part-time staff work for 15 hours or less, so she wants 'part time' to be the result for these employees and 'full time' to be the result for those who work more than 15 hours. To find these she types in the formula shown in the function bar below.

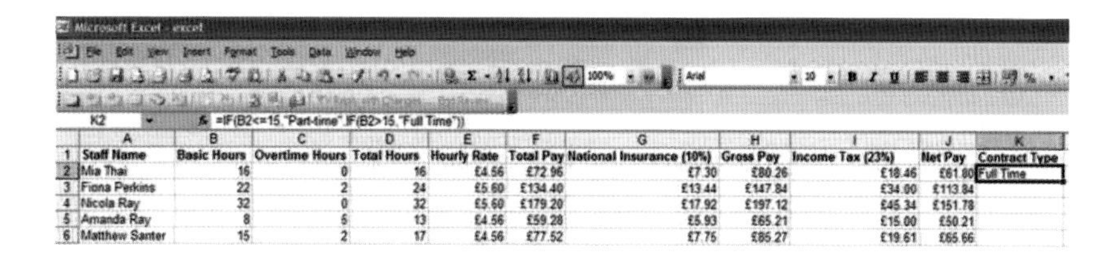

K2 =IF(B2<=15,"Part-time",IF(B2>15,"Full Time"))

	A	B	C	D	E	F	G	H	I	J	K
1	Staff Name	Basic Hours	Overtime Hours	Total Hours	Hourly Rate	Total Pay	National Insurance (10%)	Gross Pay	Income Tax (23%)	Net Pay	Contract Type
2	Mia Thai	16	0	16	£4.56	£72.96	£7.30	£80.26	£18.46	£61.80	Full Time
3	Fiona Perkins	22	2	24	£5.60	£134.40	£13.44	£147.84	£34.00	£113.84	
4	Nicola Ray	32	0	32	£5.60	£179.20	£17.92	£197.12	£45.34	£151.78	
5	Amanda Ray	8	5	13	£4.56	£59.28	£5.93	£65.21	£15.00	£50.21	
6	Matthew Santer	15	2	17	£4.56	£77.52	£7.75	£85.27	£19.61	£65.66	

As you can see from the results, she has two part-time staff and three full-time staff. Rather than retyping the formula, she can just copy and paste it when she adds a new member of staff.

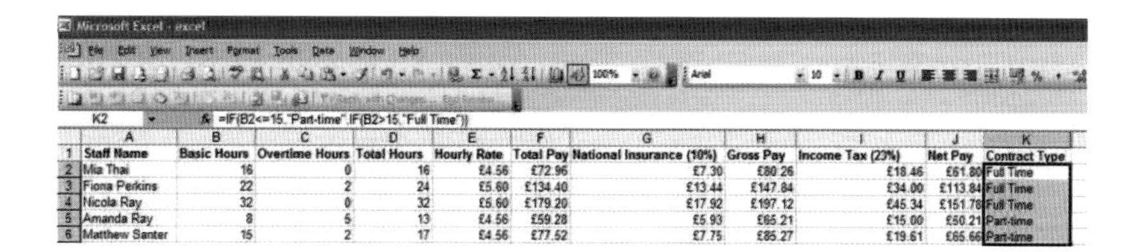

K2 =IF(B2<=15,"Part-time",IF(B2>15,"Full Time"))

	A	B	C	D	E	F	G	H	I	J	K
1	Staff Name	Basic Hours	Overtime Hours	Total Hours	Hourly Rate	Total Pay	National Insurance (10%)	Gross Pay	Income Tax (23%)	Net Pay	Contract Type
2	Mia Thai	16	0	16	£4.56	£72.96	£7.30	£80.26	£18.46	£61.80	Full Time
3	Fiona Perkins	22	2	24	£5.60	£134.40	£13.44	£147.84	£34.00	£113.84	Full Time
4	Nicola Ray	32	0	32	£5.60	£179.20	£17.92	£197.12	£45.34	£151.78	Full Time
5	Amanda Ray	8	5	13	£4.56	£59.28	£5.93	£65.21	£15.00	£50.21	Part-time
6	Matthew Santer	15	2	17	£4.56	£77.52	£7.75	£85.27	£19.61	£65.66	Part-time

As Hannah plans to update the information on a weekly basis, she will need to record the date and who has edited the information. This can be done by inserting a header and footer. Hannah decides to use a header to name her spreadsheet, as shown on the next page.

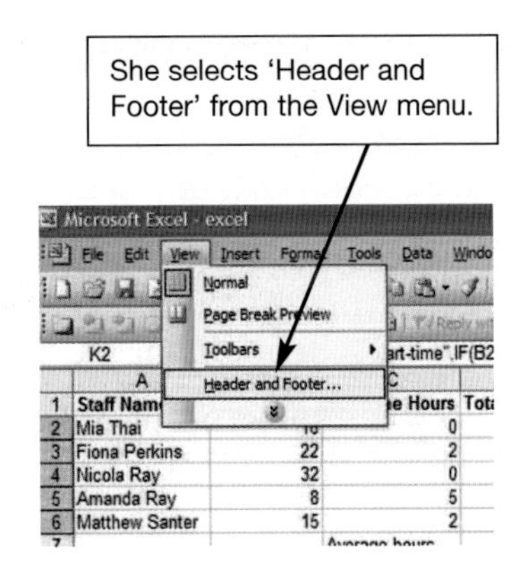

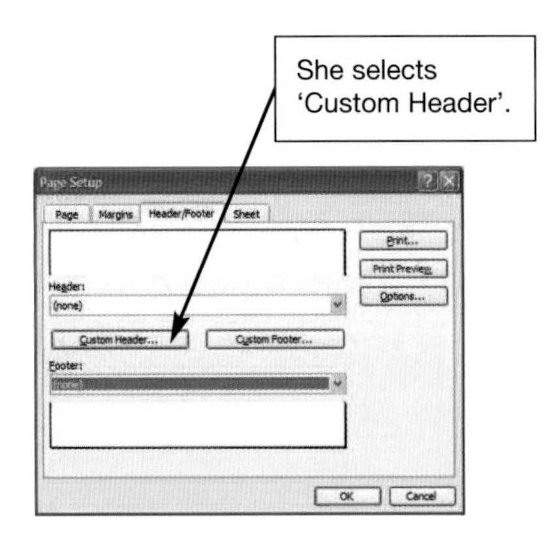

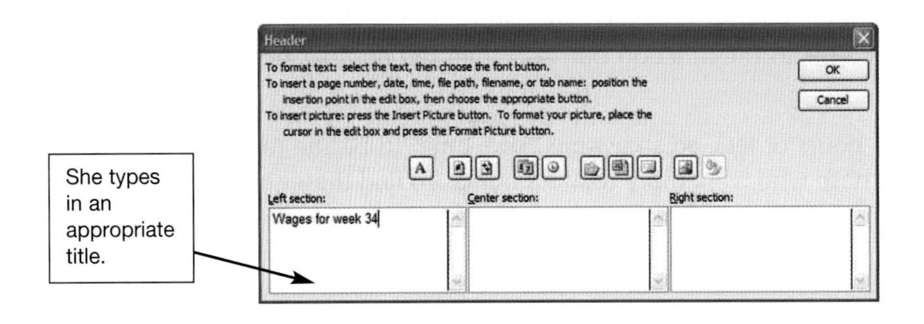

She then inserts a footer to record who updated the sheet.

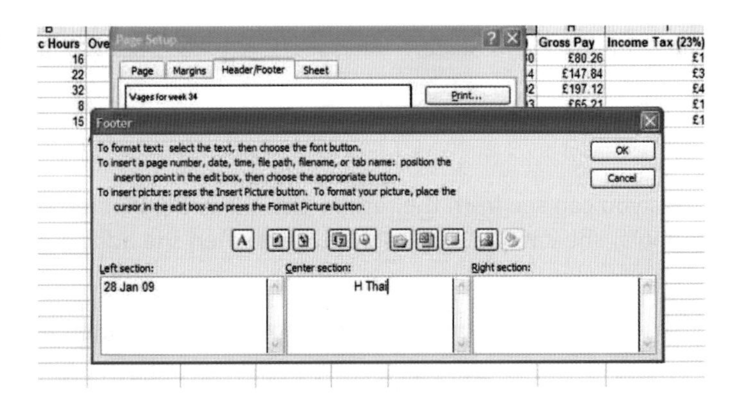

To check, she can use the 'Print Preview' to see the header and footer, which will not show in the normal view.

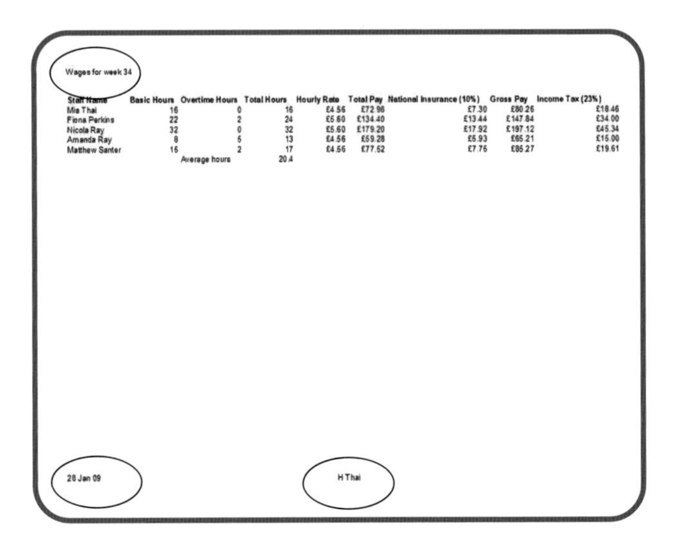

If hashes appear in a cell, this means that the cell is too narrow and the width needs adjusting. The easiest way to increase the width of the cell is to place the cursor on the line between the two cells that need increasing.

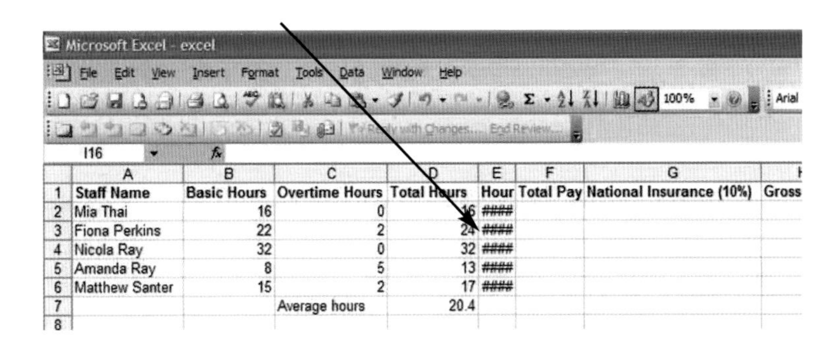

	A	B	C	D	E	F	G	H
1	Staff Name	Basic Hours	Overtime Hours	Total Hours	Hour	Total Pay	National Insurance (10%)	Gross
2	Mia Thai	16	0	16	####			
3	Fiona Perkins	22	2	24	####			
4	Nicola Ray	32	0	32	####			
5	Amanda Ray	8	5	13	####			
6	Matthew Santer	15	2	17	####			
7			Average hours	20.4				
8								

In this example, Hannah would place the cursor on the line between columns E and F. She then needs to click and drag the line across until the cell is wide enough.

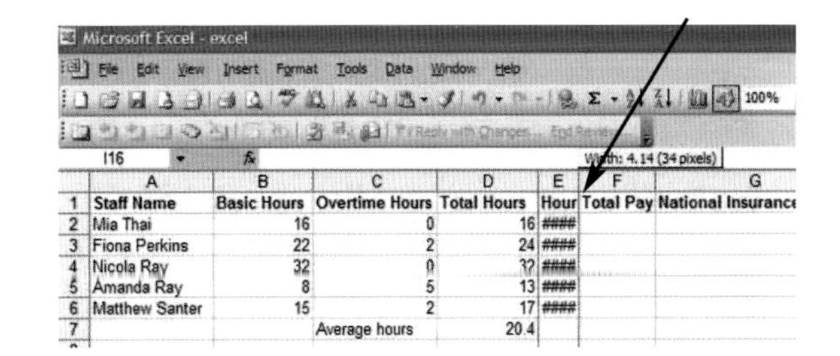

	A	B	C	D	E	F	G
1	Staff Name	Basic Hours	Overtime Hours	Total Hours	Hour	Total Pay	National Insurance
2	Mia Thai	16	0	16	####		
3	Fiona Perkins	22	2	24	####		
4	Nicola Ray	32	0	32	####		
5	Amanda Ray	8	5	13	####		
6	Matthew Santer	15	2	17	####		
7			Average hours	20.4			

Once the column width is widened, she should be able to read the figures.

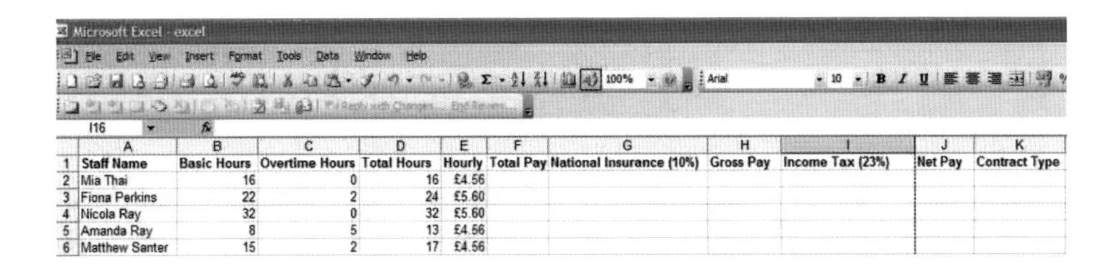

	A	B	C	D	E	F	G	H	I	J	K
1	Staff Name	Basic Hours	Overtime Hours	Total Hours	Hourly	Total Pay	National Insurance (10%)	Gross Pay	Income Tax (23%)	Net Pay	Contract Type
2	Mia Thai	16	0	16	£4.56						
3	Fiona Perkins	22	2	24	£5.60						
4	Nicola Ray	32	0	32	£5.60						
5	Amanda Ray	8	5	13	£4.56						
6	Matthew Santer	15	2	17	£4.56						

Let's go!

Activities

1 Below are the monthly sales for Bobbin Baskin's ice cream. The manager has asked you to do the following:

a) Copy the spreadsheet into appropriate spreadsheet software.

b) Insert an appropriate heading that will show the total amount of money made for each flavoured ice cream.

c) Calculate the total revenue for each ice cream.

d) Find the average number of cones sold that month.

e) Name your spreadsheet by inserting a header or footer.

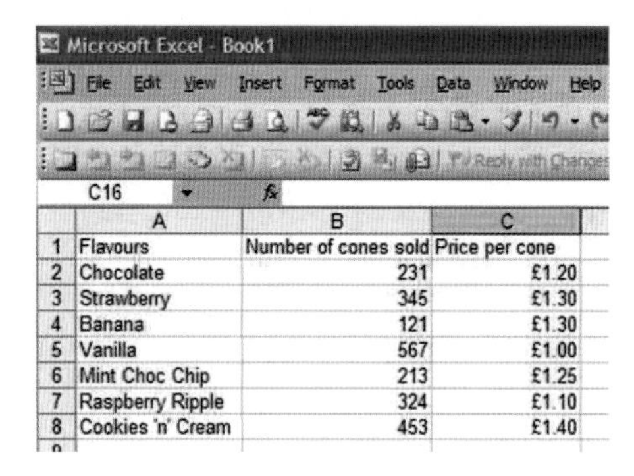

	A	B	C
1	Flavours	Number of cones sold	Price per cone
2	Chocolate	231	£1.20
3	Strawberry	345	£1.30
4	Banana	121	£1.30
5	Vanilla	567	£1.00
6	Mint Choc Chip	213	£1.25
7	Raspberry Ripple	324	£1.10
8	Cookies 'n' Cream	453	£1.40

2 May Lane Medical Centre is having problems recording the number of patients who miss, cancel or are late for their appointments. You have been asked to create a spreadsheet to record this information. You have been given information regarding the figures by month to enter into the spreadsheet. Remember to give each column an appropriate title and use a header or footer to name your sheet appropriately.

Missed appointments	Late arrivals	Cancelled appointments
Jan – 23 Feb – 12 Mar – 4 Apr – 13 May – 21 June – 10 July – 10	Jan – 41 Feb – 23 Mar – 12 Apr – 6 May – 34 June – 28 July – 9	Jan – 2 Feb – 6 Mar – 5 Apr – 10 May – 9 June – 21 July – 1

You are asked to calculate:

a) The total number of appointments that were cancelled.

b) The total number of appointments that were late.

c) The total number of appointments that were missed.

d) The average number of appointments that were missed over the seven-month period.

Summary

- Spreadsheets are extremely useful to all businesses.
- Spreadsheets can be used for a variety of purposes, with the added benefit of being able to include formulas that allow calculations to be done. However, the user needs to take care that the formula they write is accurate as this will affect their end result.
- By storing information in a spreadsheet format, it enables the user to save, edit and back up the information efficiently.

Key words

Cells – a box in the spreadsheet grid.

Cell referencing – use the co-ordinates of cells to reference them, e.g. A1 for the cell in column A, row 1, or G5 for the cell in column G row 5.

Columns – go down the page.

Rows – go across the page.

Formula – a way of calculating the information that is required.

Autosum – function on the computer to add up a range of numbers.

Autofill – by highlighting the cells you want the formula can be replicated.

Format – make changes to the cell or workbook.

Header – label at the top of the page. This will only appear in print preview or on print-outs.

Footer – label at the bottom of the page. This will only appear in print preview or on print-outs.

Give me five

1. What is a cell reference?
2. What is the symbol used to multiply?
3. What does / mean in a formula?
4. What does a formula always start with?
5. What is the difference between a row and a column?

Exam style questions

1 You have been asked to identify a certain cell on a spreadsheet. How could you do this? (2 marks)

2 What two types of data can be entered into a spreadsheet? (2 marks)

3 Katie runs a small corner shop and she wants to record all her costs and revenue on a spreadsheet. She enters her sales of 300 chocolate bars sold at 70p each into the spreadsheet. She types .70 into Cell B3, and the spreadsheet displays .7. Explain how the cell has been formatted to allow this to happen. (4 marks)

4 Katie has added a formula in cell C7 that will allow her to calculate the level of profit she will make. She wants to insert this formula up to cell K7. Explain how she can do this quickly. (2 marks)

5 Describe the ways in which any small business could utilise a spreadsheet in the operation of its business, identifying any benefits and drawbacks there might be. (4 marks)

6 What would the formula be if you wanted to find the average of cells A6 to A12? (2 marks)

7 How could the IF function be used within a spreadsheet? (2 marks)

8 Analyse the benefits of using spreadsheets in an organisation. (6 marks)

Chapter 21

Using spreadsheets to create charts

In this chapter you will learn:

- how to select data series to create charts
- how to select different charts
- how to insert titles, legends and other texts.

Getting started

Organisations use lots of data to help them monitor and review their performance. This data can often be confusing, especially if displayed as a list. Have you ever been to a presentation where the speaker used lots of figures? How did they present the information? Was it presented clearly?

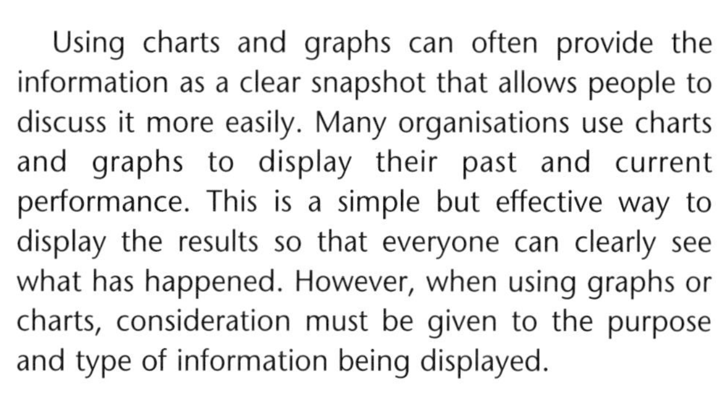

Using charts and graphs can often provide the information as a clear snapshot that allows people to discuss it more easily. Many organisations use charts and graphs to display their past and current performance. This is a simple but effective way to display the results so that everyone can clearly see what has happened. However, when using graphs or charts, consideration must be given to the purpose and type of information being displayed.

What you need to know

In this section we will look at how to create a graph and the different options available. Using appropriate software is very important. Spreadsheet software, such as Excel, allows the user to enter data and create a graph or chart based on the information they entered. Excel also has the advantage of a 'chart wizard', which guides the user through how to create a spreadsheet.

To create a graph, you will need to have information that you want to display. Hewell Swimming Leisure Centre wants to compare the weekly sales during peak and off-peak swimming times. The manager has given Amanda the data that she needs (see the table below) to create the graph.

Swimming times	Off-peak sales (£)	Peak sales (£)
Monday	121.00	56.90
Tuesday	134.00	121.00
Wednesday	120.00	67.00
Thursday	189.00	142.00
Friday	204.00	153.00
Saturday	198.00	101.00
Sunday	135.00	89.00

1 Amanda now needs to type this information into a spreadsheet, which will then look like the one below.

	A	B	C
1	Hewell Swimming Pool		
2			
3	Day	Off-Peak (£)	Peak (£)
4	Monday	£121.00	£56.90
5	Tuesday	£134.00	£121.00
6	Wednesday	£120.00	£67.00
7	Thursday	£189.00	£142.00
8	Friday	£204.00	£153.00
9	Saturday	£198.00	£101.00
10	Sunday	£135.00	£89.00
11	Total Sales	£1,101.00	£729.90

2 Amanda wants to present this information as a chart to make it easier to compare the different figures. First, she needs to highlight the data that she wants to include in the chart. Once she has selected the data, she then selects the 'Chart Wizard' from the tool bar.

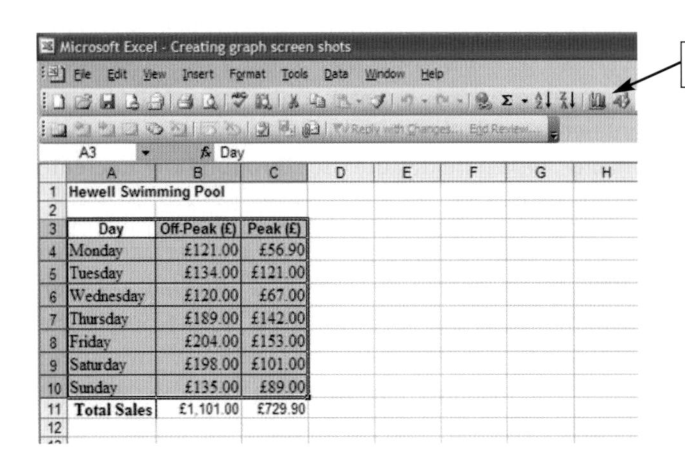

Chart Wizard

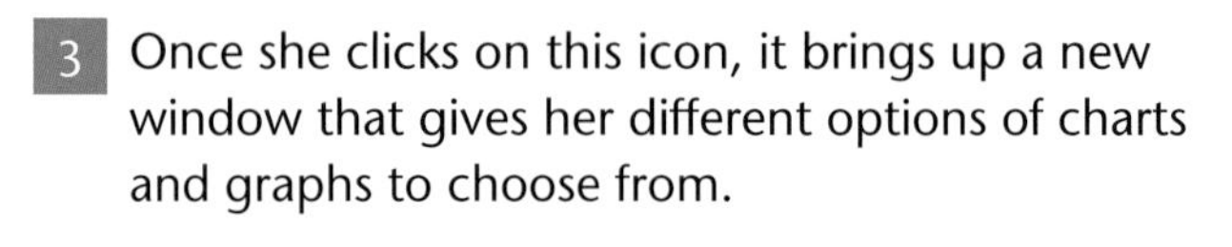
3 Once she clicks on this icon, it brings up a new window that gives her different options of charts and graphs to choose from.

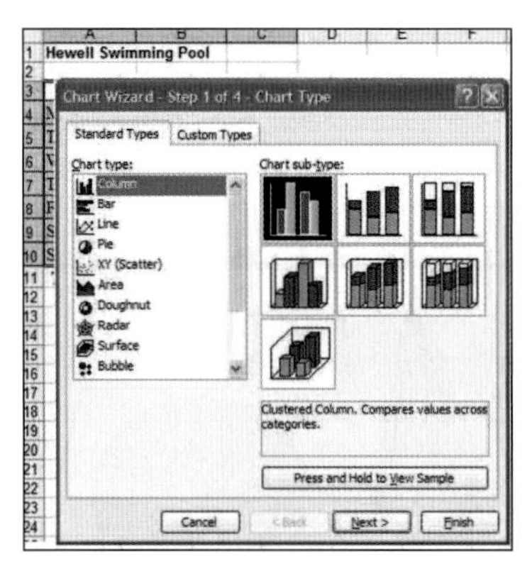

4 Amanda can preview what the chart will look like before she adds the finishing touches.

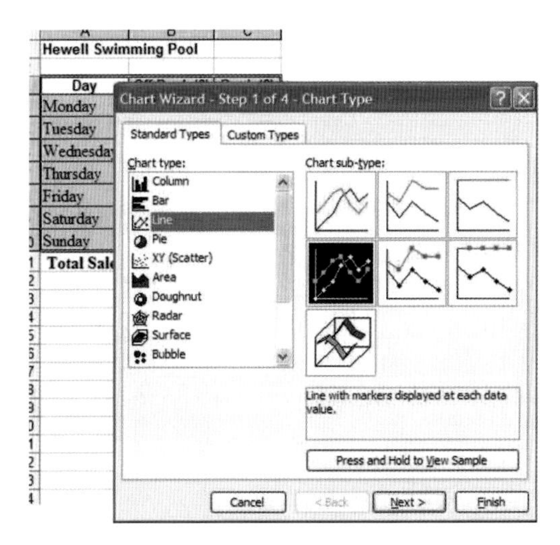

5 For this task, she decides that a column chart will be the most appropriate choice. She opts for a 3D version.

6 Once she has selected her chart she then clicks on 'Next'. A new window appears, showing her what her chart will look like.

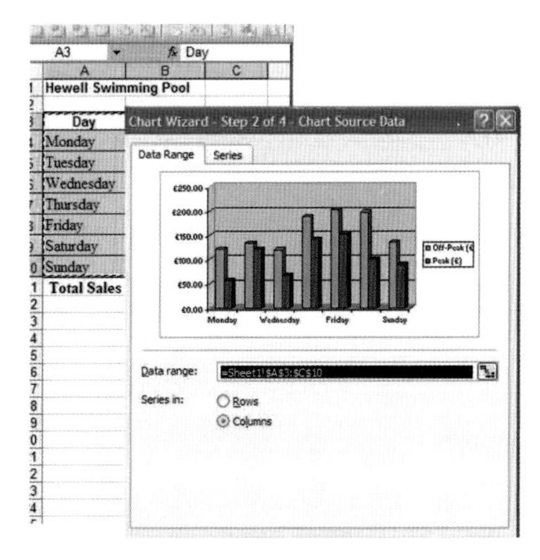

7 She is happy with the way the chart looks and clicks on 'Next'. This brings up a new window that will allow her to add axis labels and a title for her graph. It is important that any chart is given an appropriate title and axis labels. As she types the titles, it appears on screen. This is the end result once she has entered all her titles.

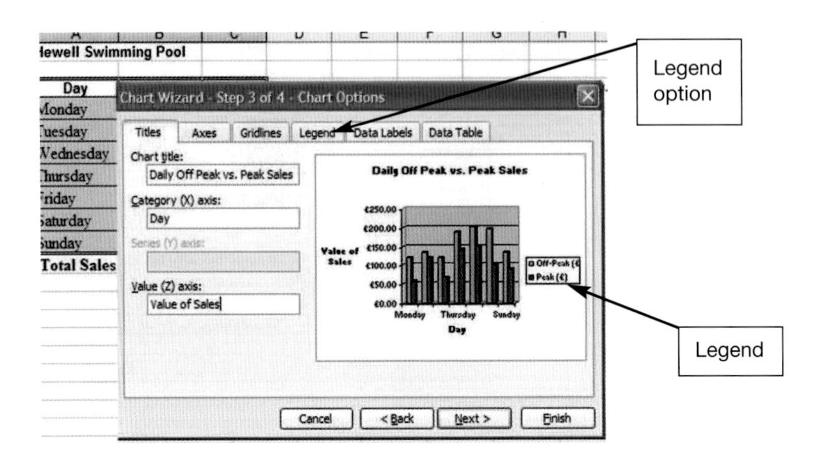

8 Amanda can move the legend key to another place or even delete it if she does not want to show it. This can be altered by selecting the 'Legend' option in the menu bar. Amanda decides to move the legend box to the bottom of the page. This is what her chart now looks like.

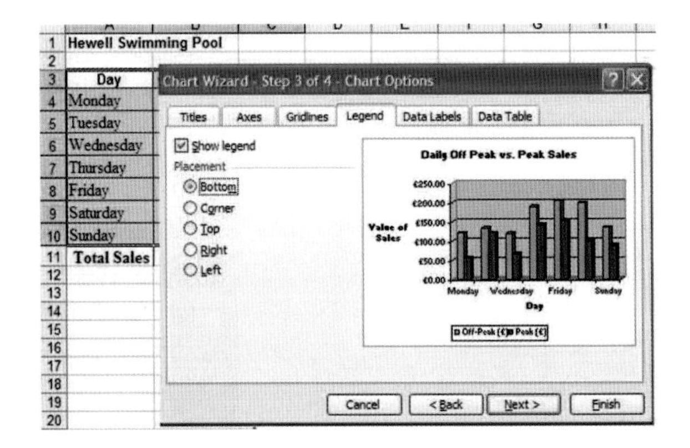

9 The last decision Amanda has to make is where to insert the finished chart. She wants to use the data in the spreadsheet she has created for another graph.

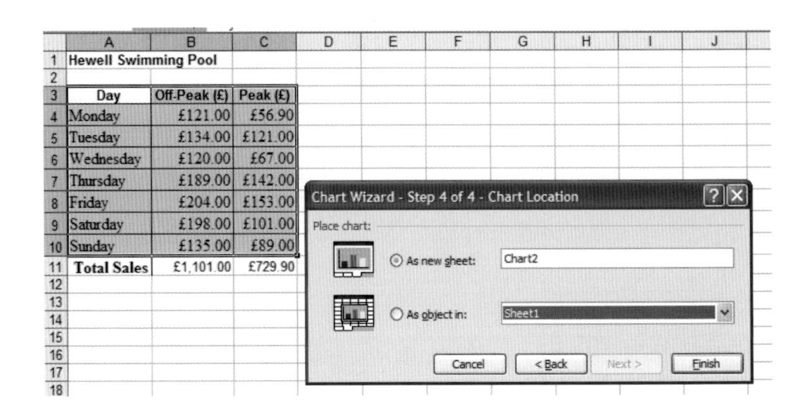

10 She opts to insert her chart as a new sheet in her workbook and selects the 'As new sheet' and clicks on the finish button. This is her final chart.

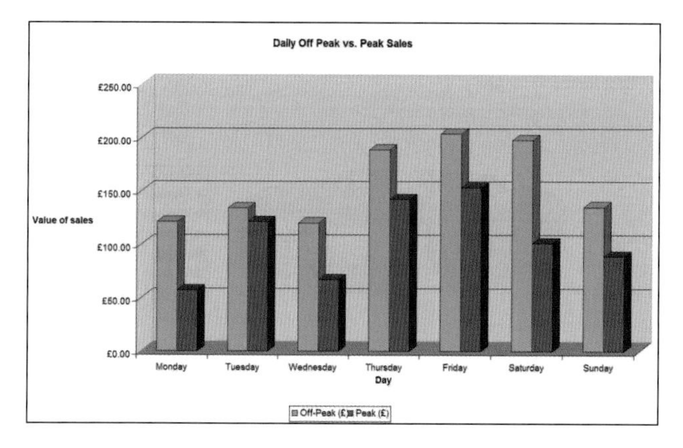

Amanda is able to copy and paste this chart with the data in different software. This is useful when she has to complete her report and presentation.

Selecting data from different columns

Sometimes the data needed for a chart are in columns that are not next to one another in the spreadsheet. The data can still be used to create a chart.

Amanda decides to create a new chart using the 'Day' and 'Peak' columns of her spreadsheet. She highlights the required cells in the 'Day' column. Then she holds down the 'CTRL' (control) button on the keyboard while she uses the mouse to select the required cells in the 'Peak' column. Cells in both columns are now highlighted, as shown here.

	A	B	C
1	**Hewell Swimming Pool**		
2			
3	**Day**	**Off-Peak (£)**	**Peak (£)**
4	Monday	£121.00	£56.90
5	Tuesday	£134.00	£121.00
6	Wednesday	£120.00	£67.00
7	Thursday	£189.00	£142.00
8	Friday	£204.00	£153.00
9	Saturday	£198.00	£101.00
10	Sunday	£135.00	£89.00
11	**Total Sales**	£1,101.00	£729.90
12			

Amanda can now use the Chart Wizard to create a chart, as before.

Choosing the chart type

There are various types of chart to choose from. Here are some of the most common, and examples of when they could be used.

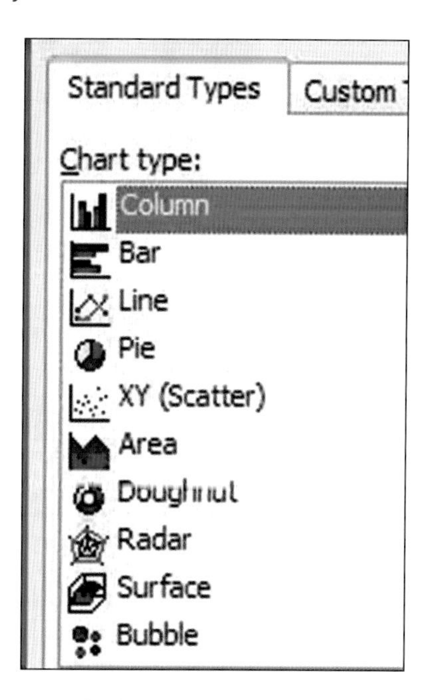

- Column: could be used to show monthly income. The user can see immediately where there are issues such as sudden changes.
- Bar: could be used to show departmental absenteeism and allow comparison between departments.
- Line: could be used to compare two versions of information, for example sales targets and actual sales. The two lines can be compared easily.
- Pie: could be used to show percentage information, such as how often suppliers meet delivery times. The percentage figures can be included on the chart, and the size of each slice shows the difference between the suppliers.
- Scatter: can be used to compare predictions with actual events, such as pupil progress. This can be difficult to read, but is very useful for analysis.

For Amanda's new chart, comparing the peak sales for different days, she chooses a 3D pie chart.

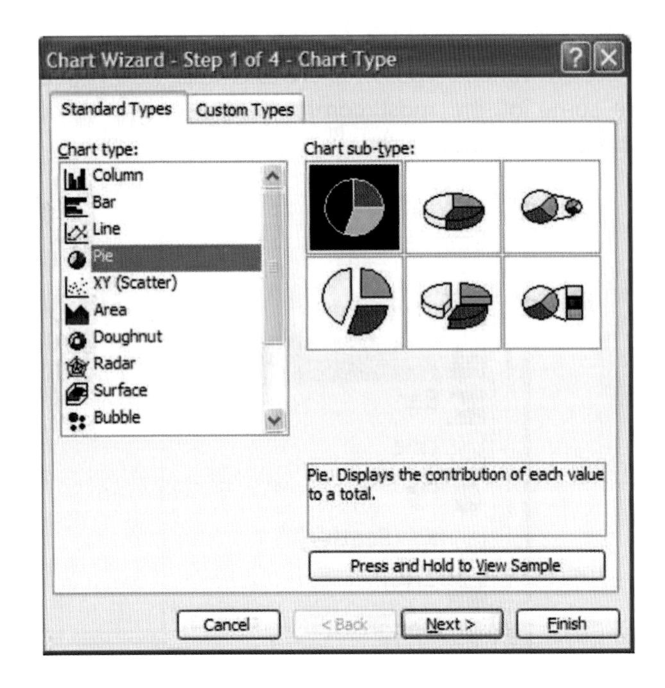

In the preview, Amanda can see that the names of the days are given in the legend.

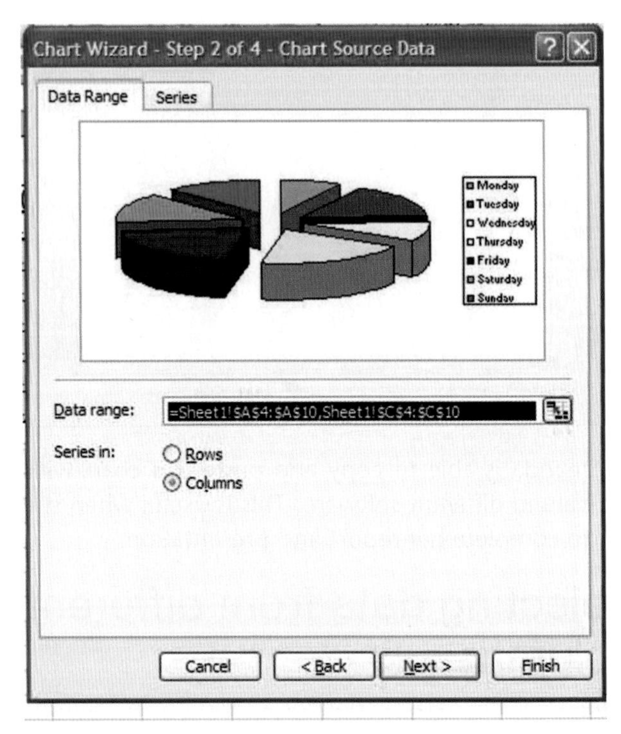

She adds an appropriate title, and labels with the sales amounts for each slice. It will be very easy to see which day had the most sales.

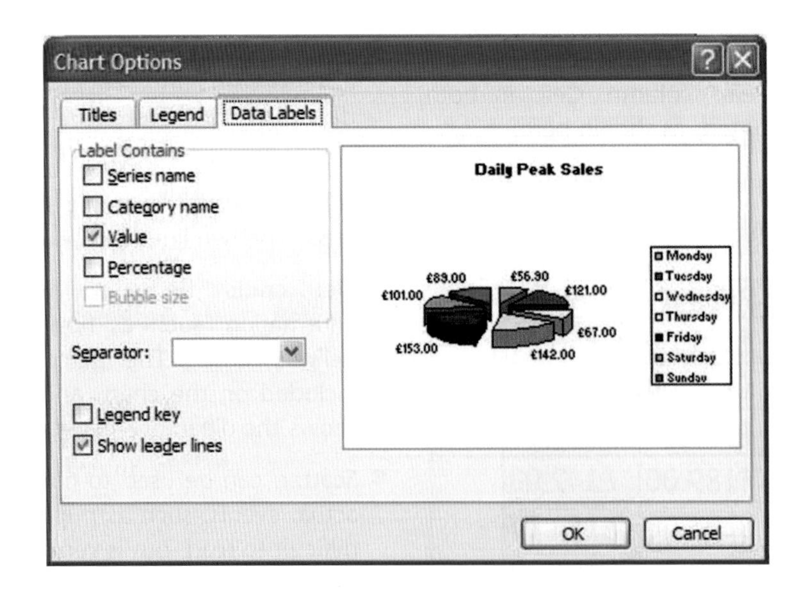

Let's go!

Activities

1 Sophie is about to start a degree in Business Studies at Aston University. However, she is a bit worried that she will not have enough money. She has written down what she plans to spend each week and has included this information in the table below.

Weekly Spend	Amount
Food	£15.00
Rent	£85.00
Heat and light	£20.00
Going out	£30.00
Books	£30.00

She wants to display the information in a chart.

Using appropriate spreadsheet software, create a column chart to present Sophie's weekly spends to her parents. Do not forget to label the axis and give the chart an appropriate title.

2 Sophie has looked at the graph that you have just created and thinks it could be presented in a better format. She wants you to use a pie chart to present her weekly spends. Using the same information from the table, create a pie chart to show her weekly spends.

Summary

- Charts are extremely useful when displaying a series of data, especially when giving a group presentation.
- There are various chart options available. Consideration should always be given to how the data will be used, its purpose and the audience before selecting a chart format.

Key words

Chart Wizard – enables the user to create charts step by step.

Axes – is the plural of 'axis'; the *x* axis (the horizontal scale) and the *y* axis (the vertical scale) identify the data that is to be presented.

Legend – the key to identify what the different sections of the bar, column or pie chart relate to you.

Column chart – a chart with blocks arranged vertically.

Bar chart – a chart with blocks arranged horizontally.

Give me five

1. Why do you need to highlight the data before you can create a chart?
2. What icon helps you to create charts?
3. Identify three different chart options available.
4. What is a legend?
5. Why do you need to give your chart an appropriate title?

Exam style questions

You have been asked to compare the different methods of transport that pupils use to get to three different schools. The information is shown in the table below.

Method of transportation	Washwood Heath	Baverstock	Lordswood
Bus	132	64	159
Car	56	45	105
Walk	246	321	65
Cycle	24	12	0
Mixture	156	109	123

1. Create a pie chart to display the results for Baverstock school. (1 mark)
2. Give the pie chart the title 'Methods of transportation to school'. (1 mark)
3. Show how the three different schools compare by creating a column graph to display the results. (1 mark)
4. Label the axes with appropriate headings. (1 mark)
5. Label the chart with an appropriate title. (1 mark)
6. Insert the chart as a new sheet. (1 mark)

Chapter 22

Creating a database

In this chapter you will learn:

- how to design and create database tables
- how to sort records
- how to search records
- how to filter records
- how to create reports.

Getting started

Databases are widely used in many organisations to keep records of their staff, customers and suppliers. The benefits of databases are that they enable organisations to edit, update and save the information without the fear of it being lost. Using databases enhances the efficiency of the business by allowing the user to create reports and search for particular information. This is very useful when scrolling through the details of hundreds of customers!

What you need to know

Databases are used to record information, with the most common being staff, customer or supplier details. It is time consuming to create a database, however, once it has been created it is an efficient method of keeping information.

How to create a database

The Flower Exchange has just refurbished its store. Hannah, the owner, wants to update the record-keeping system and would like to keep customers' details for marketing purposes. She decides to create a new database.

Hannah has a series of data capture forms that customers complete when they order their flowers. She has to enter the data from these forms into the system. However, she needs to consider the headings she wants to include in the database. These are what she has decided upon:

- Customer surname
- Customer name
- Address 1
- Address 2
- Postcode

- Contact number
- Occasion
- Date ordered.

1 Using these headings she selects appropriate database software to start. She has chosen to use Access. She selects the option of 'Blank database'.

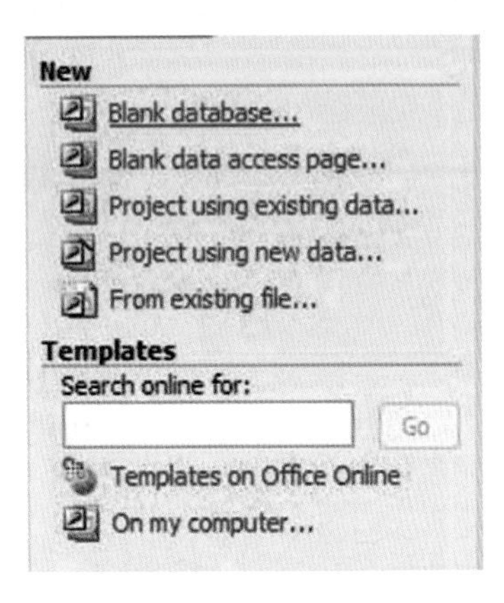

2 Hannah has to name her database. She gives it an appropriate name, 'Flower Exchange Customer DB1'. She then selects 'Create'.

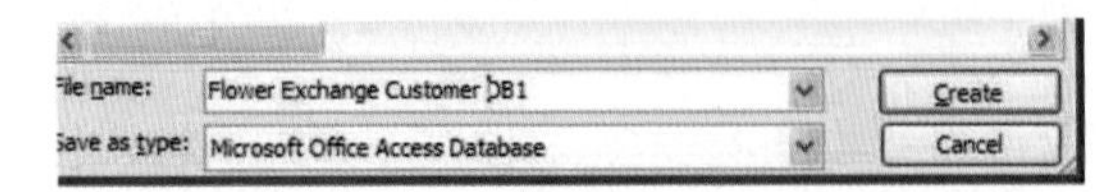

3 Hannah has different options for how she can create her database. Hannah opts to create her database in a table by entering data.

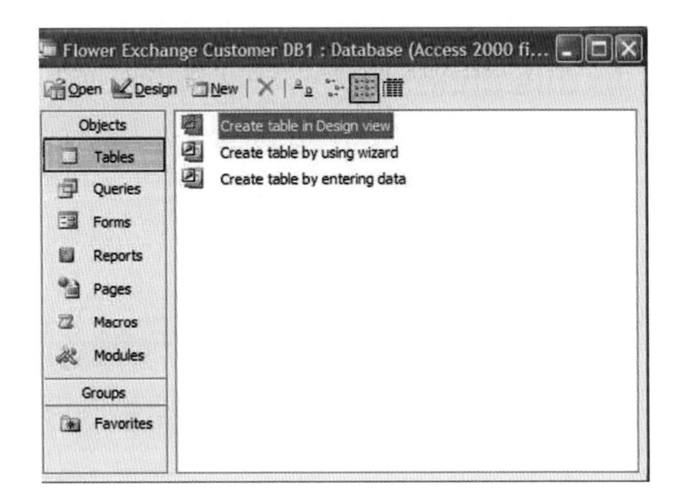

4 This opens a new window that contains a table similar to a spreadsheet.

Table1 : Table

Field1	Field2	Field3	Field4	Field5	Field6	Field7	Field8	Field9	Field10

5 Hannah has set up the database with the headings she wants to use. She now needs to enter the data.

Field1	Field2	Field3	Field4	Field5	Field6	Field7	Field8
Surname	Name	Address 1	Address 2	Postcode	Contact No	Occasion	Date Purchased

6 There are various types of data that Hannah can include. The software also allows her to limit the number of characters and the type of data that is inserted into each column. Once the information is entered, the data is then saved by assigning it an appropriate name, in this case 'Customer'.

7 Once the data has been entered, the software will ask the user to set a primary key. This is a unique code that applies to each customer. This is useful if the database has lots of records. The software will automatically assign the primary key.

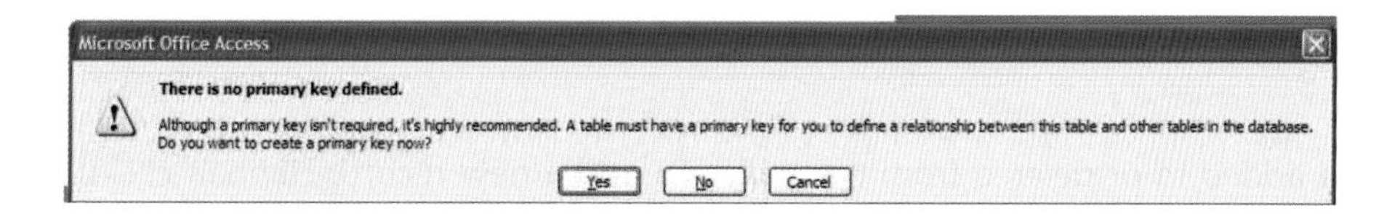

8 The data type is identified within the table. As you can see, all the data is set as text. However, Hannah can change this. For example, she can change the data type for 'Date Purchased' to 'Date/Time'.

Field Name	Data Type
ID	AutoNumber
Surname	Text
Name	Text
Address 1	Text
Address 2	Text
Postcode	Text
Contact No	Text
Occasion	Text
Date Purchased	Date/Time

9 When Hannah closes the table she can see it in the 'Tables' menu. If she double clicks this it will open up the database.

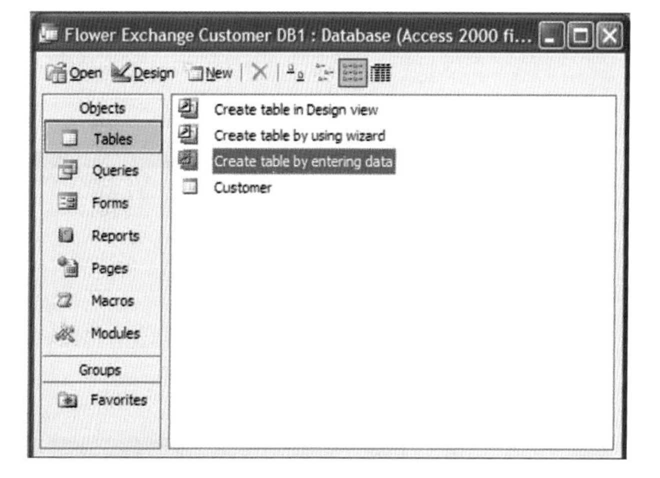

Editing the database

Hannah can now edit, update and make any changes she wishes to the database.

ID	Surname	Name	Address 1	Address 2	Postcode	Contact No	Occasion	Date Purchased
1	Brown	Jane	12 Shawhurst Lane	Hollywood	B46 2ER	0121 643724	Birthday	12/04/2008
2	Morby	Julie	34 Lime Close	Wythall	B90 1GT	0121 679934	Birthday	05/01/2009
3	Rai	Matthew	132 Holly Road	Hollywood	B45 1WS	0121 611223	Wedding	28/10/2008
4	Harris	Linda	321 May Lane	Hollywood	B45 3FD	0121 659422	Wedding	10/01/2008
5	Santer	Gwen	89 Alcester Road	Wythall	B46 9YU	0121 609351	Anniversary	25/09/2008
6	Alsam	Zeeshan	1 Simon Lane	Earlswood	B949QS	0154 532820	Thank you	03/01/2009
7	Allen	George	12 Silver Street	Wythall	B90 8PO	0121 616903	Birthday	17/07/2008
8	Lister	Emma	90 Houndsfield Lane	Wythall	B90 7PL	0121 645583	Anniversary	01/10/2008
9	Bushell	Thomas	45 Crab Mill Lane	Druids Heath	B14 5TK	0121 678093	Engagement	22/12/2008
10	Smith	Peter	45 Shawhurst Lane	Hollywood	B46 2ER	0121 698211	Birthday	12/01/09
(AutoNumber)								

Records can be added to or deleted from the table. To add a new record, Hannah clicks in the first empty row.

ID	Surname	Name	Address 1	Address 2	Postcode	Contact No	Occasion	Date Purchased
1	Brown	Jane	12 Shawhurst Lane	Hollywood	B46 2ER	0121 643724	Birthday	12/04/2008
2	Morby	Julie	34 Lime Close	Wythall	B90 1GT	0121 679934	Birthday	05/01/2009
3	Rai	Matthew	132 Holly Road	Hollywood	B45 1WS	0121 611223	Wedding	28/10/2008
4	Harris	Linda	321 May Lane	Hollywood	B45 3FD	0121 659422	Wedding	10/01/2008
5	Santer	Gwen	89 Alcester Road	Wythall	B46 9YU	0121 609351	Anniversary	25/09/2008
6	Alsam	Zeeshan	1 Simon Lane	Earlswood	B949QS	0154 532820	Thank you	03/01/2009
7	Allen	George	12 Silver Street	Wythall	B90 8PO	0121 616903	Birthday	17/07/2008
8	Lister	Emma	90 Houndsfield Lane	Wythall	B90 7PL	0121 645583	Anniversary	01/10/2008
9	Bushell	Thomas	45 Crab Mill Lane	Druids Heath	B14 5TK	0121 678093	Engagement	22/12/2008
10	Smith	Peter	45 Shawhurst Lane	Hollywood	B46 2ER	0121 698211	Birthday	12/01/09
(AutoNumber)								

She can then complete the record, with details in all the fields.

It is important for Hannah to keep the database up-to-date with accurate customer information. A customer, Mr Allen, has moved away, so Hannah decides to delete his record. She highlights the record.

ID	Surname	Name	Address 1	Address 2	Postcode	Contact No	Occasion	Date Purchased
1	Brown	Jane	12 Shawhurst Lane	Hollywood	B46 2ER	0121 643724	Birthday	12/04/2008
2	Morby	Julie	34 Lime Close	Wythall	B90 1GT	0121 679934	Birthday	05/01/2009
3	Rai	Matthew	132 Holly Road	Hollywood	B45 1WS	0121 611223	Wedding	28/10/2008
4	Harris	Linda	321 May Lane	Hollywood	B45 3FD	0121 659422	Wedding	10/01/2008
5	Santer	Gwen	89 Alcester Road	Wythall	B46 9YU	0121 609351	Anniversary	25/09/2008
6	Alsam	Zeeshan	1 Simon Lane	Earlswood	B949QS	0154 532820	Thank you	03/01/2009
7	Allen	George	12 Silver Street	Wythall	B90 8PO	0121 616903	Birthday	17/07/2008
8	Lister	Emma	90 Houndsfield Lane	Wythall	B90 7PL	0121 645583	Anniversary	01/10/2008
9	Bushell	Thomas	45 Crab Mill Lane	Druids Heath	B14 5TK	0121 678093	Engagement	22/12/2008
10	Smith	Peter	45 Shawhurst Lane	Hollywood	B46 2ER	0121 698211	Birthday	12/01/2009
(AutoNumber)								

Hannah then clicks the right mouse button. This brings up a menu of options.

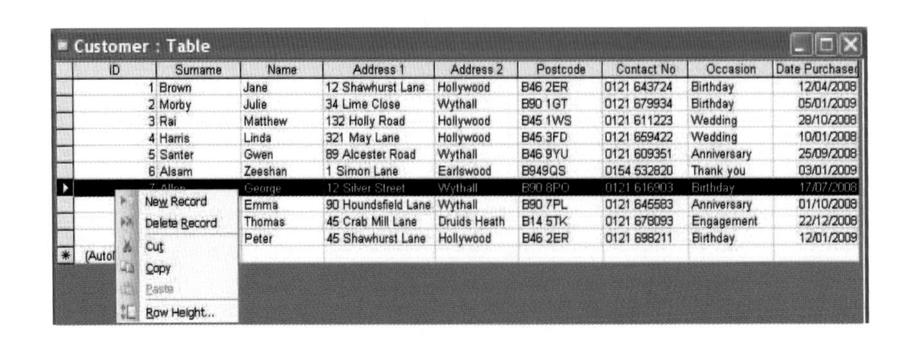

Customer : Table

ID	Surname	Name	Address 1	Address 2	Postcode	Contact No	Occasion	Date Purchased
1	Brown	Jane	12 Shawhurst Lane	Hollywood	B46 2ER	0121 643724	Birthday	12/04/2008
2	Morby	Julie	34 Lime Close	Wythall	B90 1GT	0121 679934	Birthday	05/01/2009
3	Rai	Matthew	132 Holly Road	Hollywood	B45 1WS	0121 611223	Wedding	28/10/2008
4	Harris	Linda	321 May Lane	Hollywood	B45 3FD	0121 659422	Wedding	10/01/2008
5	Santer	Gwen	89 Alcester Road	Wythall	B46 9YU	0121 609351	Anniversary	25/09/2008
6	Alsam	Zeeshan	1 Simon Lane	Earlswood	B949QS	0154 532820	Thank you	03/01/2009
7	Allen	George	12 Silver Street	Wythall	B90 8PO	0121 616903	Birthday	17/07/2008
		Emma	90 Houndsfield Lane	Wythall	B90 7PL	0121 645583	Anniversary	01/10/2008
		Thomas	45 Crab Mill Lane	Druids Heath	B14 5TK	0121 678093	Engagement	22/12/2008
		Peter	45 Shawhurst Lane	Hollywood	B46 2ER	0121 698211	Birthday	12/01/2009
(Auto								

New Record
Delete Record
Cut
Copy
Paste
Row Height...

Hannah selects 'Delete record'. A window appears, asking her to confirm that she wants to permanently delete the record. Once it has been deleted, it is impossible to bring it back!

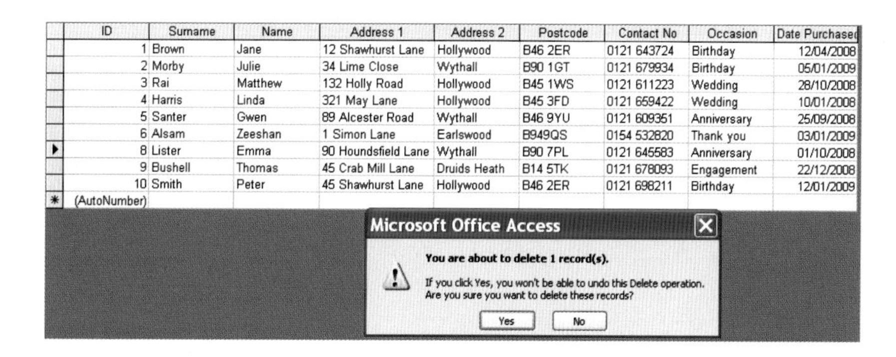

ID	Surname	Name	Address 1	Address 2	Postcode	Contact No	Occasion	Date Purchased
1	Brown	Jane	12 Shawhurst Lane	Hollywood	B46 2ER	0121 643724	Birthday	12/04/2008
2	Morby	Julie	34 Lime Close	Wythall	B90 1GT	0121 679934	Birthday	05/01/2009
3	Rai	Matthew	132 Holly Road	Hollywood	B45 1WS	0121 611223	Wedding	28/10/2008
4	Harris	Linda	321 May Lane	Hollywood	B45 3FD	0121 659422	Wedding	10/01/2008
5	Santer	Gwen	89 Alcester Road	Wythall	B46 9YU	0121 609351	Anniversary	25/09/2008
6	Alsam	Zeeshan	1 Simon Lane	Earlswood	B949QS	0154 532820	Thank you	03/01/2009
8	Lister	Emma	90 Houndsfield Lane	Wythall	B90 7PL	0121 645583	Anniversary	01/10/2008
9	Bushell	Thomas	45 Crab Mill Lane	Druids Heath	B14 5TK	0121 678093	Engagement	22/12/2008
10	Smith	Peter	45 Shawhurst Lane	Hollywood	B46 2ER	0121 698211	Birthday	12/01/2009
(AutoNumber)								

Hannah is certain that she has selected the correct record, so she clicks 'Yes'. Mr Allen's record is now gone from the table.

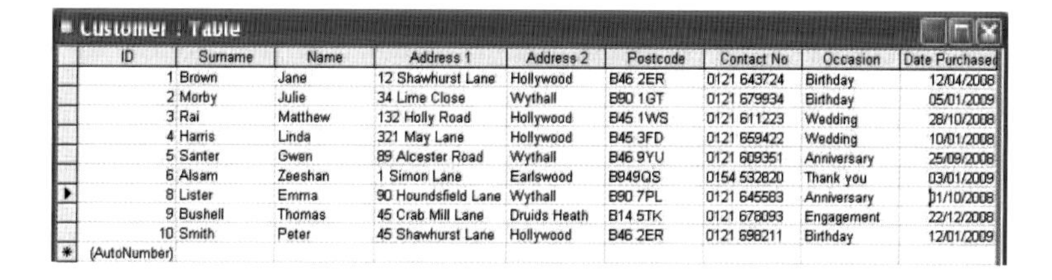

ID	Surname	Name	Address 1	Address 2	Postcode	Contact No	Occasion	Date Purchased
1	Brown	Jane	12 Shawhurst Lane	Hollywood	B46 2ER	0121 643724	Birthday	12/04/2008
2	Morby	Julie	34 Lime Close	Wythall	B90 1GT	0121 679934	Birthday	05/01/2009
3	Rai	Matthew	132 Holly Road	Hollywood	B45 1WS	0121 611223	Wedding	28/10/2008
4	Harris	Linda	321 May Lane	Hollywood	B45 3FD	0121 659422	Wedding	10/01/2008
5	Santer	Gwen	89 Alcester Road	Wythall	B46 9YU	0121 609351	Anniversary	25/09/2008
6	Alsam	Zeeshan	1 Simon Lane	Earlswood	B949QS	0154 532820	Thank you	03/01/2009
8	Lister	Emma	90 Houndsfield Lane	Wythall	B90 7PL	0121 645583	Anniversary	01/10/2008
9	Bushell	Thomas	45 Crab Mill Lane	Druids Heath	B14 5TK	0121 678093	Engagement	22/12/2008
10	Smith	Peter	45 Shawhurst Lane	Hollywood	B46 2ER	0121 698211	Birthday	12/01/2009
(AutoNumber)								

Hannah decides to add a new field to the database, recording whether customers required delivery of their order. In table view, she clicks on the column which will be next to the new field – 'Date purchased'.

ID	Surname	Name	Address 1	Address 2	Postcode	Contact No	Occasion	Date Purchased
1	Brown	Jane	12 Shawhurst Lane	Hollywood	B46 2ER	0121 643724	Birthday	12/04/2008
2	Morby	Julie	34 Lime Close	Wythall	B90 1GT	0121 679934	Birthday	05/01/2009
3	Rai	Matthew	132 Holly Road	Hollywood	B45 1WS	0121 611223	Wedding	28/10/2008
4	Harris	Linda	321 May Lane	Hollywood	B45 3FD	0121 659422	Wedding	10/01/2008
5	Santer	Gwen	89 Alcester Road	Wythall	B46 9YU	0121 609351	Anniversary	25/09/2008
6	Alsam	Zeeshan	1 Simon Lane	Earlswood	B949QS	0154 532820	Thank you	03/01/2009
8	Lister	Emma	90 Houndsfield Lane	Wythall	B90 7PL	0121 645583	Anniversary	01/10/2008
9	Bushell	Thomas	45 Crab Mill Lane	Druids Heath	B14 5TK	0121 678093	Engagement	22/12/2008
10	Smith	Peter	45 Shawhurst Lane	Hollywood	B46 2ER	0121 698211	Birthday	12/01/2009
(AutoNumber)								

With this column highlighted, she selects 'Insert' from the menu and then chooses 'Column'.

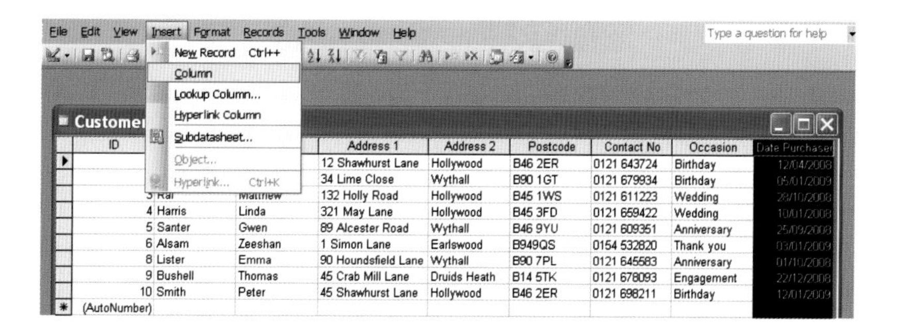

ID	Surname	Name	Address 1	Address 2	Postcode	Contact No	Occasion	Date Purchased
			12 Shawhurst Lane	Hollywood	B46 2ER	0121 643724	Birthday	12/04/2008
			34 Lime Close	Wythall	B90 1GT	0121 679934	Birthday	05/01/2009
			132 Holly Road	Hollywood	B45 1WS	0121 611223	Wedding	28/10/2008
4	Harris	Linda	321 May Lane	Hollywood	B45 3FD	0121 659422	Wedding	10/01/2008
5	Santer	Gwen	89 Alcester Road	Wythall	B46 9YU	0121 609351	Anniversary	25/09/2008
6	Alsam	Zeeshan	1 Simon Lane	Earlswood	B949QS	0154 532820	Thank you	03/01/2009
8	Lister	Emma	90 Houndsfield Lane	Wythall	B90 7PL	0121 645583	Anniversary	01/10/2008
9	Bushell	Thomas	45 Crab Mill Lane	Druids Heath	B14 5TK	0121 678093	Engagement	22/12/2008
10	Smith	Peter	45 Shawhurst Lane	Hollywood	B46 2ER	0121 698211	Birthday	12/01/2009
(AutoNumber)								

The new column is called 'Field1'. Hannah needs to give it an appropriate title. She selects 'Format' from the menu bar and then chooses 'Rename column'. This highlights the 'Field1' heading.

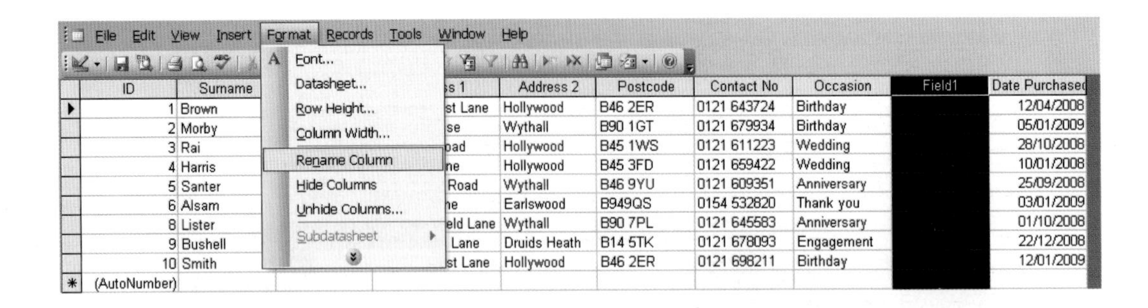

ID	Surname	Name	Address 1	Address 2	Postcode	Contact No	Occasion	Field1	Date Purchased
1	Brown	Jane	12 Shawhurst Lane	Hollywood	B46 2ER	0121 643724	Birthday		12/04/2008
2	Morby	Julie	34 Lime Close	Wythall	B90 1GT	0121 679934	Birthday		05/01/2009
3	Rai	Matthew	132 Holly Road	Hollywood	B45 1WS	0121 611223	Wedding		28/10/2008
4	Harris	Linda	321 May Lane	Hollywood	B45 3FD	0121 659422	Wedding		10/01/2008
5	Santer	Gwen	89 Alcester Road	Wythall	B46 9YU	0121 609351	Anniversary		25/09/2008
6	Alsam	Zeeshan	1 Simon Lane	Earlswood	B949QS	0154 532820	Thank you		03/01/2009
8	Lister	Emma	90 Houndsfield Lane	Wythall	B90 7PL	0121 645583	Anniversary		01/10/2008
9	Bushell	Thomas	45 Crab Mill Lane	Druids Heath	B14 5TK	0121 678093	Engagement		22/12/2008
10	Smith	Peter	45 Shawhurst Lane	Hollywood	B46 2ER	0121 698211	Birthday		12/01/2009
(AutoNumber)									

Hannah types in the title 'Delivery?' She will enter either 'yes' or 'no' in this field for each customer.

It is also possible to delete an entire field from the database. Hannah has decided that the 'Date purchased' field is not useful and should be deleted. She highlights the column and then clicks the right mouse button to bring up a list of options.

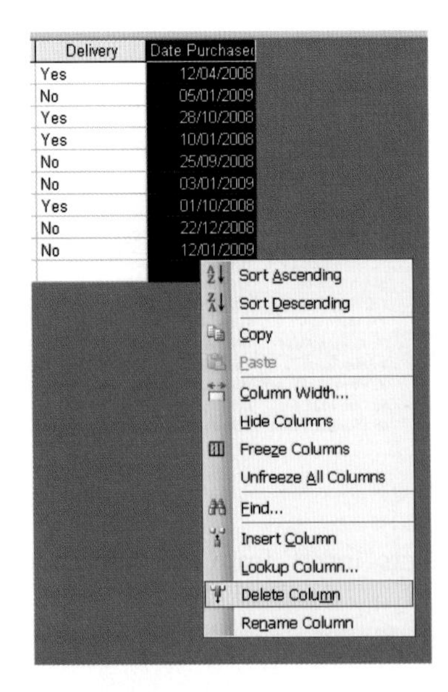

Hannah selects 'Delete column' from the list. A window appears asking her to confirm that she wants to delete the field. Remember, once it is done it cannot be undone!

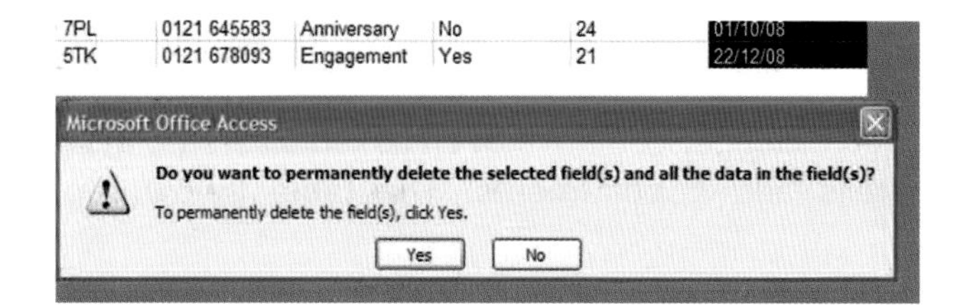

The database is not only useful to keep the records of the customers. Hannah can also sort and filter the data and use it to create reports (see Chapter 23).

Sorting

Hannah can sort her database into alphabetical order. This will be useful when the database becomes larger. She decides to sort the data by surname. To do this she highlights the data she wants to sort and selects 'Records' from the menu bar, then selects 'Sort'.

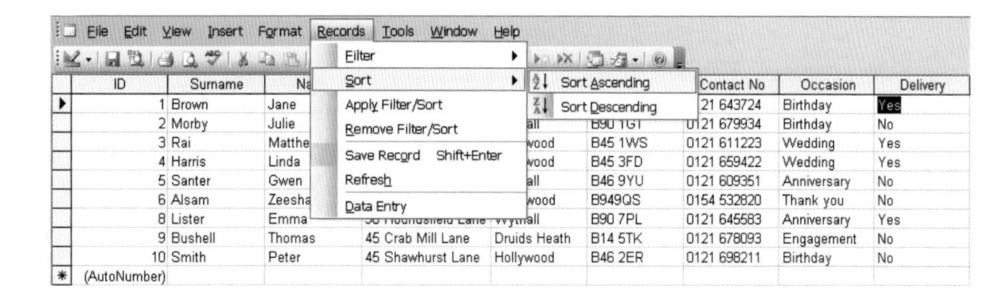

She selects 'Sort Ascending' and the records are then sorted in ascending alphabetical order, starting with A.

ID	Surname	Name	Address 1	Address 2	Postcode	Contact No	Occasion	Delivery
6	Alsam	Zeeshan	1 Simon Lane	Earlswood	B949QS	0154 532820	Thank you	No
1	Brown	Jane	12 Shawhurst Lane	Hollywood	B46 2ER	0121 643724	Birthday	Yes
9	Bushell	Thomas	45 Crab Mill Lane	Druids Heath	B14 5TK	0121 678093	Engagement	No
4	Harris	Linda	321 May Lane	Hollywood	B45 3FD	0121 659422	Wedding	Yes
8	Lister	Emma	90 Houndsfield Lane	Wythall	B90 7PL	0121 645583	Anniversary	Yes
2	Morby	Julie	34 Lime Close	Wythall	B90 1GT	0121 679934	Birthday	No
3	Rai	Matthew	132 Holly Road	Hollywood	B45 1WS	0121 611223	Wedding	Yes
5	Santer	Gwen	89 Alcester Road	Wythall	B46 9YU	0121 609351	Anniversary	No
10	Smith	Peter	45 Shawhurst Lane	Hollywood	B46 2ER	0121 698211	Birthday	No
(AutoNumber)								

Let's go!

Activities

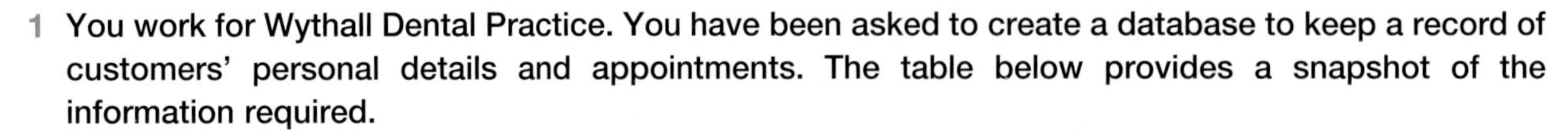

1 You work for Wythall Dental Practice. You have been asked to create a database to keep a record of customers' personal details and appointments. The table below provides a snapshot of the information required.

Surname	Name	Address	Contact no	Dentist
Smith	James	12 Heaten Road	0121 653824	Dr Mooney
Ahmed	Saima	34 Station Road	0121 694234	Dr Patrick
Tye	Bert	45 Simston Lane	0121 635921	Dr Mooney

a) Create a database using appropriate software.

b) Add the following patients to the database:

Emma Rollins, 30 Sandy Lane, 0121 659320, Dr Mooney

Paul Petals, 5 Evergreen Drive, 0121 603895, Dr Patrick

Kaitlyn Thai, 27 Lime Street, 0121 688954, Dr Mooney

c) Sort your database by surname in ascending order.

Summary

- Today information is vital to the running of a business, so the use of database has many benefits for any organisation.
- In the past, holding large of amounts of information took a lot of space, and recording the information was time consuming.
- Using a database has reduced the need for filing cabinets. Sorting and searching for information can be carried out with the click of a button.
- With the many functions that database software offers, the keeping, maintaining and monitoring of data is much more efficient.

Key words

File – a group of records on a topic.

Record – details of one entry into the database, e.g. details of an applicant for the job.

Field name – the name given to a set of information, e.g. Surname.

Data type – the type of information that is being stored in the cell, e.g. text, currency.

Primary key – unique code give to each record in the database.

Field heading – the title given to the column containing the data.

Sort – a facility on the database to organise the data in ascending or descending order.

Give me five

1. What is a database?
2. Other than text, what other type of data can be entered into a database?
3. What is the purpose of a primary key?
4. What are the benefits of using the report function?
5. Explain the benefits of using the filter function.

Exam style questions

You work for a local music shop, MusicForYou, which has just opened in your area of town. There are no records yet of any data and as you have computer skills the manager has asked if you could sort out the following issues.

1. The manager is keen to keep all the staff records in a simple but efficient format, so that it is easy to transfer the information onto the computer. Design a data capture form that could be used to collect staff details. You will need to include the following information:
   - name
   - address
   - postcode
   - telephone number
   - mobile number
   - next of kin

   plus four other pieces of information that you think are relevant. (10 marks)
2. Explain two benefits of using a form to collect this information. (4 marks)
3. You have been asked by the local Youth Club to give them a list of the top ten CDs being sold each week. The manager of the store has devised a simple form below which he thinks would be suitable to gather the information.

Name of CD	Artist/Artists	Number Sold

   You realise that this is not going to work, as the shop sells over 7000 CDs each week.

   a) Describe the type of equipment you would need to use within the store to find the information on the top ten bestselling CDs.

   b) How would you collect the information once the new equipment had been purchased?

Chapter 23

Interrogating a database

In this chapter you will learn:

- how to export a database into spreadsheet software
- how to use the information to create a mail merge.

Getting started

The information in a database can be used for many different purposes. Many businesses often need to send letters and promotional materials to their customers. Instead of sending generic letters, companies who value their customers will send personalised standard letters. This can be done easily by using a mail merge. Businesses can also export the information they store in a database into spreadsheet software. This is especially useful if the database holds staff information and the business wants to incorporate the personal details with the wage information.

What you need to know

Remember Hannah from the Flower Exchange? With her customer database, she can filter the data and use it to create reports; she can also use it to create a mail merge.

Filter

Hannah can filter the records to find specific information. For example, she may want to find out the people who ordered flowers for birthdays.

1 To do this she selects 'Filter' from 'Records' menu in the menu bar.

File Edit View Insert Format Records Tools Window Help

Filter
Sort
Apply Filter/Sort
Remove Filter/Sort
Save Record Shift+Enter
Refresh
Data Entry

Filter By Form
Filter By Selection
Filter Excluding Selection
Advanced Filter/Sort...

ID	Surname	Na				No	Occasion	Delivery
6	Alsam	Zeesha				20	Thank you	No
1	Brown	Jane				24	Birthday	Yes
9	Bushell	Thoma				93	Engagement	No
4	Harris	Linda		wood	B45 3FD	0121 659422	Wedding	Yes
8	Lister	Emma		all	B90 7PL	0121 645583	Anniversary	Yes
2	Morby	Julie		all	B90 1GT	0121 679934	Birthday	No
3	Rai	Matthew		wood	B45 1WS	0121 611223	Wedding	Yes
5	Santer	Gwen	89 Alcester Road	Wythall	B46 9YU	0121 609351	Anniversary	No
10	Smith	Peter	45 Shawhurst Lane	Hollywood	B46 2ER	0121 698211	Birthday	No
(AutoNumber)								

2 She selects 'Advanced Filter' and this opens a new window. As you can see, she has a small drop-down menu that allows her to select the different field headings. She can decide how she wants to filter the information. She clicks on 'Occasion'.

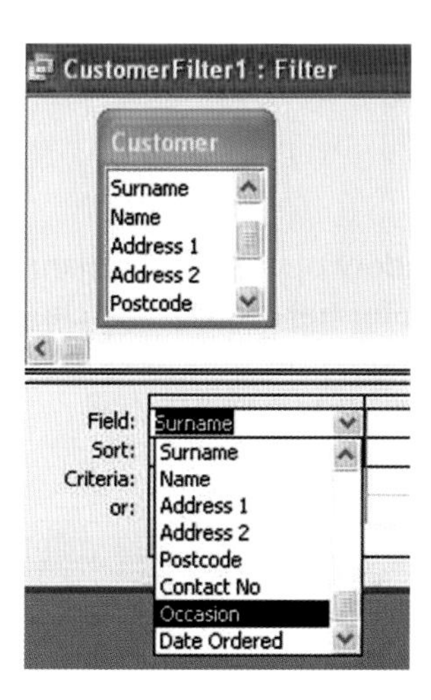

3 She then sets the criteria she wants to filter, in this case 'Birthday'.

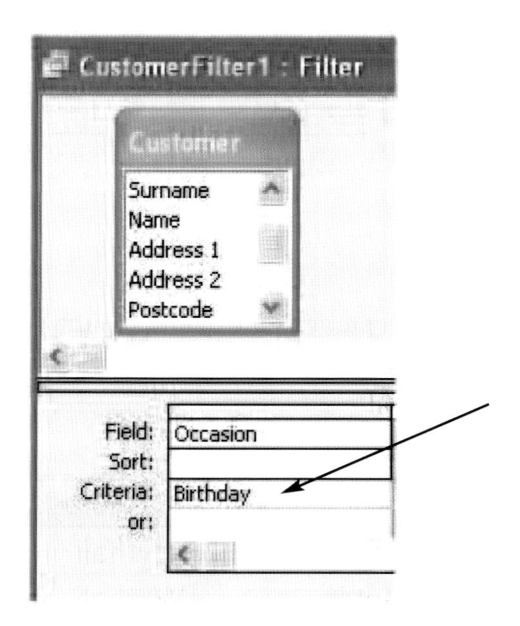

4 She then selects the 'Apply Filter' option in the 'Filter' menu. She can also include other criteria to filter.

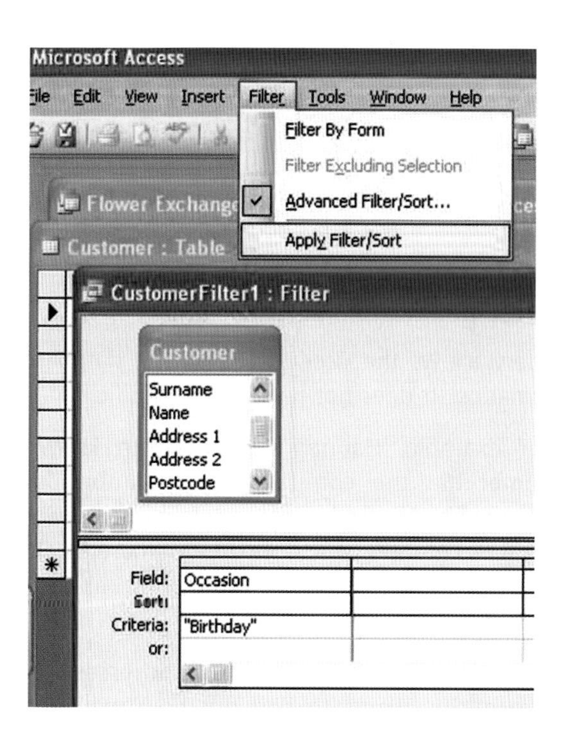

5 Once Hannah selects 'Apply Filter', the information is then displayed and she can see all the customers who ordered flowers for a birthday.

	ID	Surname	Name	Address 1	Address 2	Postcode	Contact No	Occasion	Delivery
▶	10	Smith	Peter	45 Shawhurst Lane	Hollywood	B46 2ER	0121 698211	Birthday	No
	2	Morby	Julie	34 Lime Close	Wythall	B90 1GT	0121 679934	Birthday	No
	1	Brown	Jane	12 Shawhurst Lane	Hollywood	B46 2ER	0121 643724	Birthday	Yes
*	(AutoNumber)								

Query

A query allows the user to search the database for information. It does not have to be specific.

For example, Hannah may want to know if a customer has the correct contact number in the database. She would insert the telephone number as the query criterion; if it is in the database, it should come up with the other information about that customer.

Hannah includes customers' addresses in her database. She wants to find out how many of the customers live close to the shop.

1 She selects 'Queries' from the main window of the database.

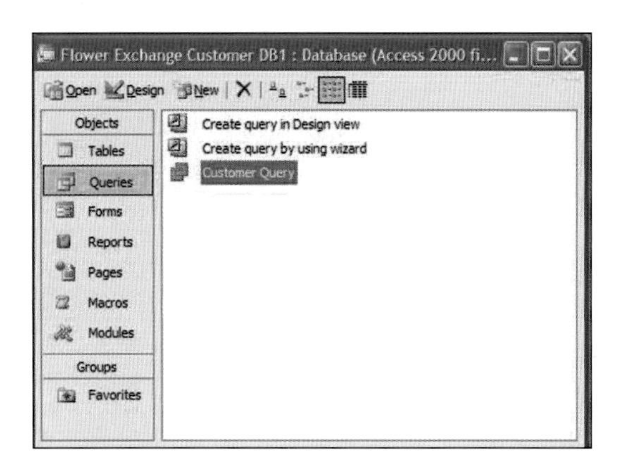

2 A new window opens, where Hannah can select the criteria for her search. She chooses to include the fields 'Surname' and 'Address 2' in her results, and limits it to 'Wythall'.

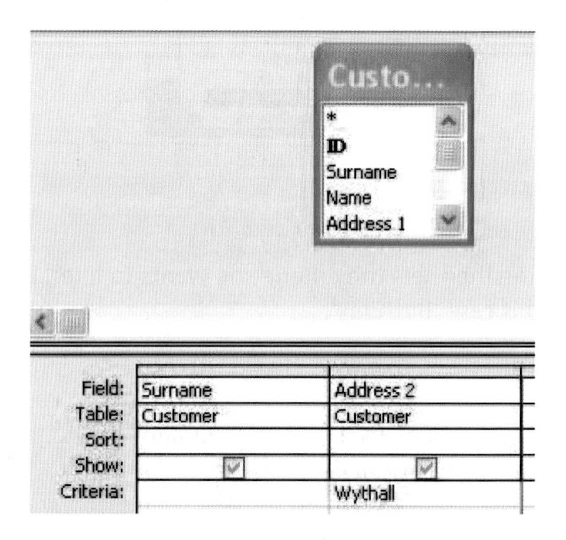

3 Hannah previews the query, and she can see that the search has selected the information she requested.

	Surname	Address 2
▶	Morby	Wythall
	Santer	Wythall
	Lister	Wythall
*		

Reports

Hannah can also produce reports using information entered into the database. In order to do this, she will complete the following steps.

1 First Hannah selects the 'Reports' option and this will bring up a new window. This offers a list of data headings ('Fields') so that she can choose what to include in the report.

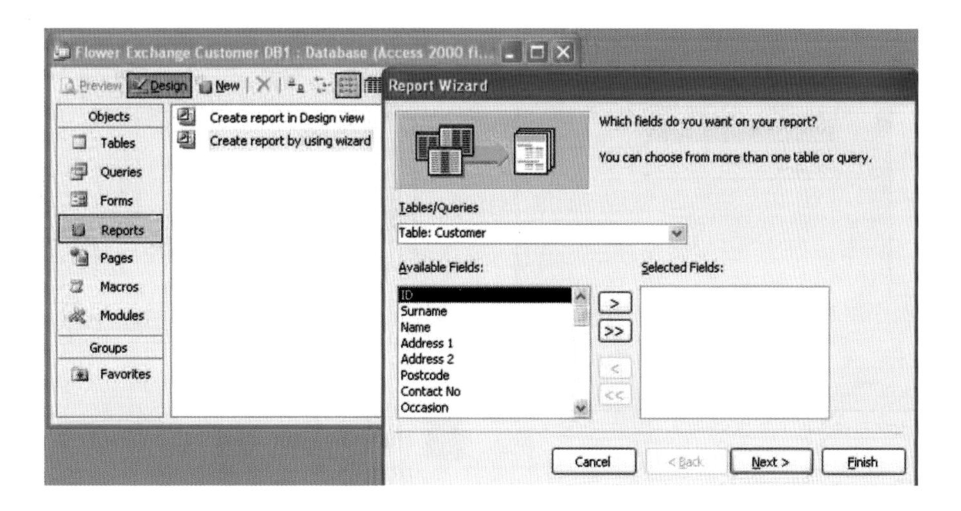

2 Hannah chooses the headings from the 'Available Fields' list and adds them to the 'Selected Fields' box.

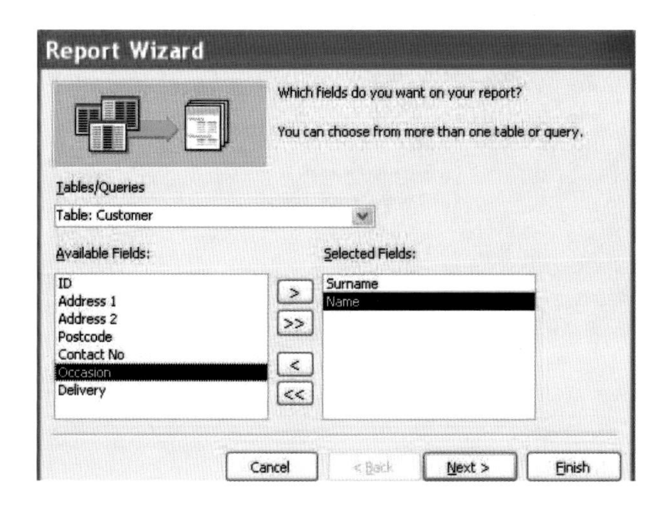

3 She then clicks on 'Next'. The next step is to decide how she wants the report to be organised. She is given the option to select the headings ('Grouping levels') she wants to include.

4 Once she has selected the headings she wants, Hannah can sort the records in the report according to any of these headings. For this purpose, she decides to sort by surname.

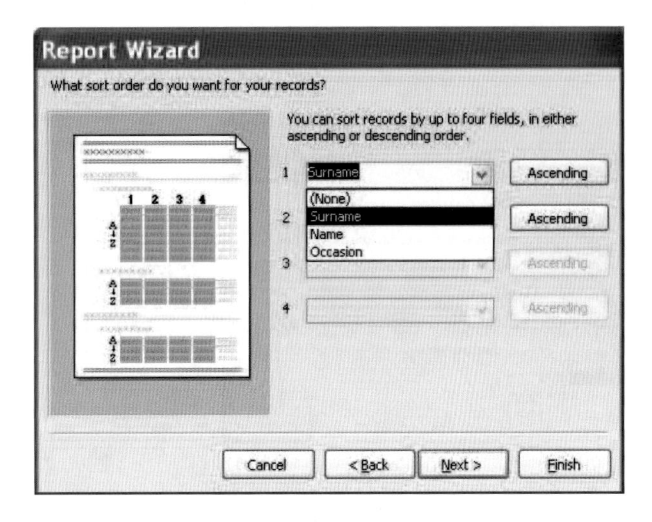

5 Hannah now has to decide how she would like the report laid out. The layout is pre-set as 'Tabular', which means it will be shown as a table.

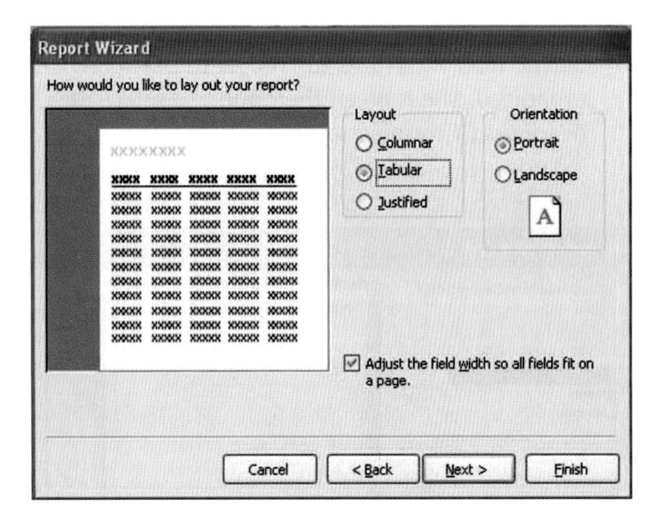

6 Hannah can also add colour and different format styles to her report. In this section, she has opted to go for a 'Casual' format.

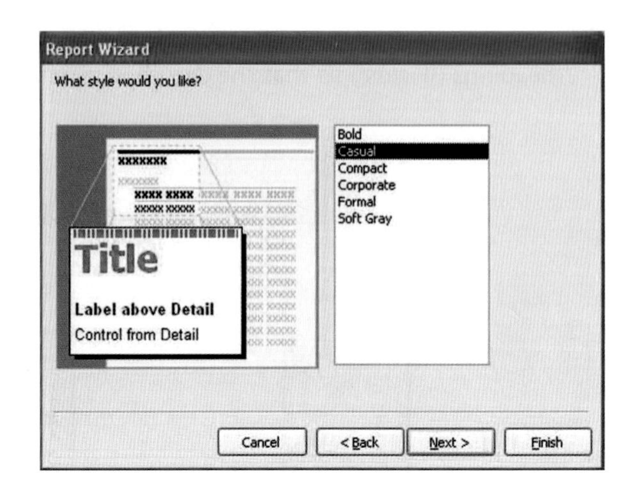

7 Hannah then gives the report an appropriate title.

8 Once she is happy with the report she just needs to select 'Finish'.

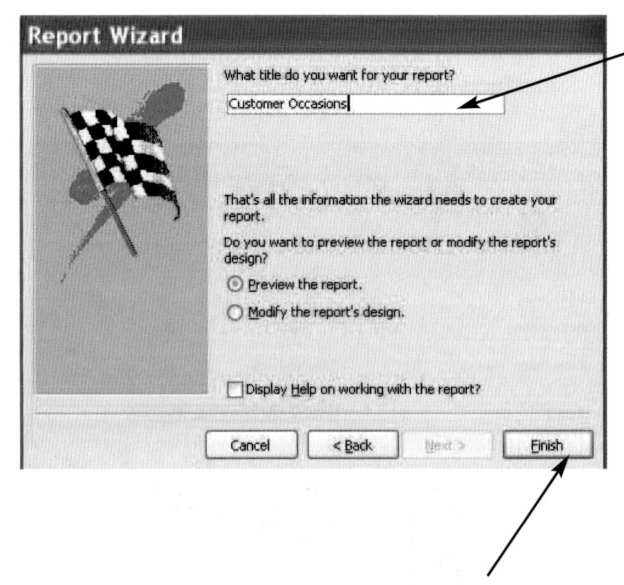

This is what her completed report looks like.

Customer Occasions

Surname	Name	Occasion
Alsam	Zeeshan	Thank you
Brown	Jane	Birthday
Bushell	Thomas	Engagement
Harris	Linda	Wedding
Lister	Emma	Anniversary
Morby	Julie	Birthday
Rai	Matthew	Wedding
Santer	Gwen	Anniversary
Smith	Peter	Birthday

Reports are useful when summarising information. Imagine a large organisation like Toyota. The production and logistics team would need to have regular meetings about the number of cars to be built that month and the number of parts being held in stock. The report function allows the user to select specific information to take to these meetings and show a snapshot of what has happened. It avoids the user having to scroll through lots of data that is not relevant. If an appropriate format is chosen, the report can look very professional. However, the user needs to take care that they select the correct data, or the report will be no use!

Exporting the database

The information from a database can be exported easily into a spreadsheet. Hannah now wants to export the information from the database so that it can be used in a spreadsheet. She knows that once the information has been exported into the spreadsheet there are many ways that it can be used, such as mail merging the customer information. To export the database into a spreadsheet Hannah carries out the following steps.

1. Hannah highlights the customer database and then right clicks. This opens a drop-down menu, from which she selects 'Export'.

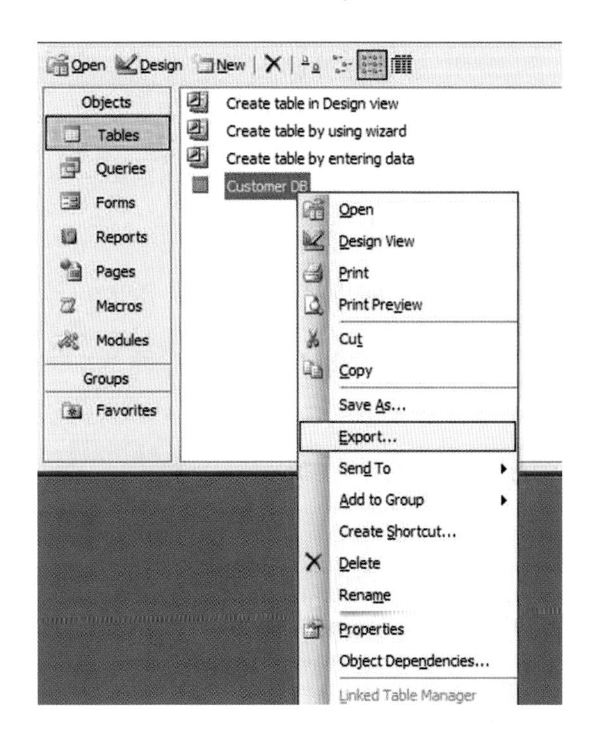

2. She saves the information in an appropriate area. To export the data as a spreadsheet, she needs to change the format the information is saved in. In this case, she saves it as an Excel format.

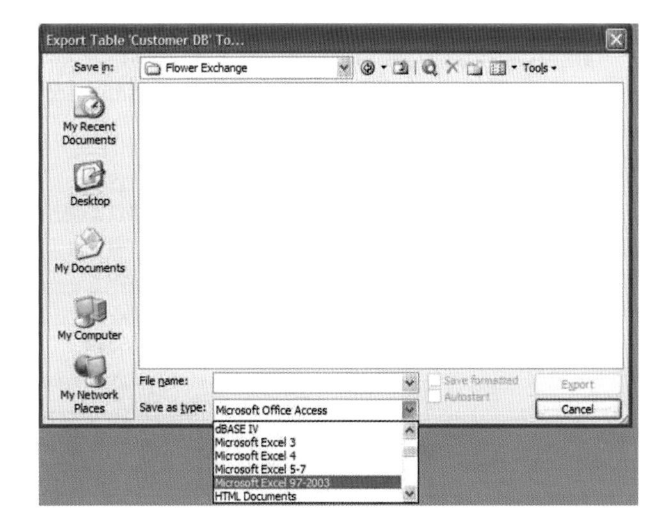

3 She also gives the file an appropriate name. Once she has named the file 'Customer', she clicks on 'Export'.

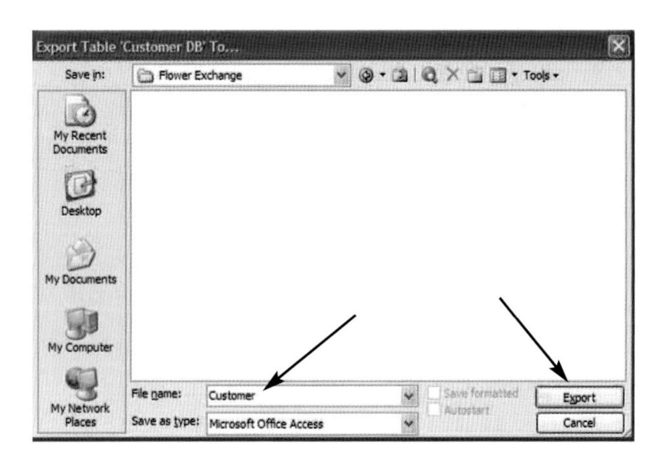

4 Hannah should now be able to see her file saved as an Excel document, with the name she gave it.

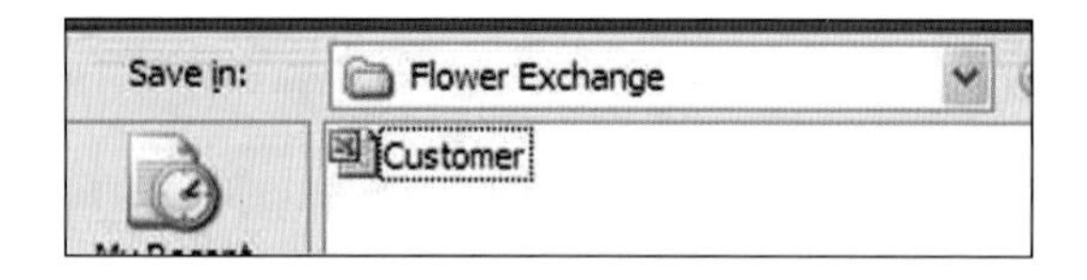

5 From here, if she double clicks on the file it will open, showing the information that was in the database.

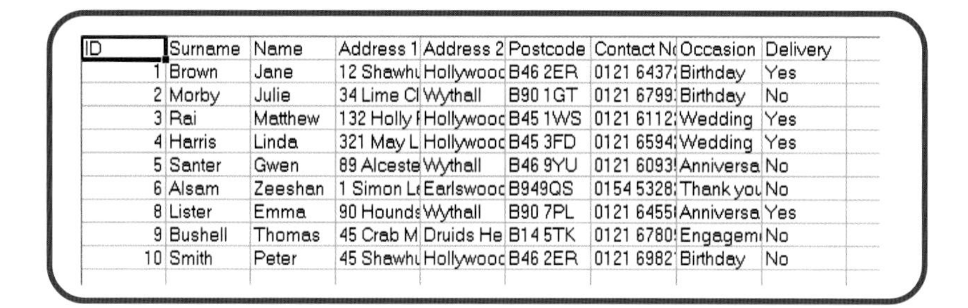

ID	Surname	Name	Address 1	Address 2	Postcode	Contact N	Occasion	Delivery
1	Brown	Jane	12 Shawhu	Hollywooc	B46 2ER	0121 6437	Birthday	Yes
2	Morby	Julie	34 Lime Cl	Wythall	B90 1GT	0121 6799	Birthday	No
3	Rai	Matthew	132 Holly	Hollywooc	B45 1WS	0121 6112	Wedding	Yes
4	Harris	Linda	321 May L	Hollywooc	B45 3FD	0121 6594	Wedding	Yes
5	Santer	Gwen	89 Alceste	Wythall	B46 9YU	0121 6093	Anniversa	No
6	Alsam	Zeeshan	1 Simon L	Earlswooc	B949QS	0154 5328	Thank you	No
8	Lister	Emma	90 Hounds	Wythall	B90 7PL	0121 6455	Anniversa	Yes
9	Bushell	Thomas	45 Crab M	Druids He	B14 5TK	0121 6780	Engagem	No
10	Smith	Peter	45 Shawhu	Hollywooc	B46 2ER	0121 6982	Birthday	No

6 As you can see, some of the information cannot be seen, as the cell width is too narrow. This can be amended easily by highlighting all the data, then going to 'Format' on the menu bar and selecting 'Column'. She can then choose 'AutoFit Selection' and this will change all the columns so that they show all the data.

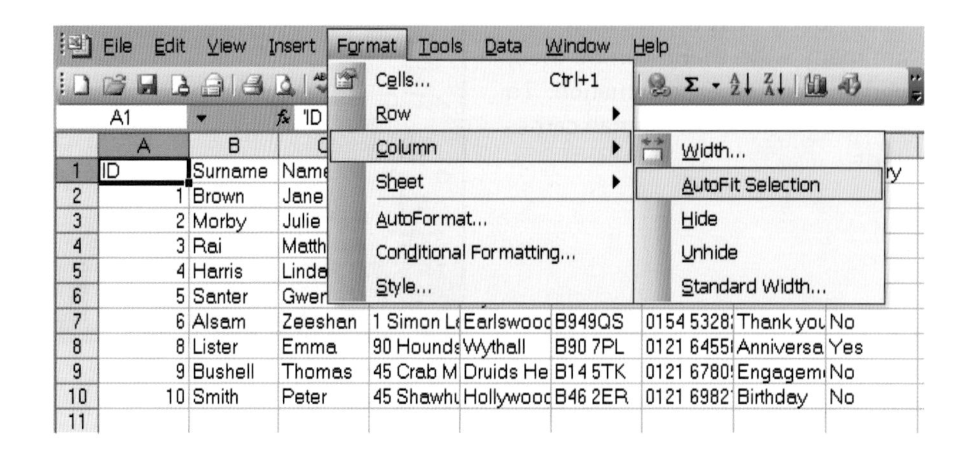

All the information within each cell can now be seen.

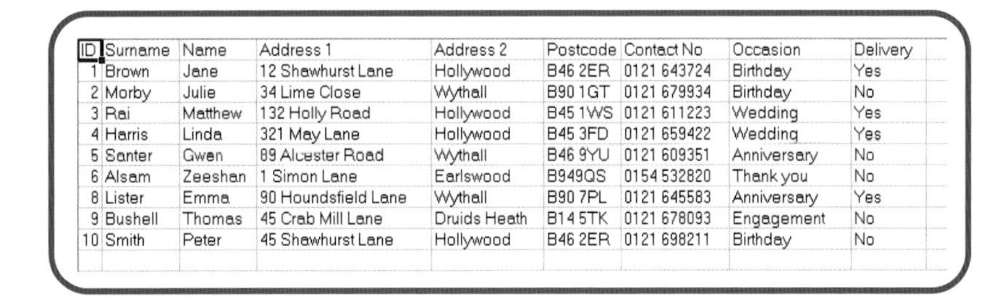

ID	Surname	Name	Address 1	Address 2	Postcode	Contact No	Occasion	Delivery
1	Brown	Jane	12 Shawhurst Lane	Hollywood	B46 2ER	0121 643724	Birthday	Yes
2	Morby	Julie	34 Lime Close	Wythall	B90 1GT	0121 679934	Birthday	No
3	Rai	Matthew	132 Holly Road	Hollywood	B45 1WS	0121 611223	Wedding	Yes
4	Harris	Linda	321 May Lane	Hollywood	B45 3FD	0121 659422	Wedding	Yes
5	Santer	Gwen	89 Alcester Road	Wythall	B46 9YU	0121 609351	Anniversary	No
6	Alsam	Zeeshan	1 Simon Lane	Earlswood	B949QS	0154 532820	Thank you	No
8	Lister	Emma	90 Houndsfield Lane	Wythall	B90 7PL	0121 645583	Anniversary	Yes
9	Bushell	Thomas	45 Crab Mill Lane	Druids Heath	B14 5TK	0121 678093	Engagement	No
10	Smith	Peter	45 Shawhurst Lane	Hollywood	B46 2ER	0121 698211	Birthday	No

7 To make the headings stand out, Hannah makes them bold so that they are easier to see.

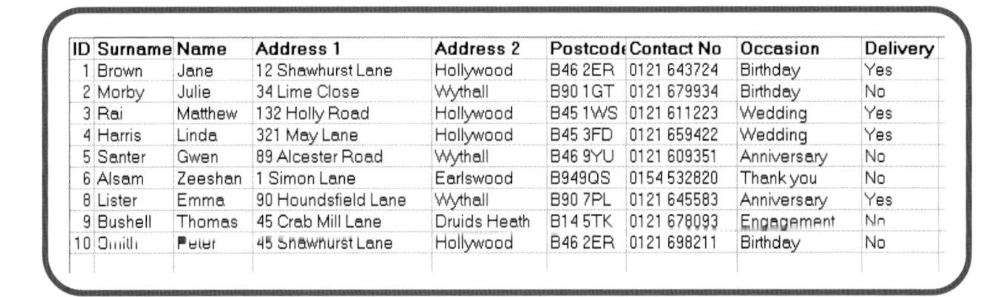

ID	**Surname**	**Name**	**Address 1**	**Address 2**	**Postcode**	**Contact No**	**Occasion**	**Delivery**
1	Brown	Jane	12 Shawhurst Lane	Hollywood	B46 2ER	0121 643724	Birthday	Yes
2	Morby	Julie	34 Lime Close	Wythall	B90 1GT	0121 679934	Birthday	No
3	Rai	Matthew	132 Holly Road	Hollywood	B45 1WS	0121 611223	Wedding	Yes
4	Harris	Linda	321 May Lane	Hollywood	B45 3FD	0121 659422	Wedding	Yes
5	Santer	Gwen	89 Alcester Road	Wythall	B46 9YU	0121 609351	Anniversary	No
6	Alsam	Zeeshan	1 Simon Lane	Earlswood	B949QS	0154 532820	Thank you	No
8	Lister	Emma	90 Houndsfield Lane	Wythall	B90 7PL	0121 645583	Anniversary	Yes
9	Bushell	Thomas	45 Crab Mill Lane	Druids Heath	B14 5TK	0121 678093	Engagement	No
10	Smith	Peter	45 Shawhurst Lane	Hollywood	B46 2ER	0121 698211	Birthday	No

Mail merge

The information that has been saved from the database into a spreadsheet can now be used to create a mail merge. Hannah has a standard letter, shown here, that she wants to send out to all the customers.

23rd January 2009

Flower Exchange
Drakes Cross
Wythall
B46 7HU

Dear

For your loved one!

Flowers say a million words! Why not send your loved one a bouquet to remind them how special they are to you.

We at the Flower Exchange would like to offer all our valued customers a special offer for Valentines day.

All orders received by February 10th 2009 will be upgraded to our Gold range bouquet when a Silver range bouquet is purchased - priced at £25.00. This special offer will include:

Free delivery on Valentine's day
Free balloon
Free card
Free box of chocolates

We would like to wish you a Happy Valentines and look forward to seeing you soon.

Yours sincerely

These are the steps that Hannah will follow to carry out the mail merge:

1 To start the mail merge, she selects 'Tools' from the menu bar, then 'Letters and Mailings' and then 'Mail Merge'.

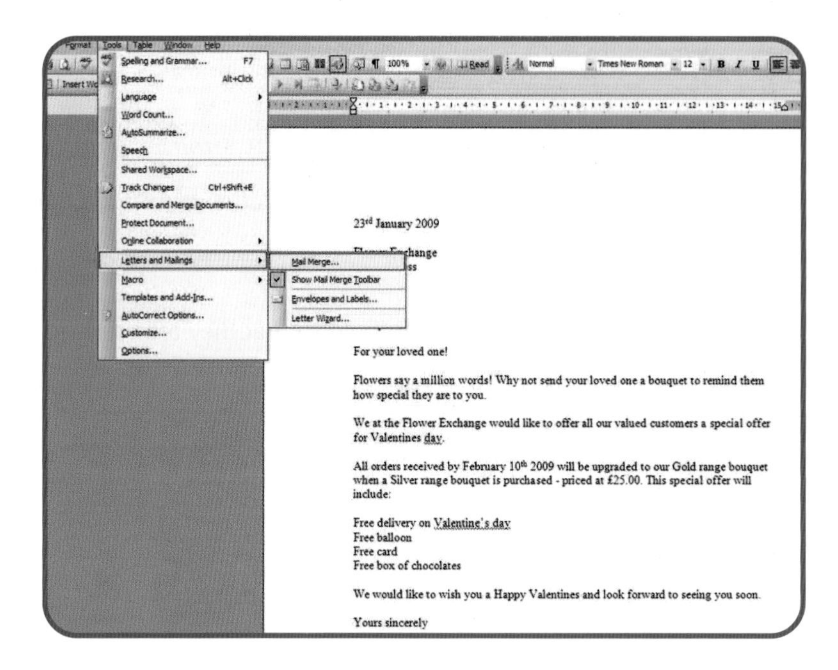

2 This brings up the different merge options. Hannah selects 'Letters'.

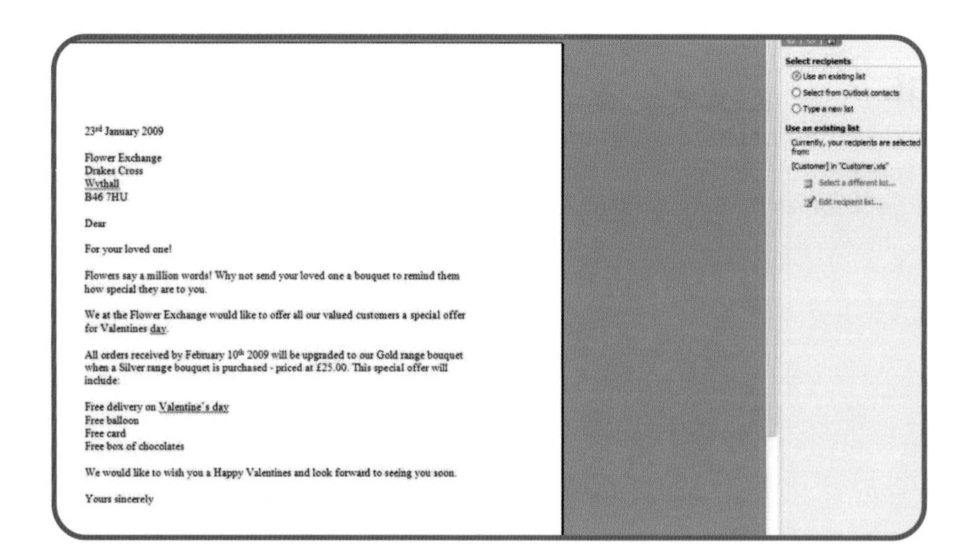

Hannah then needs to select the source of the information she wants to merge with the letter. She selects the Excel document that she has saved previously.

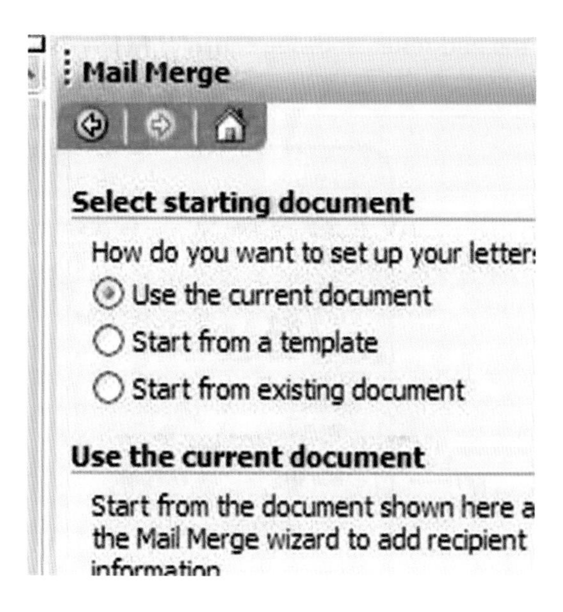

Hannah inserts the headings she wishes to include in the letter.

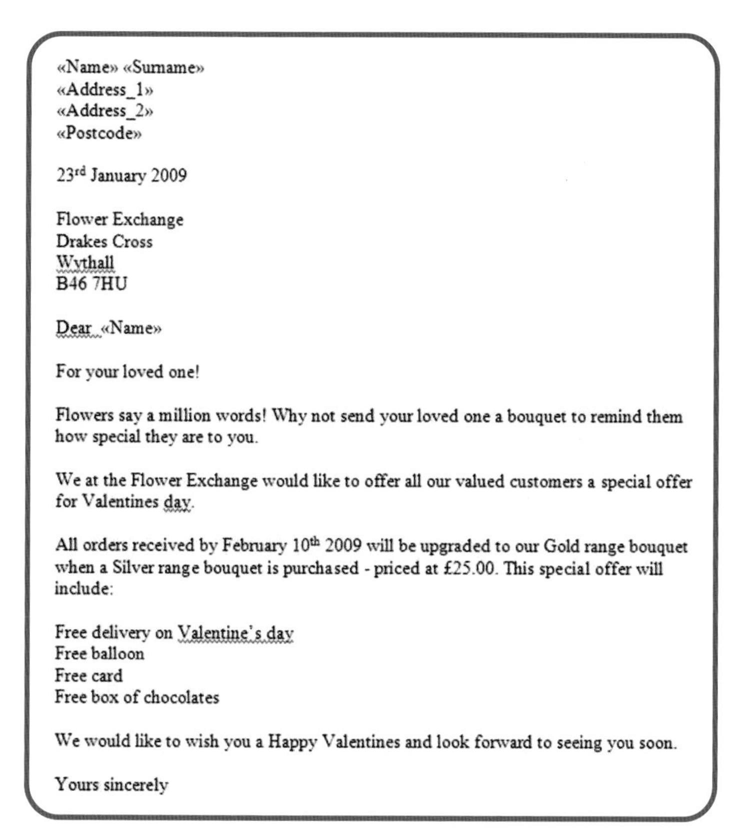

«Name» «Surname»
«Address_1»
«Address_2»
«Postcode»

23rd January 2009

Flower Exchange
Drakes Cross
Wythall
B46 7HU

Dear «Name»

For your loved one!

Flowers say a million words! Why not send your loved one a bouquet to remind them how special they are to you.

We at the Flower Exchange would like to offer all our valued customers a special offer for Valentines day.

All orders received by February 10th 2009 will be upgraded to our Gold range bouquet when a Silver range bouquet is purchased - priced at £25.00. This special offer will include:

Free delivery on Valentine's day
Free balloon
Free card
Free box of chocolates

We would like to wish you a Happy Valentines and look forward to seeing you soon.

Yours sincerely

This is the end result, showing the information that Hannah exported from the database to the spreadsheet and finally used in the letter.

Jane Brown
12 Shawhurst Lane
Hollywood
B46 2ER

23rd January 2009

Flower Exchange
Drakes Cross
Wythall
B46 7HU

Dear Jane

For your loved one!

Flowers say a million words! Why not send your loved one a bouquet to remind them how special they are to you.

We at the Flower Exchange would like to offer all our valued customers a special offer for Valentines day.

All orders received by February 10th 2009 will be upgraded to our Gold range bouquet when a Silver range bouquet is purchased - priced at £25.00. This special offer will include:

Free delivery on Valentine's day
Free balloon
Free card
Free box of chocolates

We would like to wish you a Happy Valentines and look forward to seeing you soon.

Yours sincerely

Let's go!

Activities

1 Carrefour Gym has just opened next door to the supermarket in Maypole. You have been asked to create a database of gym members, from the information in the table below, which can then be exported into an Excel file.

Title	Initial	Surname	Address	Postcode
Mr	E	Edwards	24 Thistle Lane	B14 3TR
Miss	P	Flanders	76 Acorns Road	B15 8YU
Mrs	H	Simpson	64 Mary Road	B14 2ER
Mr	J	Robinson	90 Riddings Road	B15 2WD

a) Create the database.

b) Export your database into spreadsheet software.

c) Edit the cells to ensure that all the information is shown clearly.

2 a) Write a standard letter that can be sent to each customer about the changes to the membership fee.

b) Send this letter to the customers using mail merge.

3 a) Using the information below, create a database for the different pupils in the different forms.

Name	Surname	Form	Tutor
Richard	Griffiths	8N	HTH
Jasmine	Henry	8N	HTH
Haris	Ahmed	8O	MPE
Rameez	Ali	8T	HFI
Michael	Rouke	8C	RNA
Abu	Mustafa	8N	HTH
Basma	Fadil	8S	RBA
Neelam	Hussain	8S	RBA
Mohammed	Aqeel	8C	RNA

b) Sort the database by form in ascending order.

c) Create a report using the following headings:

Name

Surname

Form

d) Filter the database on the tutor field. Look for RBA.

Summary

- Integrating a database is extremely useful when the same information is used for different purposes.
- Being able to export the information into another software format can often save time.
- The database can hold personal details, and the spreadsheet will enable the user to use this data to carry out calculations and create charts. The same information can also be used in mail merges.

Key words

Query – using the database to find out certain information.

Filter – a facility on the database to narrow down the information so that only particular data is shown.

Report – provides an overview of information in the database, based on selected field headings.

Mail merge – combining a list of names and addresses from one program with another to make a standard personalised letter.

Bold – a thicker, darker version of text that makes it stand out from the rest.

Export – take from one place to another.

Give me five

1. What does export mean?
2. Why would you want to export information from a database to a spreadsheet?
3. How do you format the cells to show all the information?
4. Why would you use mail merge?
5. What benefits are there to using mail merge?

Exam style questions

The Hair Room has announced a special reduction throughout the month of February. You have been asked to transfer the information from the client database to a spreadsheet so that the information can be used to send out a promotional letter.

1 a) Using the information below, create a database. (2 marks)

Title	Initial	Surname	Address	Stylists
Mr	P	Sanders	21 May Lane	Abbey
Miss	T	Harris	46 Swan Road	Gina
Miss	H	Smith	56 Holly Croft	Abbey
Mrs	G	Powers	89 Lister Road	Emma
Miss	H	Allen	190 Peterbrook Road	Emma

b) Save your database with an appropriate name. (1 mark)

c) Export your database into spreadsheet software. (1 mark)

d) Edit the spreadsheet to ensure all the information fits. (1 mark)

2 The Hair Room wants you to write a short note to all the customers. In the note you must explain that Abby and Gina are leaving the company and that Emma will now be their stylist. (2 marks)

3 Mail merge the note, sending it to customers who ONLY have Abbey or Gina as their stylists. (2 mark)

Chapter 24

Creating graphics

In this chapter you will learn:

- how to create graphics
- how to edit graphics
- how to combine text and graphics.

Getting started

Organisations want to make their business stand out from others. This is especially important for small businesses, which have to compete with more well-known companies. Customers are often attracted by the logos and graphics associated with that brand name.

If your teacher were to name some name brands, would you instantly picture an image? What symbol would you associate with Nike? Did you say a tick? How about Cadburys? Is it the purple background with a white swirl?

By having a distinctive logo, the organisations are creating a corporate image that makes people remember their name. They will invest large amounts of money in this and will hire a specialist design company to develop and design a logo that customers will remember. But how does a small business compete?

What you need to know

The development of graphics software has enabled small businesses to create simple yet effective designs without spending too much money. There is different software available to suit the skills of different user. A very simple and easy software to use is Paint. Users can draw freehand, add shapes and even manipulate existing designs to suit their needs.

Creating and using graphics

Hollywood Fish Bar has recently undergone a refurbishment. They want to redesign their logo so that it reflects what they do. The owner, Jane Rouke, has decided to create her own using Paint. Read the steps below to see how she is able to use simple shapes and freehand functions to create her logo.

1 Jane has used Paint to create a design that is unique to her business. The graphic below has been created using simple lines and shapes. The eye has been filled in using the 'Fill' option.

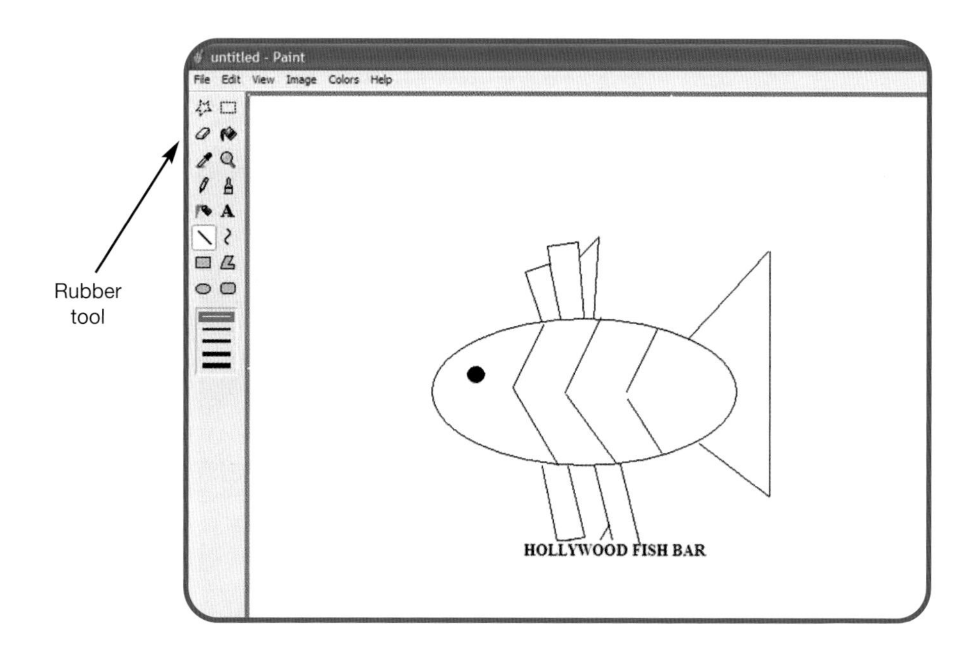

2 Jane can edit this image by using the rubber. She can also add more colour. As you can see, Jane has coloured in part of the fish and a chip.

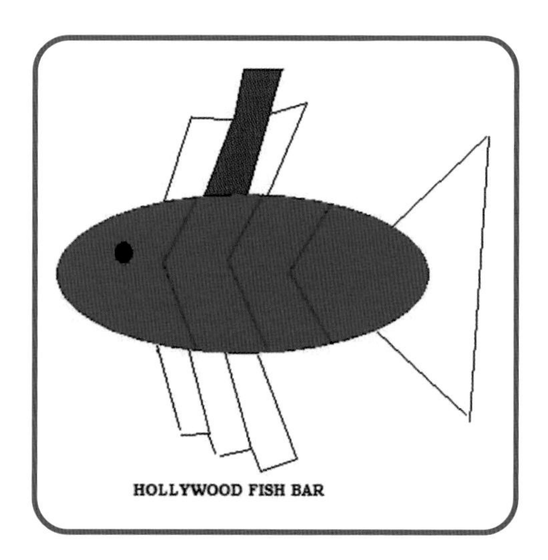

3 Jane can also resize the image and even import it into another document. For example, if she wanted to create a promotional flyer she could copy and paste the logo into desktop publishing software. To do this Jane draws round her image and then selects 'Cut'. She could also select 'Copy' if she wished to keep the original in the graphics software as well as exporting a copy.

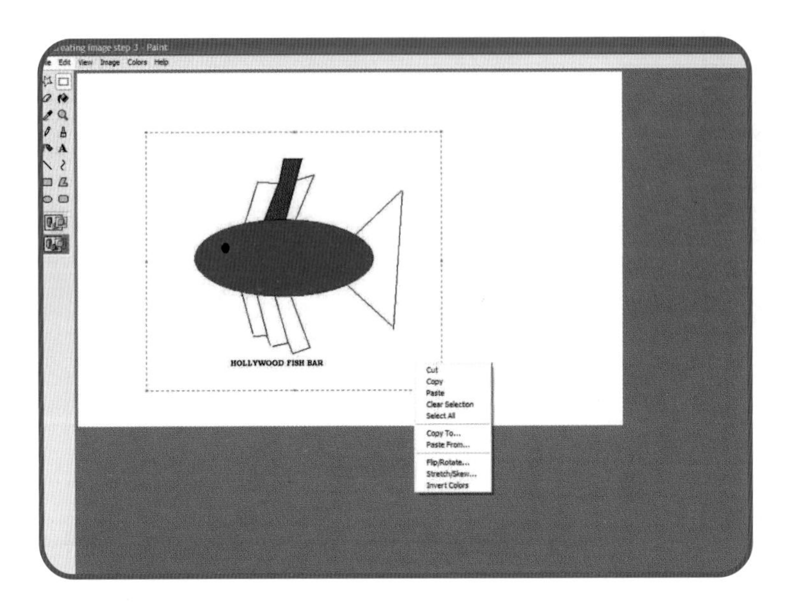

4 She then opens the appropriate software, in this case Publisher, and selects 'Paste'.

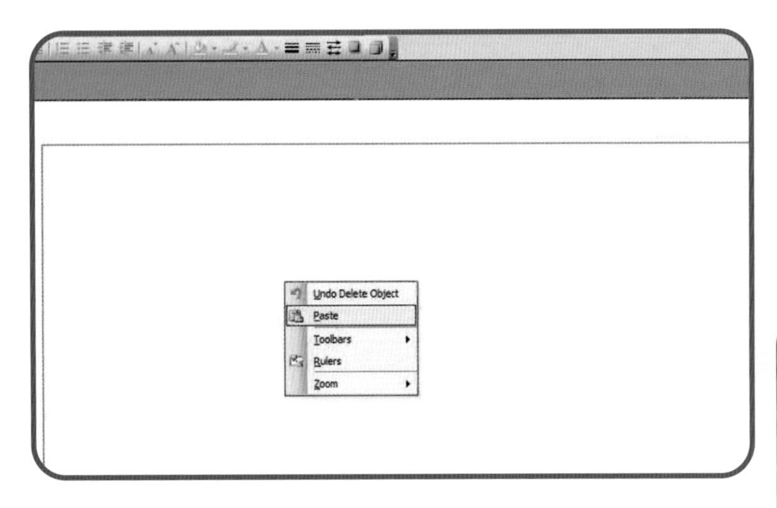

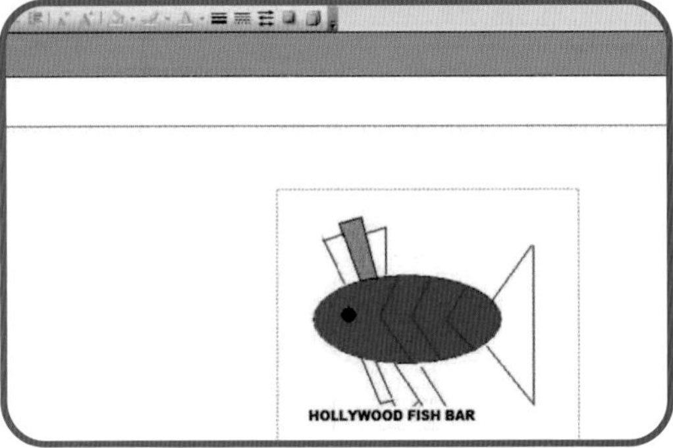

5 Jane can resize her image if necessary. As you can see, Jane has decided to move and resize her image to the top middle of the page.

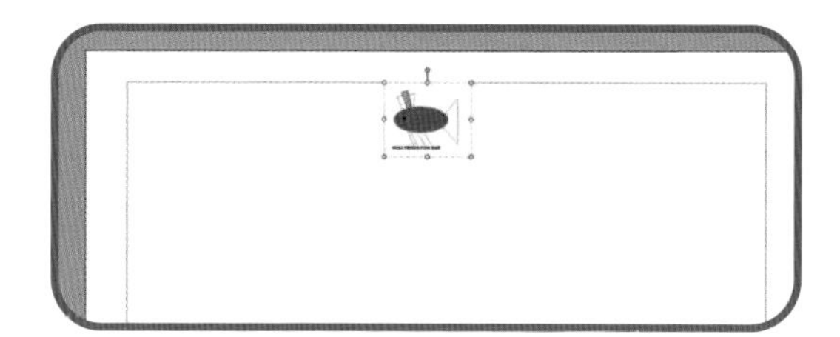

Let's go!

Activities

1 Your doctor's surgery wants you to design a new logo for the business. You have been asked to use shapes and lines only. You can use colour and text to identify the name. Use drawing software such as Paint to practise creating a logo. Alternatively, you can use desktop publishing software to practise using graphics tools.

2 Using the logo you designed in activity 1, make two changes to your logo. Show screen shots of the steps you have taken.

3 Import the logo you amended in activity 2 into different software. Resize the logo so it will fit on a letter. Take screen shots to show the steps you have taken.

Summary

- Graphics can often make a document more eye catching and appealing.
- A simple graphic can be just as effective as a complex design.
- It is important for the user to consider what the business actually does and the image it wants to portray to its customers.

Key words

Resize – make the image smaller or larger.

Edit – alter the appearance of the original image.

Crop – cut around the image to get rid of unwanted background.

Shading – adding a light colouring to the image.

Freehand – using the mouse and tool to replicate hand drawing.

Geometric shapes – include squares and rectangles; shapes that can be filled with colour and put together to create an image.

Call outs – can be used to replicate someone speaking or thinking.

Give me five

Identify five different functions in drawing software.

Exam style questions

1. Give ONE reason why a small business would want to create a graphic to support its image? (2 marks)
2. Explain the benefits of using a drawing software package to create graphics. (6 marks)
3. Analyse the reasons why a small business would design its own logo instead of hiring a specialist company. (8 marks)

Chapter 25

Using presentation software

In this chapter you will learn:

- how to create a business presentation
- how to create transitions and animations
- how to modify presentations
- how to create presenter notes
- how to create handouts.

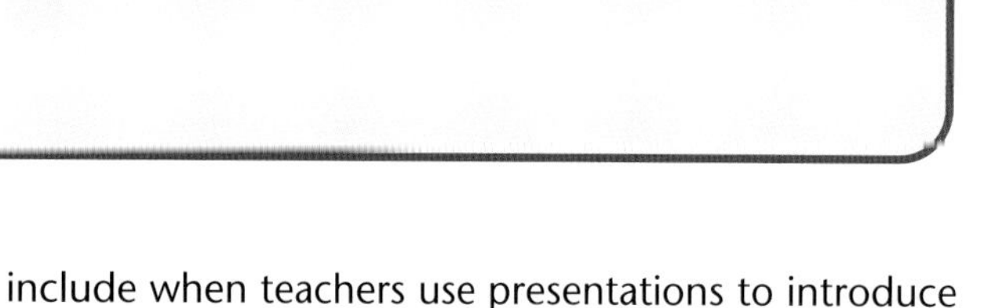

Getting started

Presentations are given for many different reasons, such as communicating information or trying to persuade someone to do something. Examples include when teachers use presentations to introduce a new topic or a salesperson tries to get you to buy something. Businesses now use presentations on a more regular basis as the technology is so readily available.

Most presentations are given by a speaker who introduces slides which are projected onto a large screen. This means that the audience can see the information on the screen while the speaker gives more detailed spoken information.

What you need to know

The most popular presentation program is Microsoft PowerPoint. Many homes, schools and businesses use Microsoft Office on their computers and PowerPoint is one of the programs which is incorporated with the Office collection. PowerPoint is now used more in schools than blackboards or whiteboards as a method of teaching. It is easy to change and add information to an already prepared presentation, which makes it much easier to use.

Getting started with PowerPoint

1 Open the program by clicking on the PowerPoint icon.

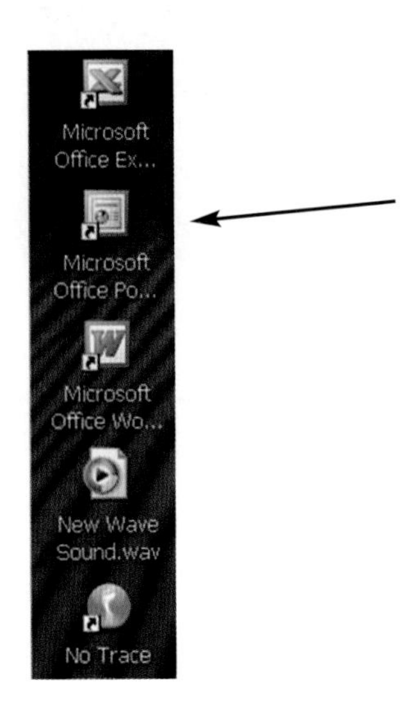

2 When the program opens up, the first page will look like this.

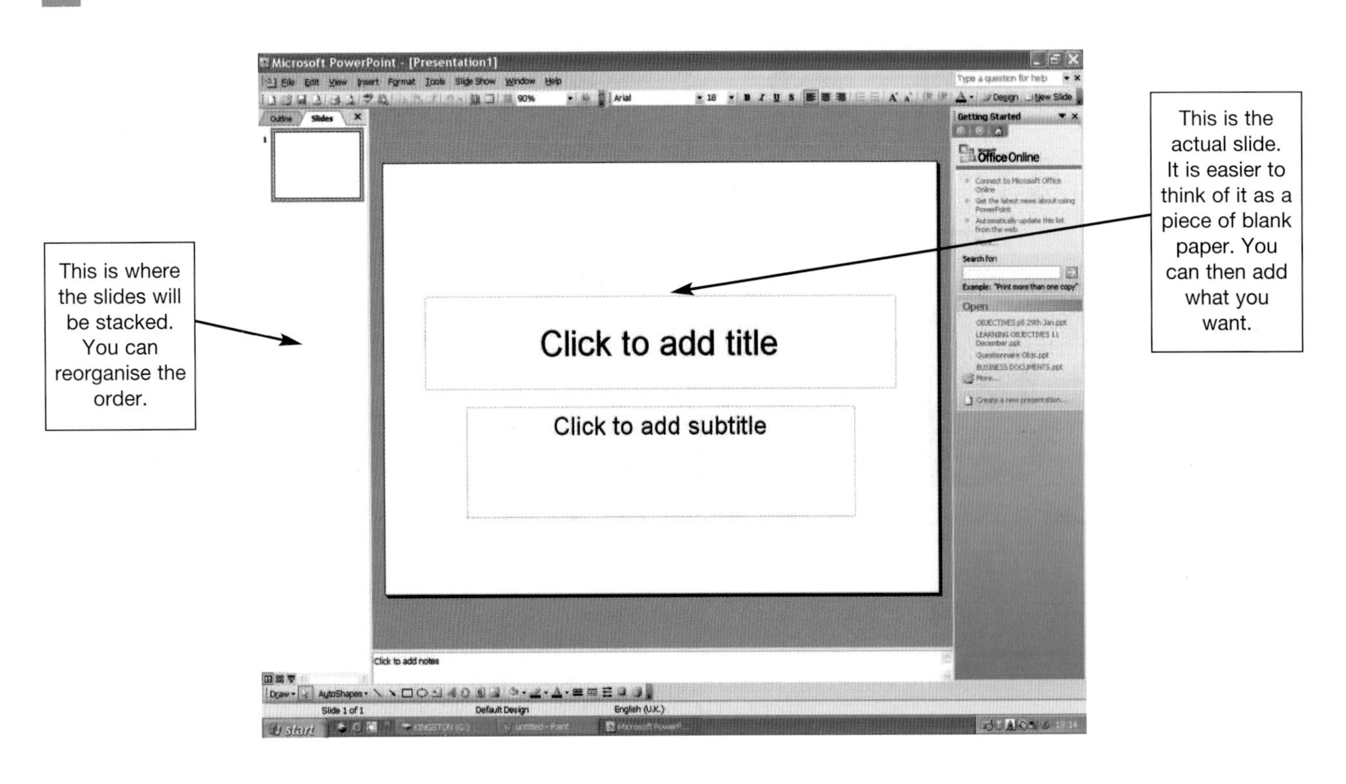

3. You are now ready to begin creating your own presentation. You can see that the program helps you by suggesting that you click on the box to add your title or subtitle.

4. Clicking on the 'View' menu tab gives you several options in which you can view your screen.

   - 'Normal View, Outline View' will show all the titles and text for each slide.
   - 'Slide Sorter View' can be used to reorganise the sequence of the slides.
   - 'Slide Show' allows you to watch the presentation.

5. There are guidelines to help you position your items on the slides. Go to 'View', then 'Grids and Guides', then select 'Display drawing guides on screen'. These will not be shown during your presentation.

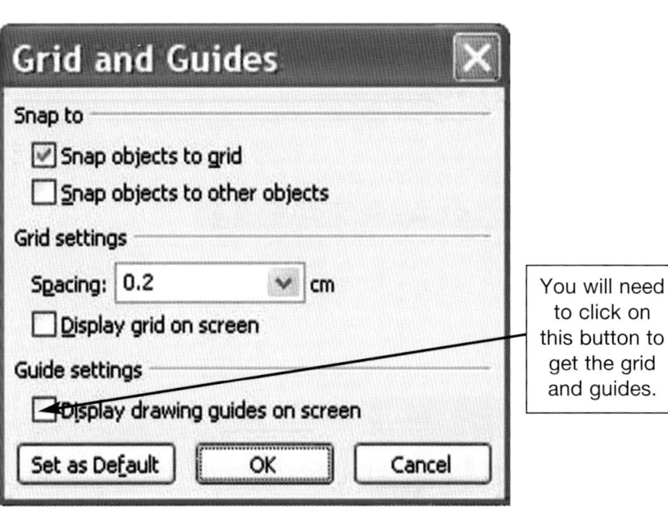

Adding colour to your presentation

You may wish to have a colour scheme to your presentation. However, it is important when creating a business presentation that the colour scheme is chosen to reflect the topic being considered or the corporate image of the business. Care should be taken not to reduce the effect of the message because the colour scheme takes over the presentation. For example, having a black screen with coloured writing on may not be very clear. Also, using a variety of different colours for each slide might look nice on screen but can distract from the presentation. The people watching the presentation will be looking at the colour rather than the details of the presentation.

To choose your colour:

1. Go to 'Format' and then select 'Slide Design'.

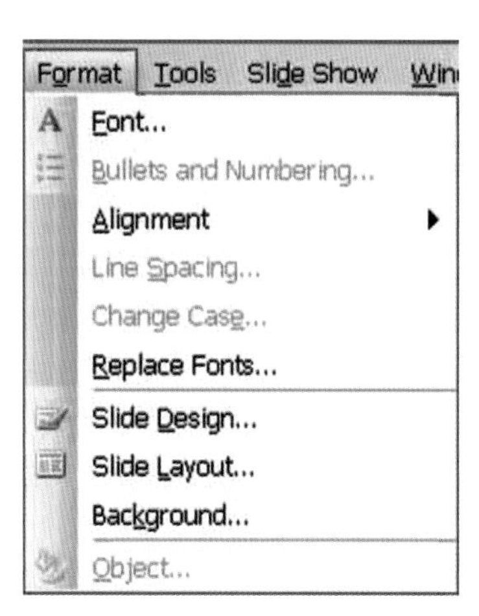

2. Now choose 'Color Schemes' (colour is spelt without the 'u' because an American company designed the program and they spell the word differently). You will see from the section below that there are many standard colour schemes to choose from.

3 You can use one of the standard colour schemes or customise your own. Even if you choose one colour now you can always change your mind and alter it later. If you wish to create your own colour scheme, select 'Edit Color Scheme'.

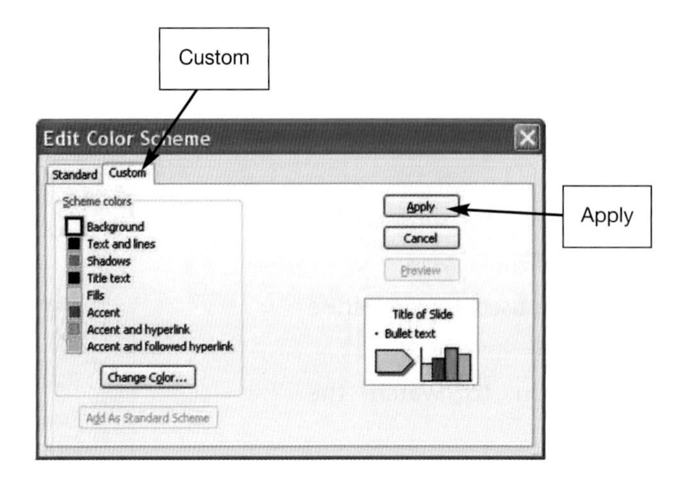

Creating your title page

Now that you have decided on the colour scheme you can begin to add your text to the presentation. You can use the main fonts and sizes or you can add more to your presentation by using the WordArt Gallery.

1 Click on the 'WordArt' icon.

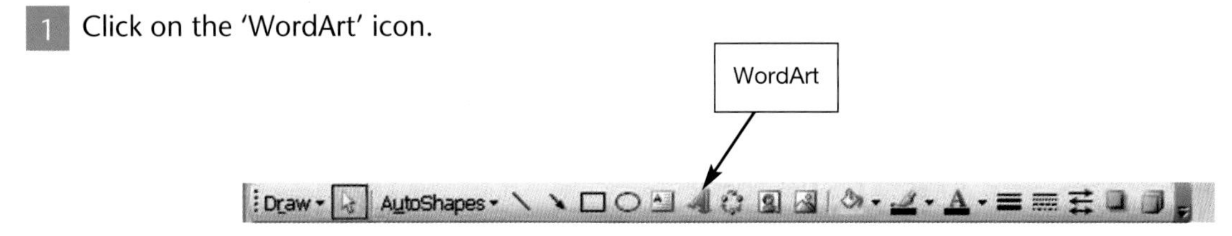

The WordArt Gallery will then appear.

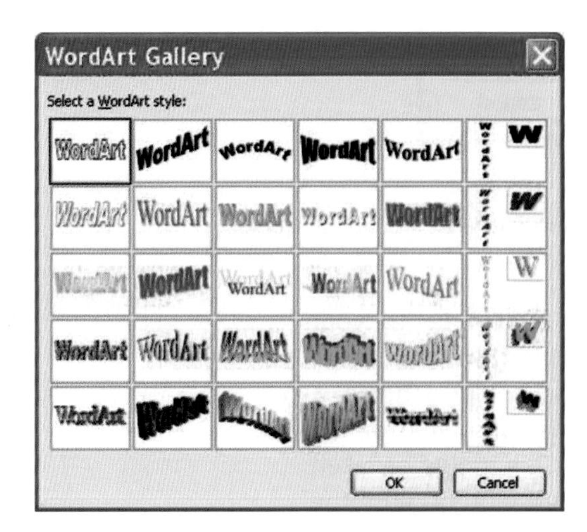

2 You can then select whichever style you prefer for your heading or title. Remember that you can change the font size, style and colour to personalise your work.

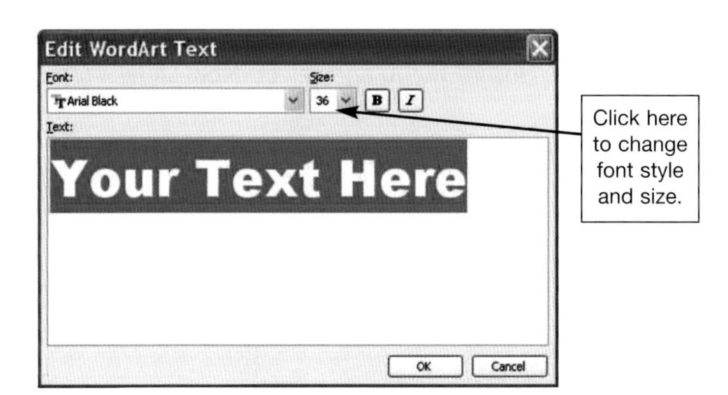

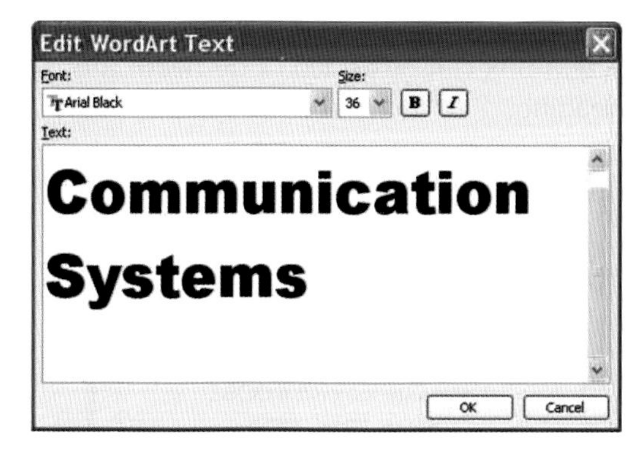

3 When creating a heading, remember that it is a heading and not a statement and therefore should not be too long.

Business & Communication Systems

4 You can add colour to your heading and also change the size and height of the heading by using the WordArt toolbar.

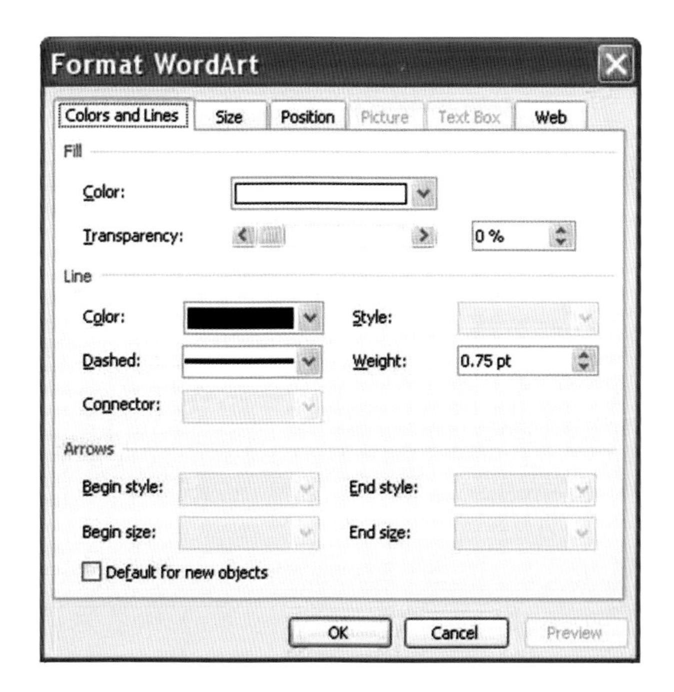

5 The final version of your heading could look like this.

BUSINESS & COMMUNICATION SYSTEMS

6 By using the tool bar at the bottom you can shade your work, change the colour and alter the heading as much as you like.

7 A text box can be added underneath the heading.

Adding slides

Now that the title page is complete, a new page (slide) can be added.

1 Go to 'Insert' menu and select 'New Slide'.

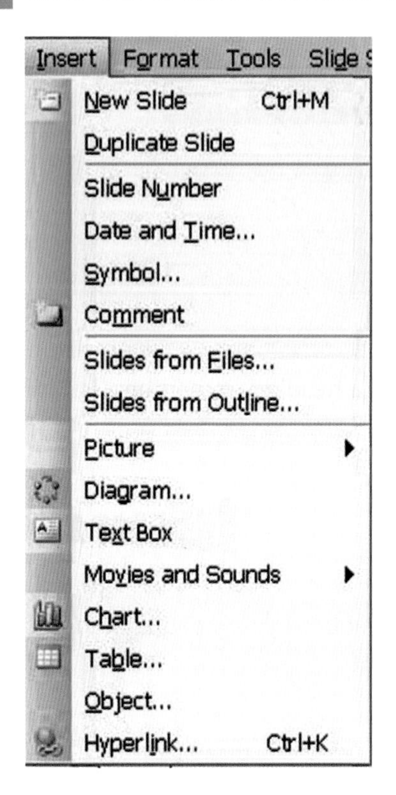

2 This will add a new slide.

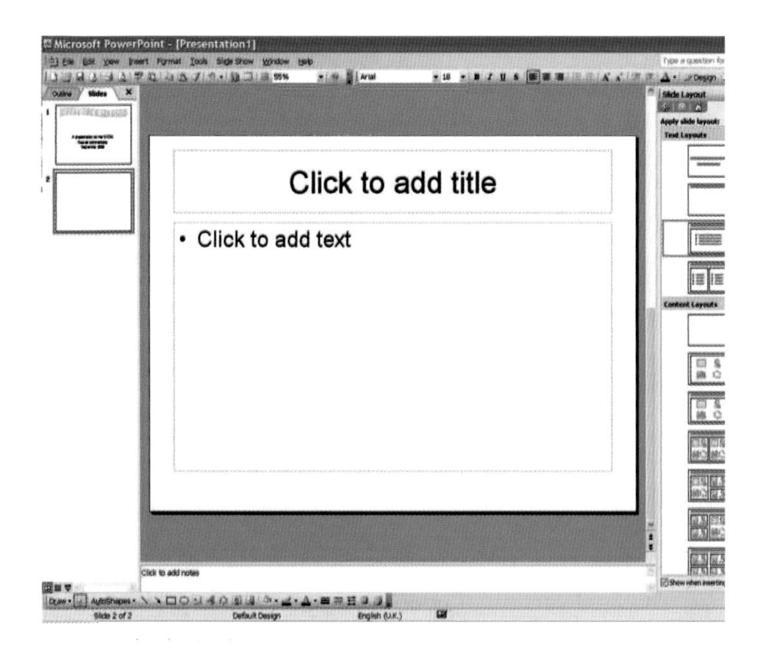

You will see that the new slide has the same background that you chose for the title page. The number of slides you have in your presentation is shown on the left-hand side of the screen. This is a good way to keep track of the number of slides you have created and a view of what they look like.

3 Each slide will have a title and a text box.

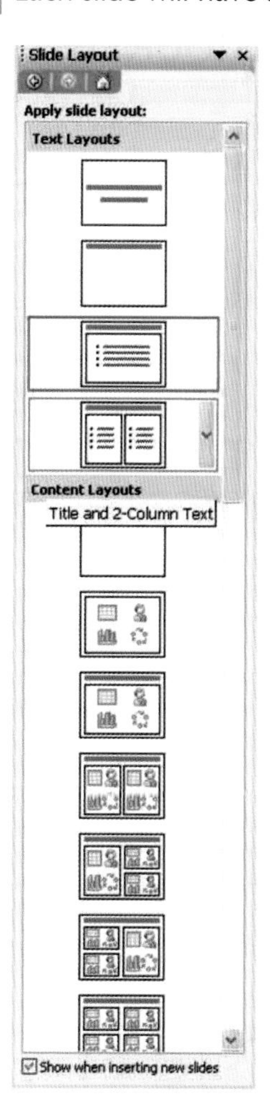

4 When you insert a slide you can either use a blank side or use one of the many standard layouts from the 'Slide Layout' menu. They give you a good idea of what you can do. Depending on your skill and experience of the program, you may feel happier using one of the templates rather than creating your own.

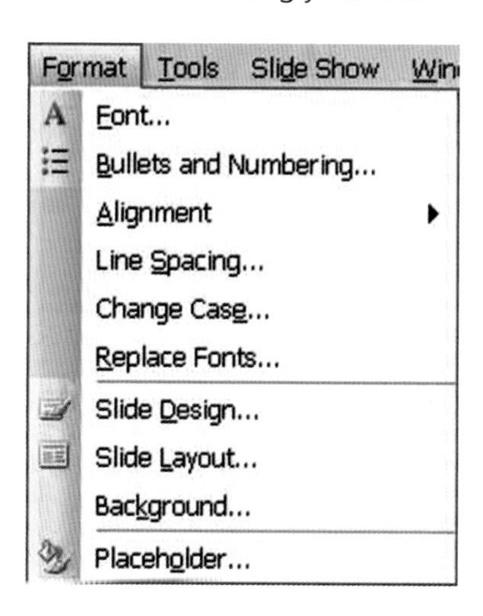

Adding detail

More detail can now be added to your presentation, along with clipart, charts and many other facilities that the program offers.

To add bullet points go to 'Format' and select 'Bullets and Numbering'. You can select the format as shown here.

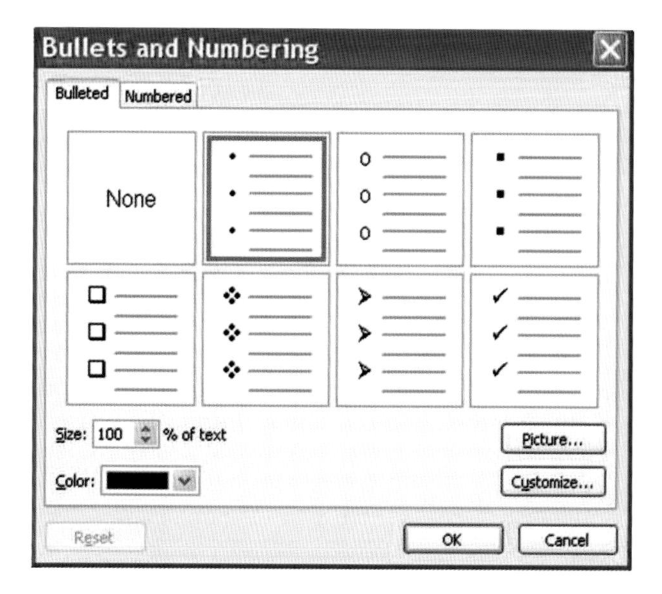

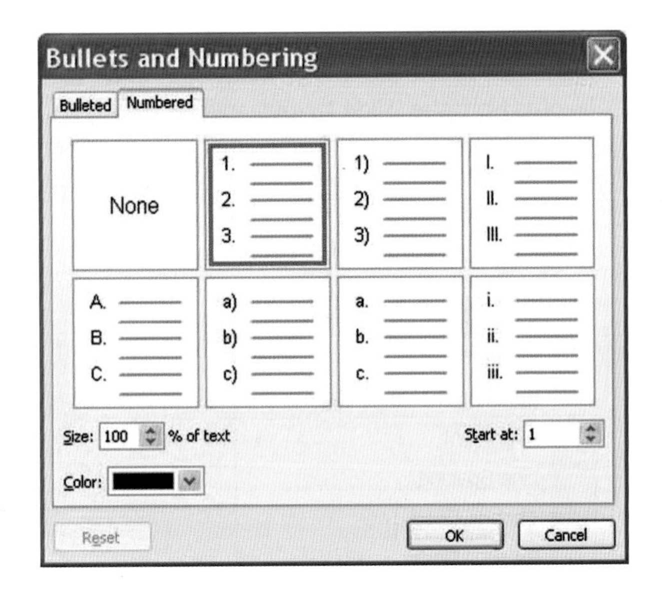

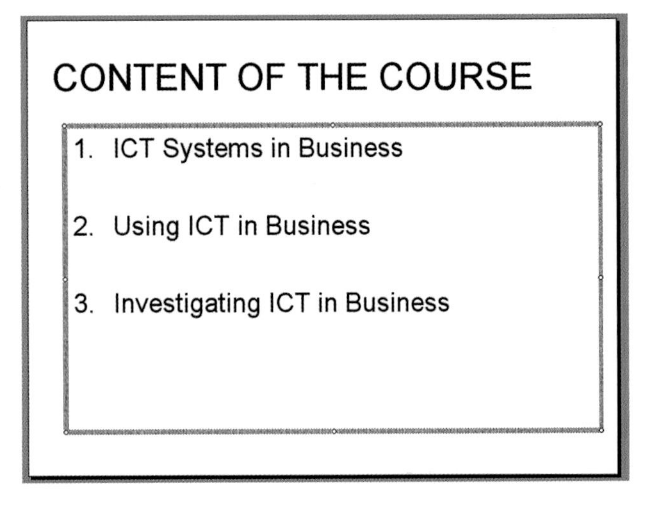

Now that you have added bulleted or numbered items you may want to enhance your presentation with clipart or pictures. You do this by going to 'Insert' and selecting 'Picture', then 'From File'. You locate the picture you want from the folder where you have saved the pictures and then select 'OK'.

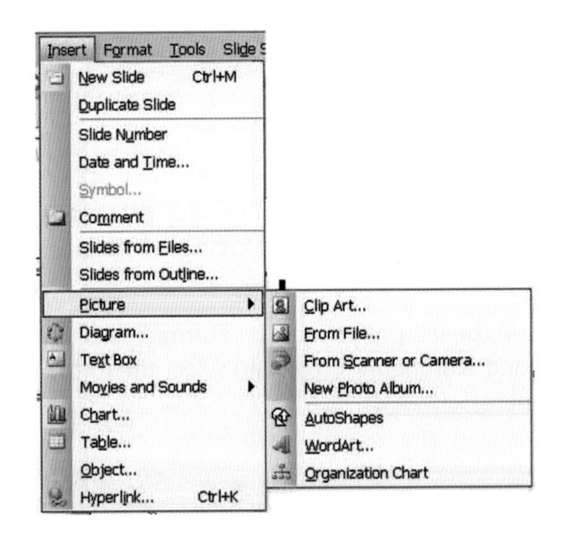

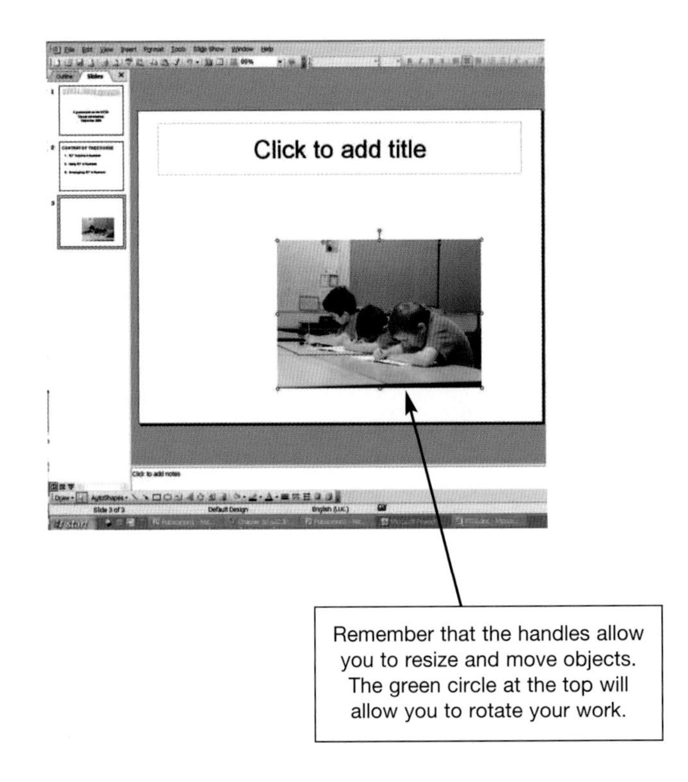

To add a picture from 'Clip Art' is very similar: click on 'Inset', 'Pictures', but choose 'Clip Art' instead of 'From File'. You can also add pictures, text from other sources, such as another presentation, a Word document or even the internet. You can simply 'Insert' the words or pictures from wherever your items are saved.

Adding a chart is just as easy. Click on 'Insert', then 'Chart'.

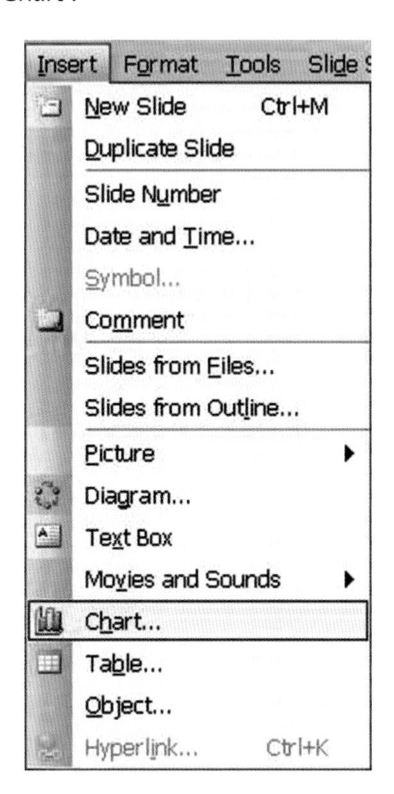

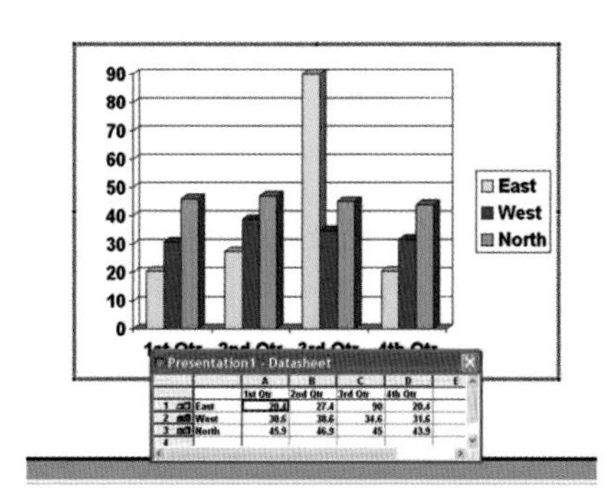

You can either create your chart in the spreadsheet program Excel or amend the standard chart that has been inserted. You can move the chart around and decide where you want it on the slide. You can also add explanatory text beside your chart.

You can add a logo to every page of your presentation by inserting the logo graphic on the master slide. Click on the 'View' menu, then 'Master' and then 'Slide Master'. Then insert the image by going to 'Insert' and selecting 'Picture', then 'From File'. After inserting the graphic, close the master view. The logo will appear on all the slides in the top right-hand corner.

Making slides into a presentation

Once you have created your series of slides, you can now begin to make them into a presentation. The advantage of this presentation program is that the speaker is in control and can decide when each frame on a slide appears; for example, each bullet point in a list should appear on screen at just the right moment. Your presentation should contain short, carefully worded sentences and paragraphs – as a rule, there should be no full pages of text. This means that the text will remain large and clear so that everyone can see it properly, even those sitting at the back of the room.

You can use animation effects to make the frames arrive on screen in different ways. For example, a line of text can appear one word at a time, or the whole line can fly into place from one side. However, as with colour and other formatting features, it is important not to let the animation distract from the content of the presentation, so do not overuse it.

Again, there are standard animation schemes supplied on the software, or you can customise your own. Animation can keep your presentation lively or draw attention to a particular point.

1 Select 'Custom Animation' from the 'Slide Show' menu.

2 To animate your slide show, select the item you wish to animate by clicking on it. Choose how you want to animate the item and choose the type of animation you want, as shown here.

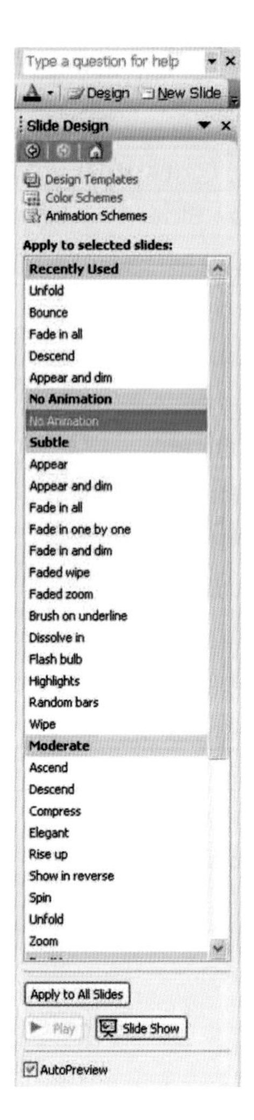

3 It is important that you are consistent in your presentation (keeping fonts and colours the same). Remember that animation can be used for headings as well as text boxes. It is also possible to change the order in which your items appear and the timing of the animations.

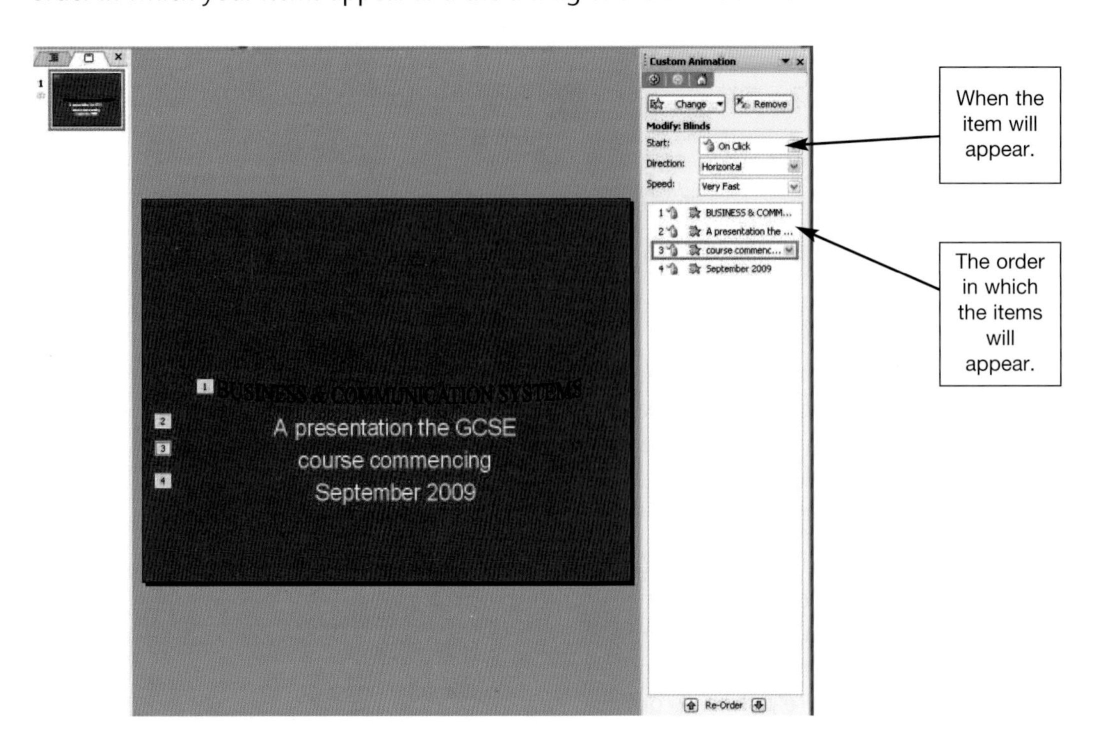

When you have finished preparing the presentation you can add a slide transition effect. This is an effect that will happen between each slide.

1 Go to the 'Slide Show' menu and select 'Slide Transition'.

2 Choosing the transition effect you want is easy – it will be demonstrated on the slide.

3 You then need to decide the speed at which you want it to happen: 'Slow', 'Medium' or 'Fast'. Bear in mind the content and audience of your presentation; 'Fast' is not always going to be appropriate. Select 'On mouse click' or set a time limit for the slides to change automatically.

4 Select 'Apply to All Slides'.

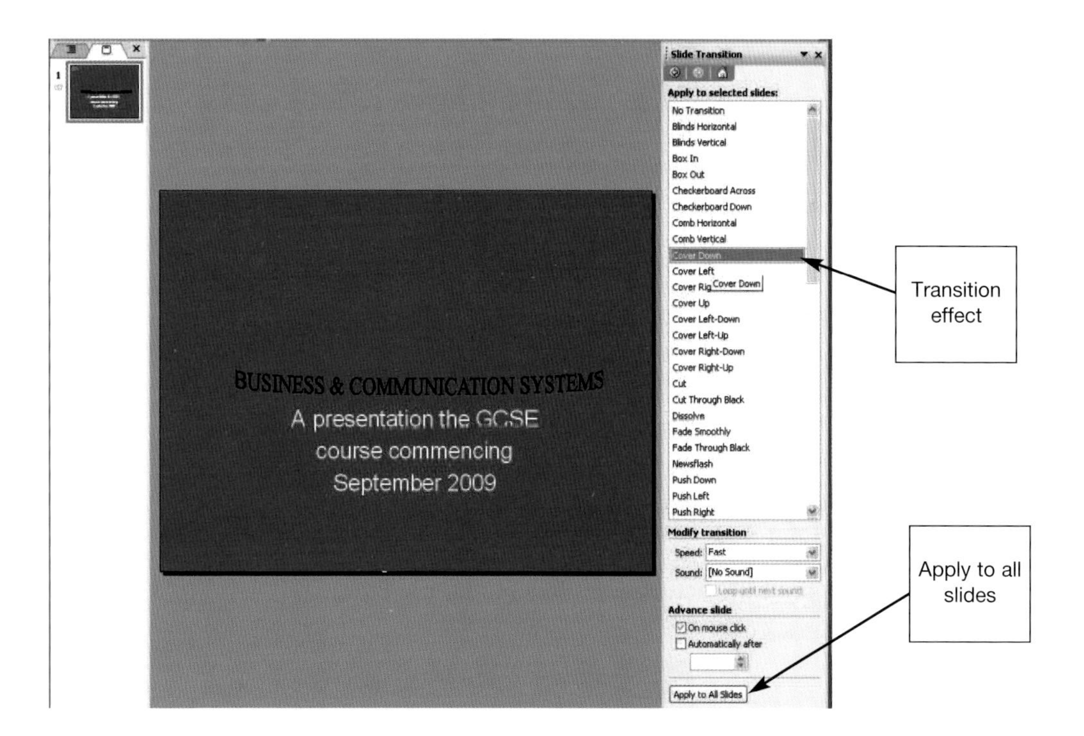

Using your presentation

You have now created your presentation, but how are you going to use it? If you are actually going to give the presentation then you will need to prepare what you are going say with each slide. This program will allow you to make notes at the bottom of each slide so that you have something as a prompt to help you.

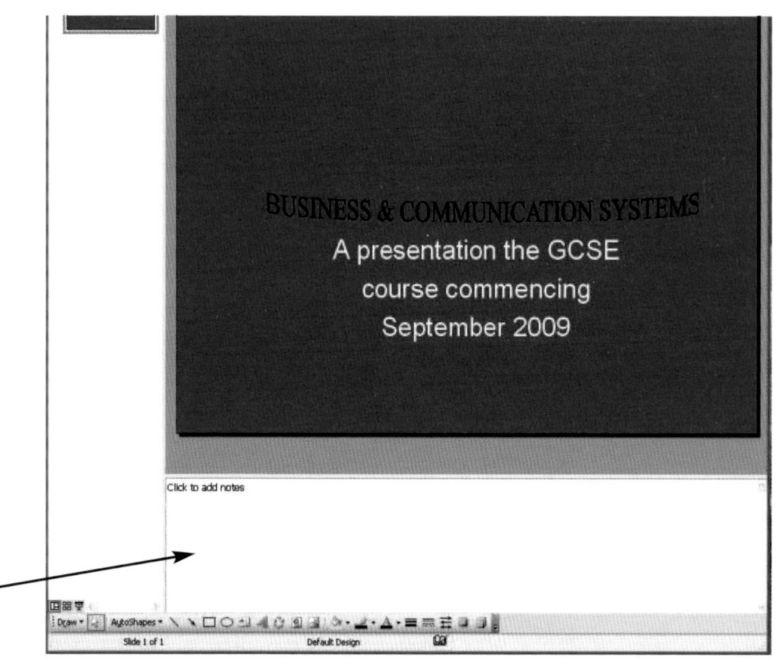

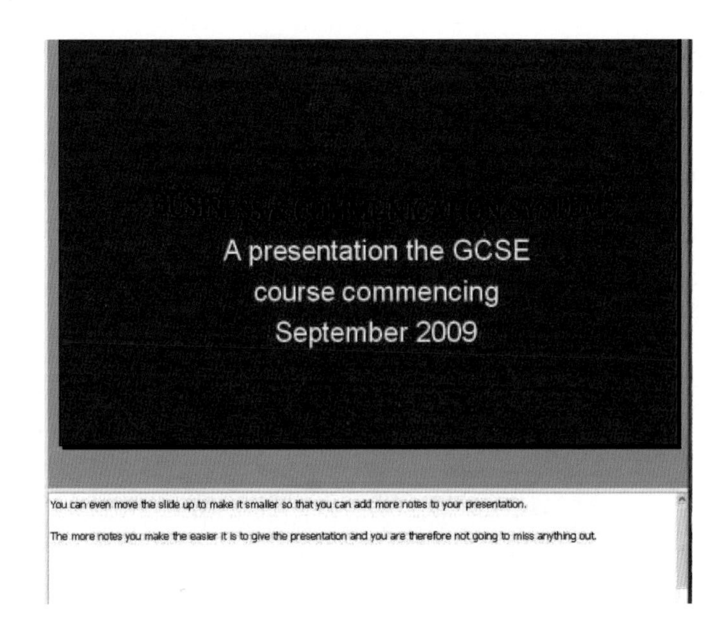

By clicking on the bottom of the slide you are able to move the slide up the screen, allowing you to see clearly the notes you have made. The more notes you make the better your presentation will be, as you are less likely to forget anything.

Printing

Once you have completed your notes there are a variety of ways to print your presentation. Most presenters will offer at least two if not three ways of doing this.

The first way is to just print the actual slides by clicking on 'Print'.

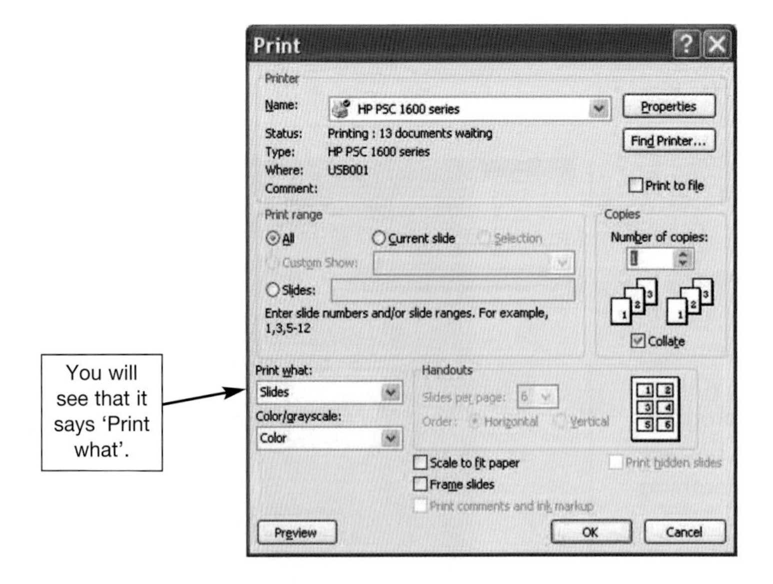

The second method is to print off the slides with the presenter's notes underneath. You again click on 'Print' and then select the drop-down menu for 'Print what'.

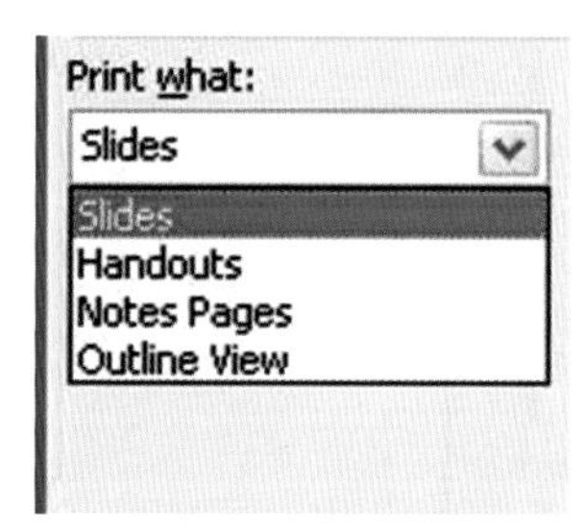

You will see that there are several options to choose from.

- Slides – which are the actual slides and they will print on a page each.
- Handouts – this will print the number of slides you want on each page.
- Notes page – this will print the notes the presenter has written to go with the presentation.
- Outline view

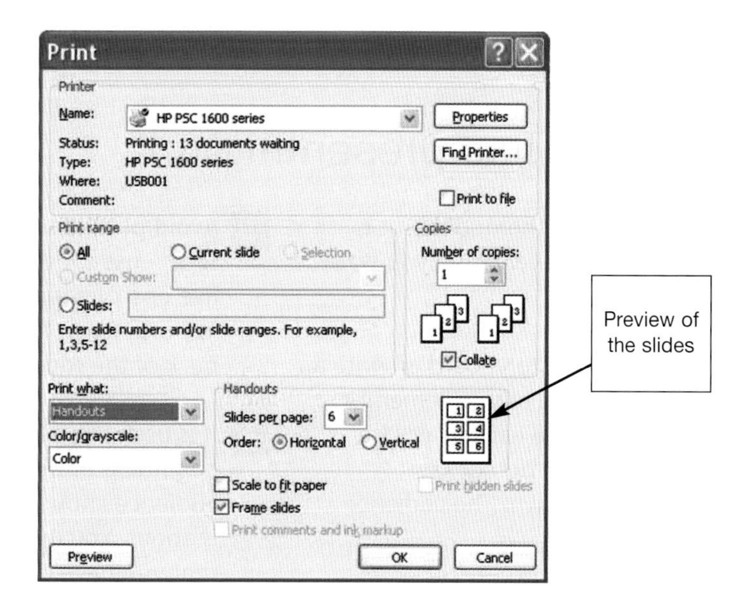

In the screen shot below 'Handouts' has been selected with three slides on each page. You can see a small preview of what it will look like on the right-hand side.

You can select a number of slides with lines on the right-hand side so that your audience can make notes, as shown below.

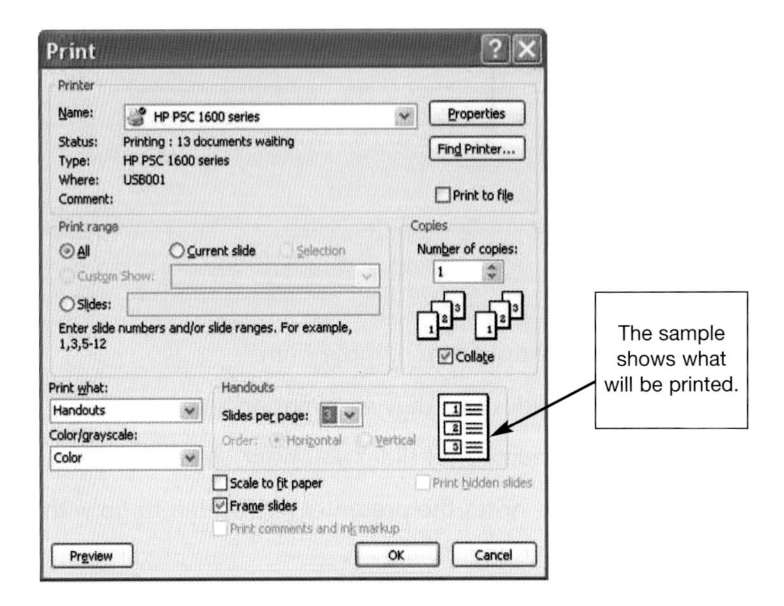

Tips on giving a good presentation

1. Prepare and plan your work thoroughly – it is important that you include everything you want to discuss.

2. You might want to create a storyboard or write a script of what you would like to say. Remember, the more notes you make the easier it will be and it does not matter if you do not say everything that is written down. The audience will not know.

3. Keep the slides simple – too much fuss, colour and animation can distract the audience from the content of the presentation. Take care to use fonts that are easy to read.

4. Use an 'Opening' so that people know what the presentation is about and a 'Closing' slide to remind them of the key points at the end. Also remember to introduce yourself at the beginning.

5. Avoid putting too much information on each slide – use short sentences with a maximum of five or six lines per slide. Remember the importance of font size so that the people at the back of the room can read the text easily.

6. It is useful to have a contents page at the beginning of the presentation so that the audience knows exactly what your presentation is about. You can then refer back to it to ensure that you have covered everything you intended to.

7. Practise your presentation several times. It is sometimes useful to get someone else to check through your slides to see if you have made any errors – spelling mistakes stand out more on a slide show than they do in written work. Check!

8. Remember to keep looking at your audience rather than your notes – they want to see your face, not the top of your head.

Let's go!

Activities

1. Write a simple, step-by-step guide to using a presentation program.
2. Give some advice on using colour in presentation.
3. Many students like to use animation in their presentations. What concerns might be pointed out about using animation in a presentation?
4. Draw up a plan for a presentation to the school's senior management team about a Leavers' Prom to be held next year.
5. Create the presentation, including notes to use when it is given.

Summary

- Presentations have been transformed by the use of presentation programs that give people a professional and effective method of delivering information.
- The audience has its own copy of what it has seen and can make its own notes.
- Information can be combined with text, charts and diagrams and makes the presentation more interesting for both the presenter and the audience.

Key words

Blank slide – a slide with nothing on it.

Slide sorter – a function for changing the order of the slides.

Animation – effects that can make a presentation more interesting.

Handles – (when activated) allow the user to change use and remove the frame.

Template – a slide layout that has already been created and comes with the software.

Transition – the movement from one slide to another.

Give me five

1 If you have not used Microsoft PowerPoint before, then open it up and create a presentation of at least four slides.
2 Add pictures and text from another file into your presentation, together with a clipart picture.
3/4 Try animating your presentation using at least two different styles.
5 Print off your presentation with four slides to one page.

Exam style question

You work in your local department store where presentations are a common method of informing people of many different things. You work in the Administration Office and often create presentations for a variety of tasks. A new employee, Lesley, has joined the company. She has very little experience using this program and has asked for your help.

1 Explain what might influence your choice of colour scheme in a presentation. (2 marks)

2 You have been asked to give Lesley some pointers on using PowerPoint for presentations. Draw up a list of Do's and Don'ts for her. (10 marks)

3 You have been asked by the manager to give help to resolve some problems they are having in one of their branches. The manager has provided you with the following data:

Customer Complaints in 2008

Quality of service (sales)	10%
Speed of service (sales)	30%
Quality of service (Customer service)	2%
Speed of service (Customer service)	2%
Product knowledge	15%

Design a presentation of 6–12 slides, based on the figures above. Use the data to find a focus for your presentation. The presentation should be for the staff and should aim to provide training in an area that you feel is appropriate.

Your presentation must:

- use Microsoft Powerpoint, or any comparable presentation software
- include analysis of relevant business issues
- include at least one chart to illustrate a point
- include at least one graph based on the data
- use illustration such as clipart or graphics. (25 marks)

Chapter 26

Web authoring

In this chapter you will learn:

- how to create a web page
- how to create hyperlinks
- how to animate text.

Getting started

The development in technology has created easy access to a global market for any business that wishes to reach it. The increase in internet usage has enabled potential customers to find almost anything! In a highly competitive market, a business would be seriously hampered if they did not consider the benefits that a website could bring. However, they might be concerned about the cost of setting up and maintaining the website. This is an issue, but the potential increase in the market share, and ultimately the sales that could be generated, might make up for it. So how could a small business create a web page effectively?

What you need to know

Small businesses have limited finance when considering ways to increase their profile. However, with the development of software, creating a website does not have to be expensive. Many of the software packages offer a wizard, enabling the user to follow step-by-step instructions. Consider the benefits to one small business from a new website.

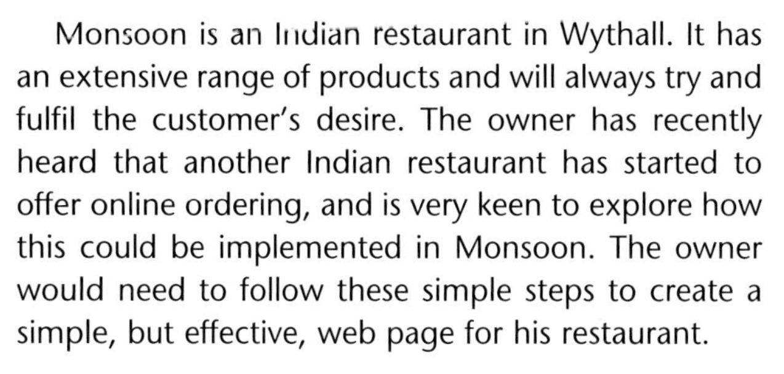

Monsoon is an Indian restaurant in Wythall. It has an extensive range of products and will always try and fulfil the customer's desire. The owner has recently heard that another Indian restaurant has started to offer online ordering, and is very keen to explore how this could be implemented in Monsoon. The owner would need to follow these simple steps to create a simple, but effective, web page for his restaurant.

Selecting the software

There are a range of web creation software packages that can be used to create a web page and these range from beginner to expert level. For a simple website created by a beginner, software such as a desktop publisher is ideal, although it does have limitations. It can create an effective web page, but it does not allow the user to animate the text.

In this chapter, Microsoft Publisher is used to demonstrate how a simple web page can be created. Flash is then used to demonstrate how animation can bring a web page to life.

Publisher enables the user to select a range of templates. There is one for websites. A series of templates will appear and all the user needs to do is select one that they like.

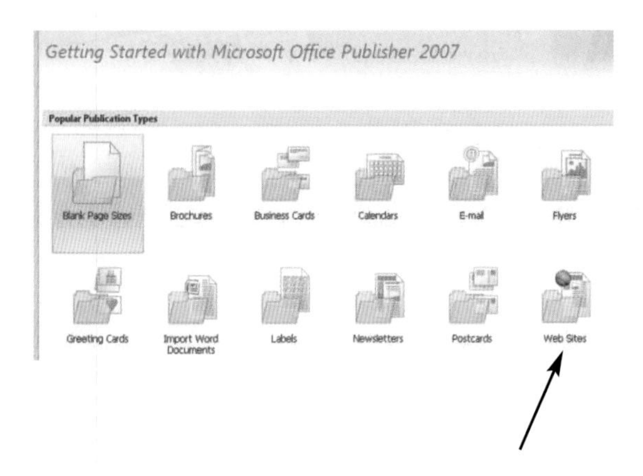

Once the user has selected a template they can then start inserting the necessary information. Below is an example of how the information for Monsoon has been included.

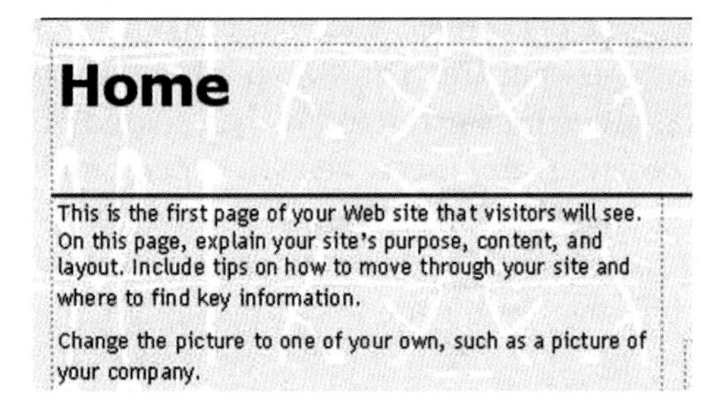

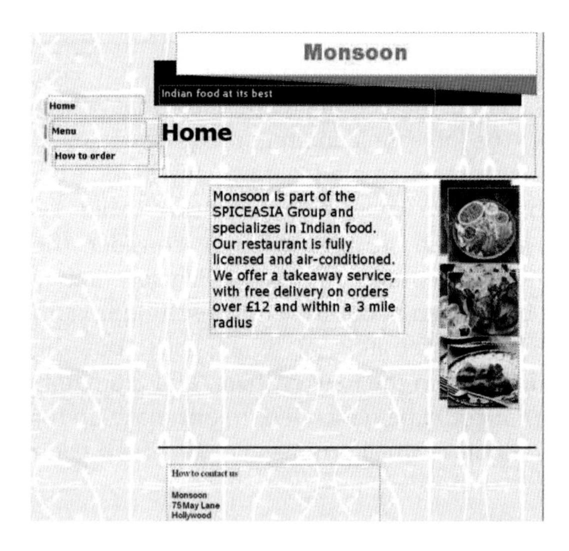

You can format all parts of the template. For example, the owner of Monsoon wants the colour scheme to include red, making the page more eye-catching. The background can be changed easily.

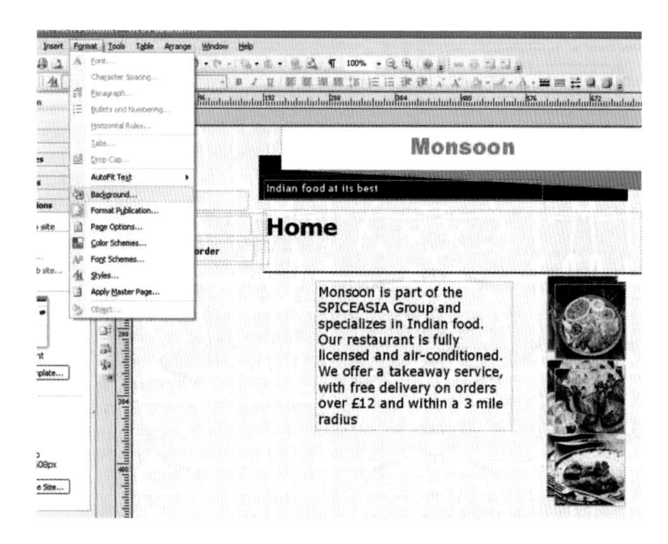

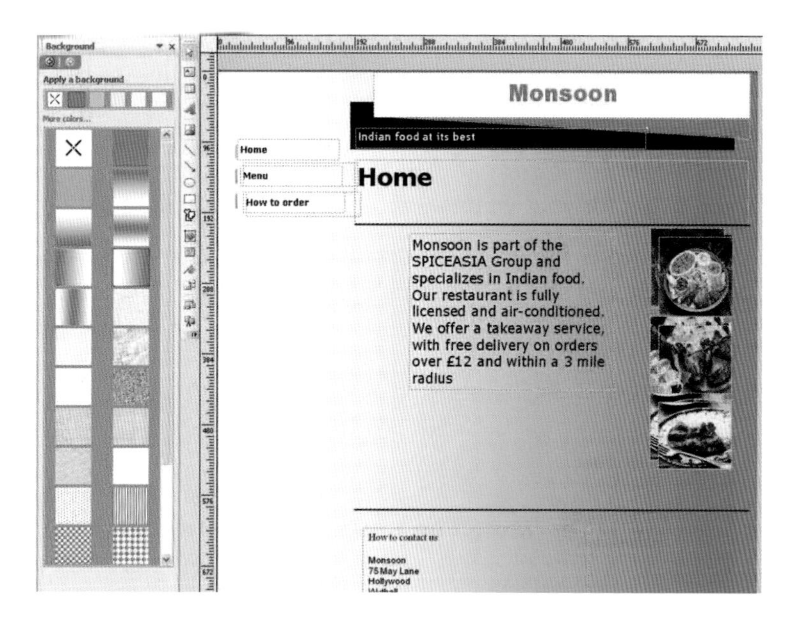

You can add as many pages to the website as you wish. All you need to do is select 'Add webpage'. The program will ask you what title you would like to call the page, offering some standard options. If the option selected is 'Blank', this means you can call the page anything you like.

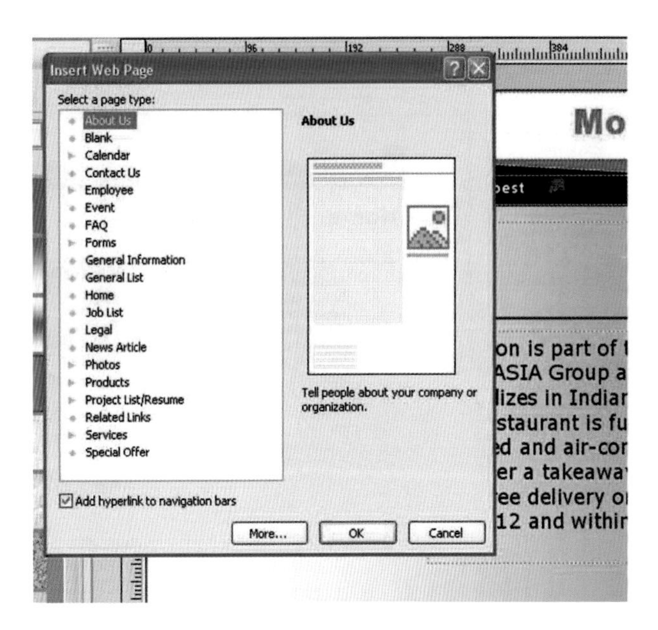

Creating hyperlinks

Once you have created some pages for your website, you can create hyperlinks between the pages.

Choose the text which will have a hyperlink. Select 'Insert' from the menu bar, and then 'Hyperlink'. Alternatively, right-click on the text and select 'Hyperlink', as shown here.

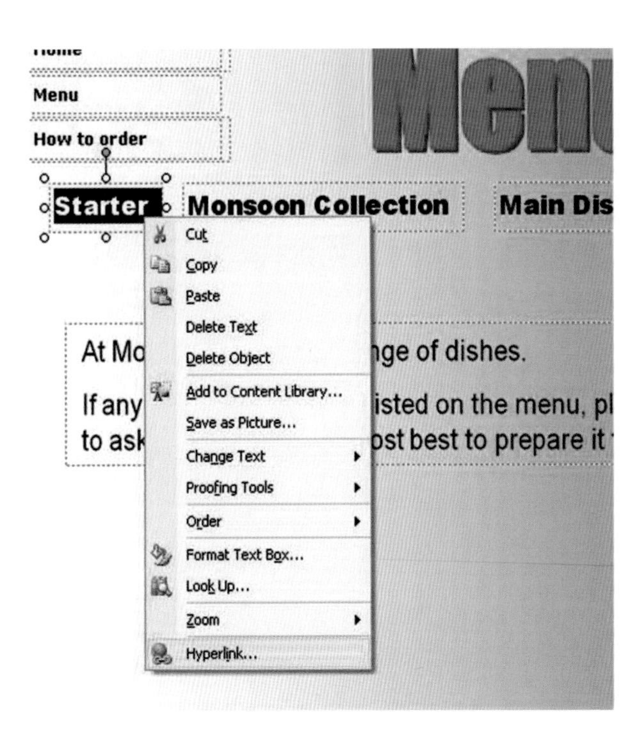

At this point, you can change the title of the page to which you are linking. Select the page number and then click 'Change title'. Change the title to something appropriate, because users of your website will be able to see it in the titlebar.

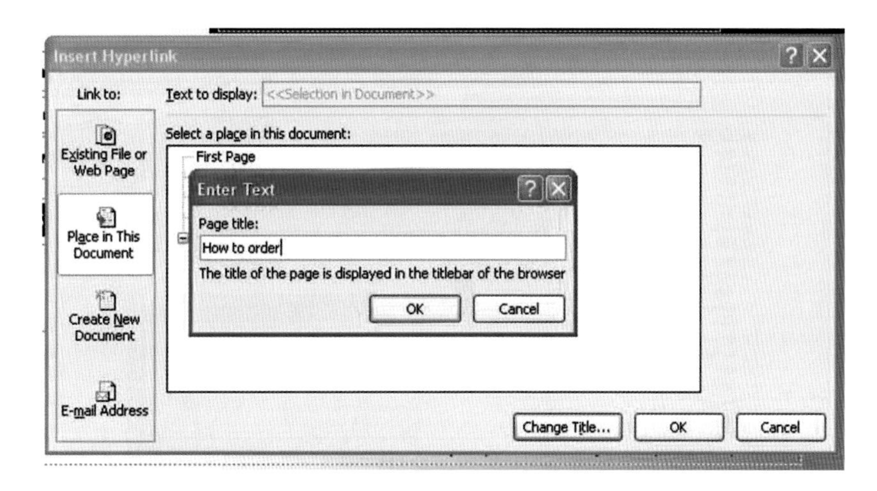

As you can see here, the pages of the Monsoon website have been given appropriate titles. This makes it easier to create hyperlinks between them.

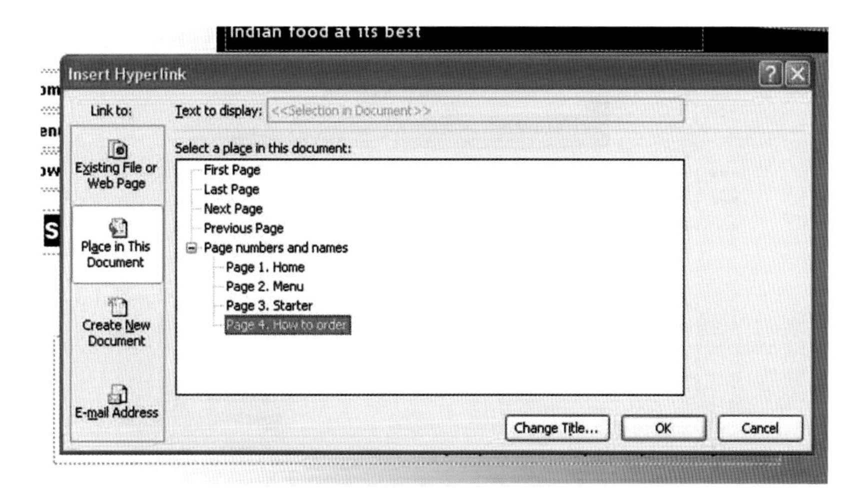

Previewing the website

You can preview your web pages over the web. This is useful because you can check that the hyperlinks are correctly linked to the right pages. Select 'File' and then 'Web page preview'. The website will then appear in an internet browser window, as shown below. You can use the navigation bar to move around the site, and click on the hyperlinks to test them.

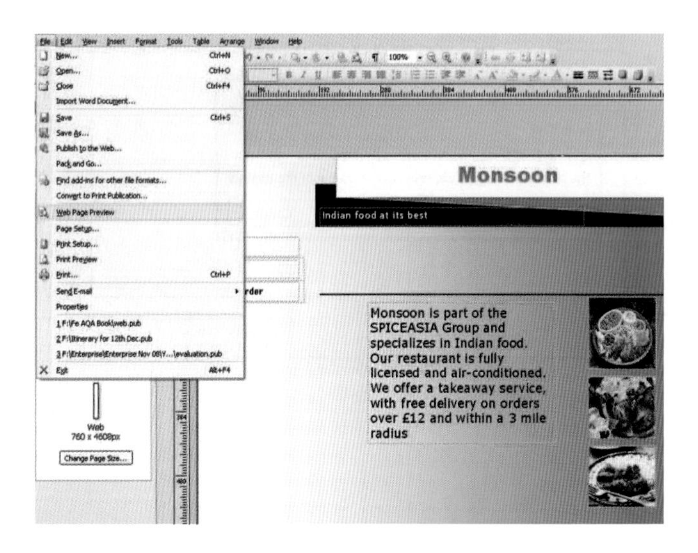

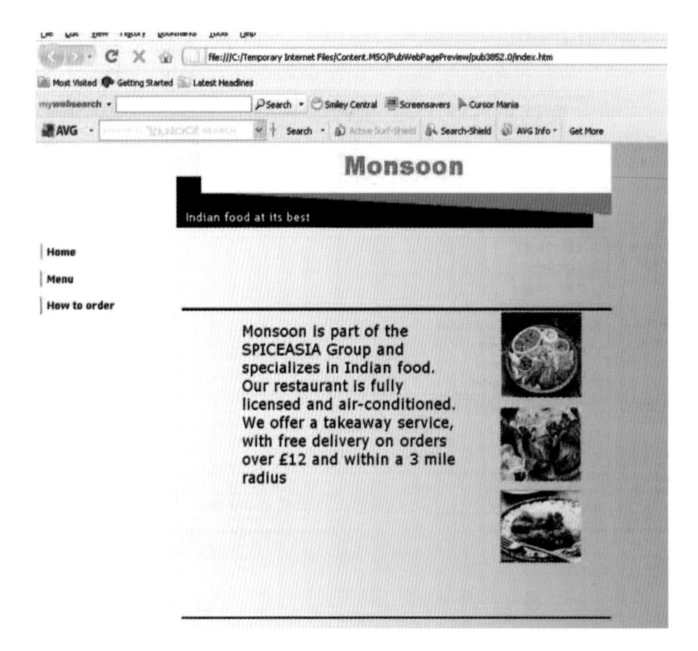

Creating animations for a web page

There are many different programs that you can use to create an animation for your web page. You will need to look carefully at each one to see which one is better for your needs. You can research the programs available by using help guides from the internet.

You will need to consider the following before making your decision as to which one to use:

- What is the purpose of the animation?
- What are the better features of the program and which are not as good?
- How easy is it to improve the animation?

There are many other reasons you may personally have for choosing one as opposed to another.

What you need to know

What is animation? It is actually a number of objects joined together in such a way that they look as if the object is moving across or up and down the page. You may have created your own flip book when you were younger by drawing several different images on the page of a book; when you flip through the pages of the book it gives the effect that the image is moving.

Creating an animation

You can use Flash Macromedia to create an animation. There are five steps:

1. Create an object.
2. Insert the required number of keyframes into the timeline.
3. Set the starting position of the object in the first keyframe.
4. Set the ending position of the object in the second keyframe.
5. Tween the motion of the object between the keyframes.

The following pages show this process in more detail. To begin, click on the screen to create a new document.

Once you have opened the program your document will look like the one below.

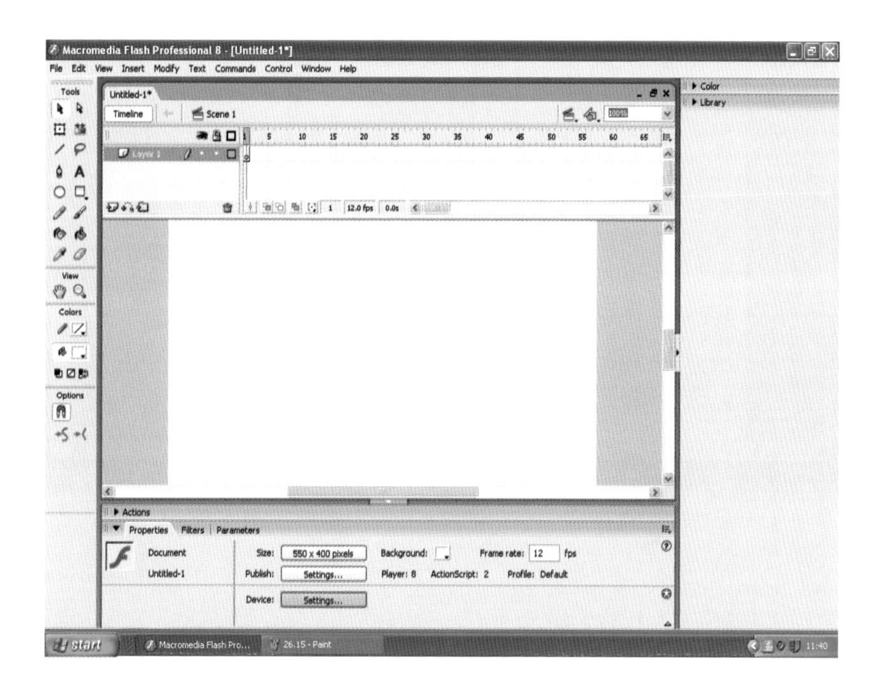

If you go to the left-hand side of the screen you will see the tool bar which will allow you to create your animation.

Using the tool bar you can choose the shape you want to use, along with all the other features that are available, such as the rubber, different fonts and so on.

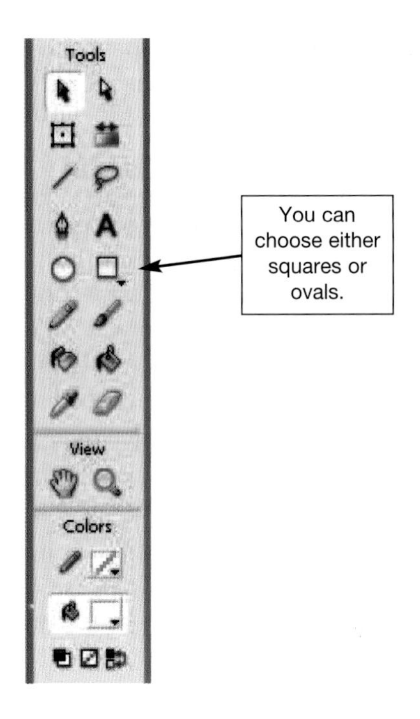

The animation has a timeline, shown at the top of the screen.

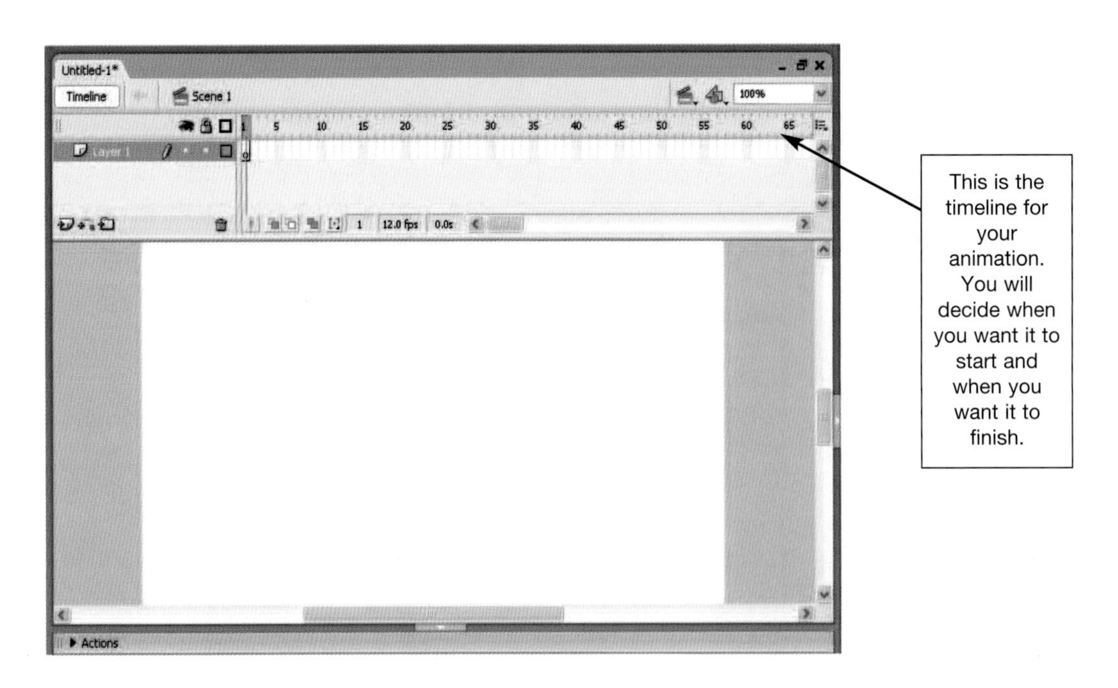

If you click on 'Insert' you can decide when you would like your animation to start and finish.

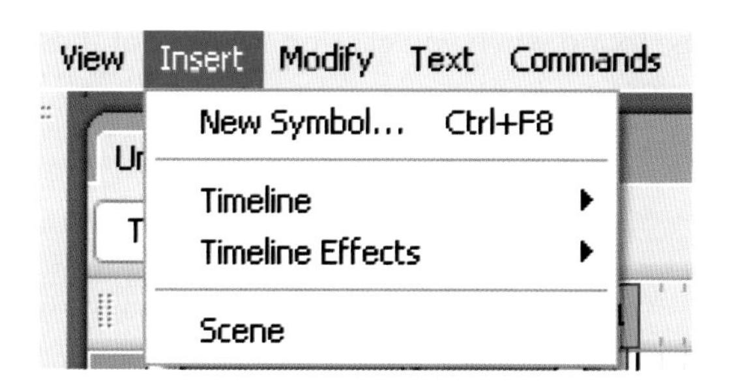

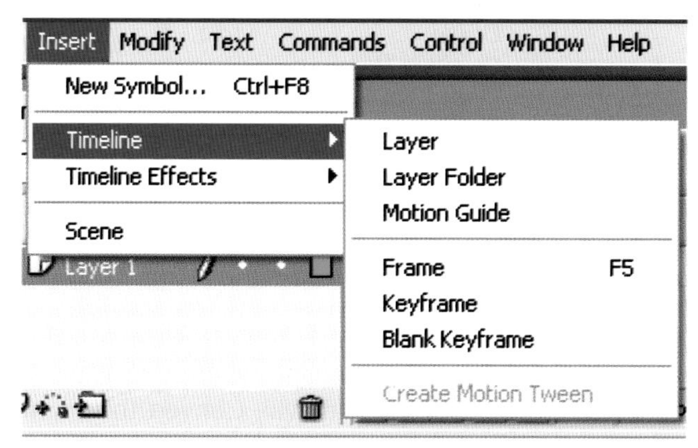

When you begin to create your animation it is really like looking at a stage. Imagine that an actor (your animation) is going to perform on this stage.

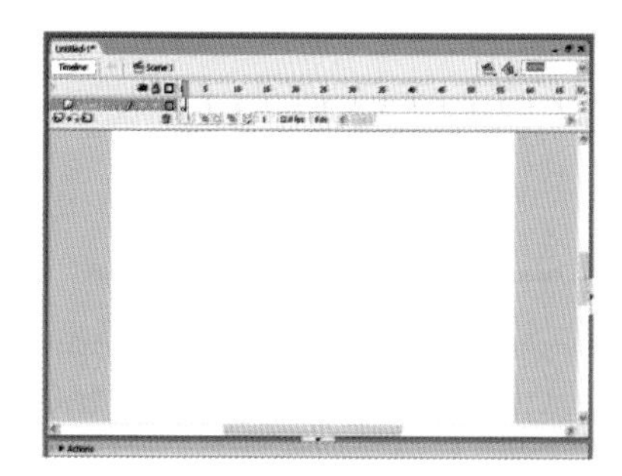

The white part is the stage and the grey area around is the paste board, where you can place all the objects that you want to show (like the props for a play). However, these will only be shown when you put them on the stage (on the white part of the screen). You can zoom in on the paste board to have more space on the screen to begin to plan your work.

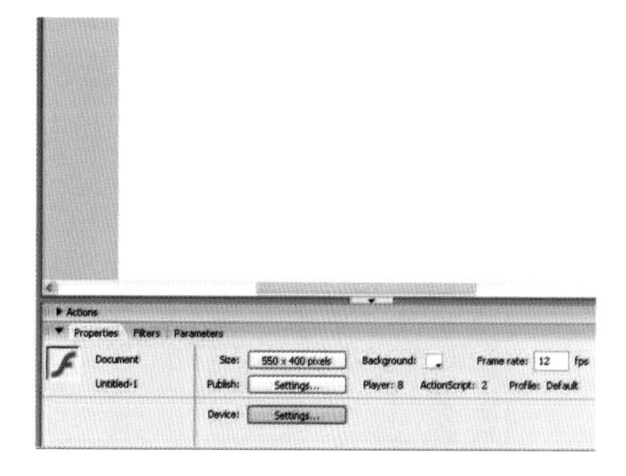

Below you will see the properties panel, which can be found at the bottom of your screen. Here you can choose the size, background and frame rate for your animation. The properties will change depending on what you have chosen to do.

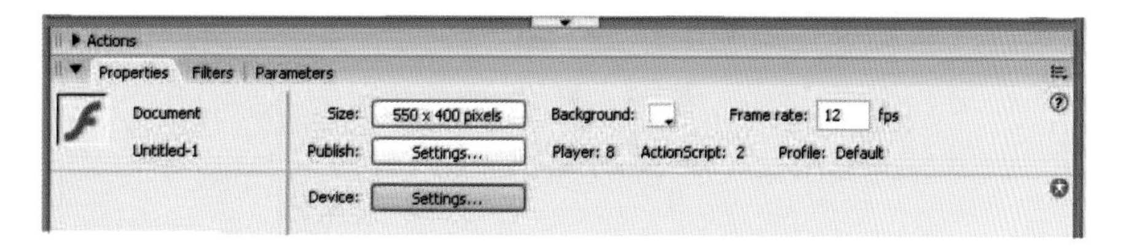

If you go to the toolbar and click on the oval, the properties will change to show you what you can do with the oval. You can then click and drag out the size of the oval you want on your 'stage'.

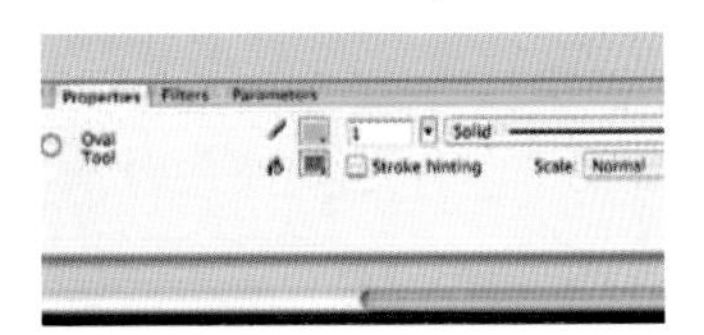

You can see below how the properties have changed now that you have clicked on the oval.

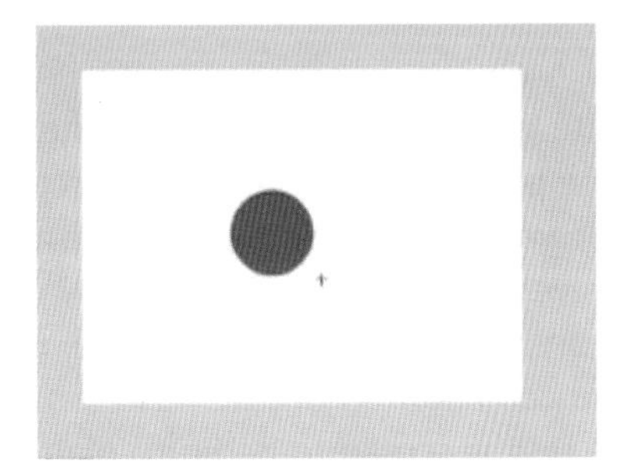

You can change the colour of the oval by clicking on Properties again, selecting the colour chart and choosing exactly the colour you want.

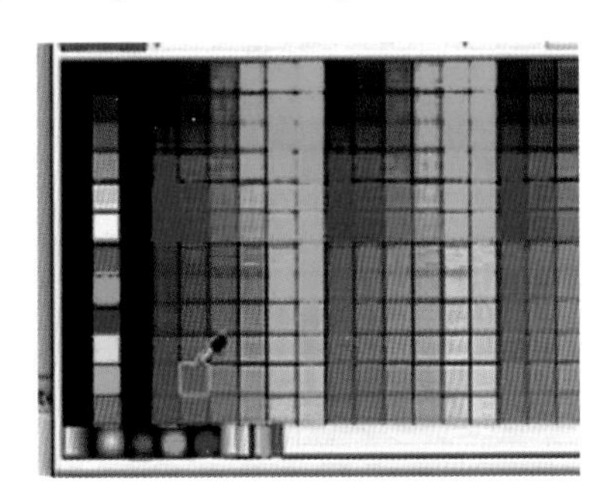

On the right-hand side of the screen there are panels which include many other features that you can use to help improve your animation. Other panels can be found when you click on Window at the top of the page.

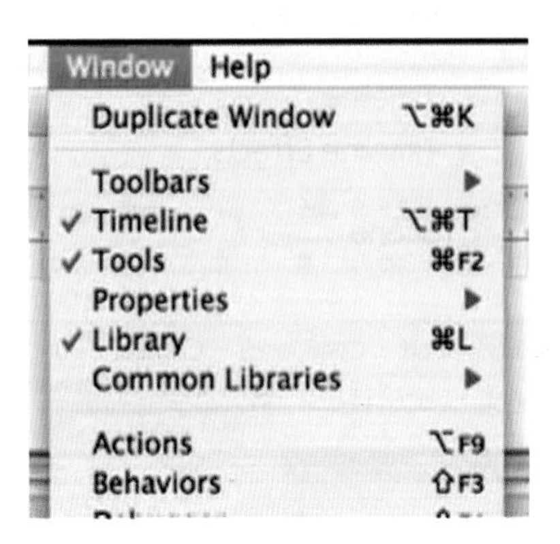

Having used the drawing tools to create an oval, we will now make it move across the stage.

The oval was created in Frame 1. Now select a frame further along the timeline where you want to define a new position for the oval. Convert this frame to be a keyframe by selecting Insert, Timeline and then Keyframe (or press the Function key F6).

For example, if you are using a frame rate of 12 frames per second, Frame 12 represents a position in the animation that is one second after the start. Frame 24 is two seconds after the start, and so on. So if you wanted something to change after two and a half seconds you would insert a keyframe at Frame 30.

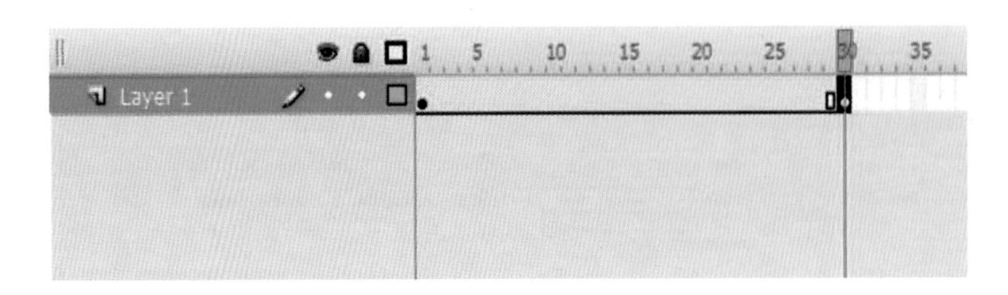

Select Frame 1 on the timeline and use the selection tool to position the oval at the starting position. Then select Frame 30 on the timeline and use the selection tool to position the oval at the ending position.

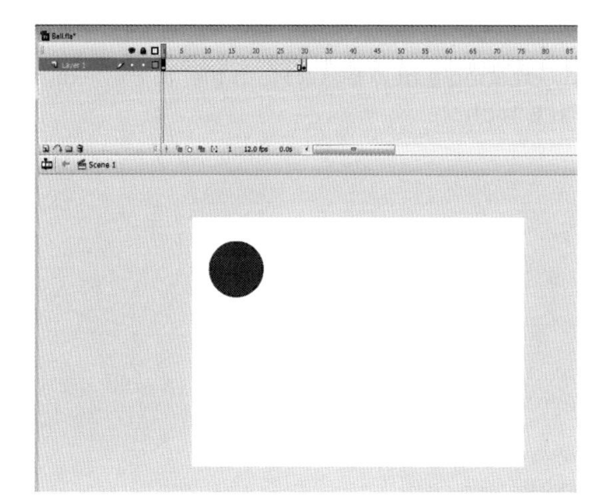

Frame 1: start position

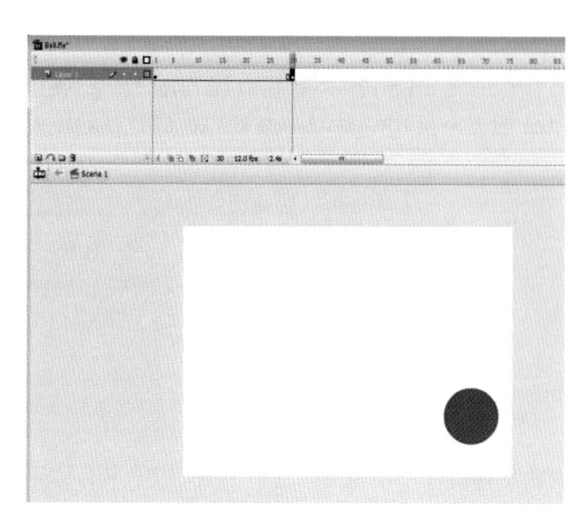

Frame 30: end position

A motion tween (or a shape tween) is chosen using the Properties panel at the bottom of the screen.

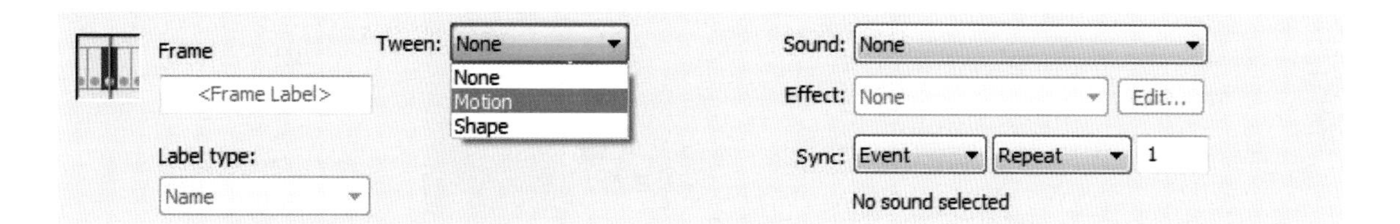

Once the tween has been added, it is shown as an arrow on the timeline between the keyframes.

You could also set the oval object to 'bounce' around the stage, by adding more keyframes for each change of direction. Reposition the oval where you want it to be in each keyframe, and add a motion tween to the timeline between each keyframe.

Use the Control menu or press Enter on the keyboard to preview what the final animation will look like.

Animating text

If you want to include moving text on a web page, first create it as an animation. Then insert the animated text file into the web page using your web authoring software. Suitable animation file formats are .gif or .swf.

To produce an animated text banner for a web page, start by creating a new blank Flash file. In this example, the size of the stage has been set to 600 pixels wide × 160 pixels high.

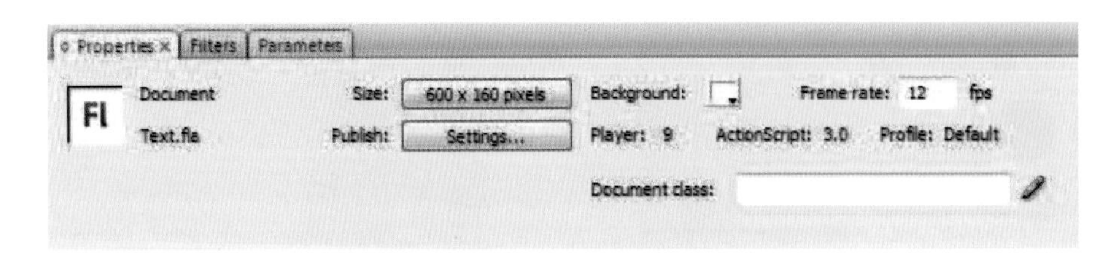

Text is added using the text tool from the toolbar.

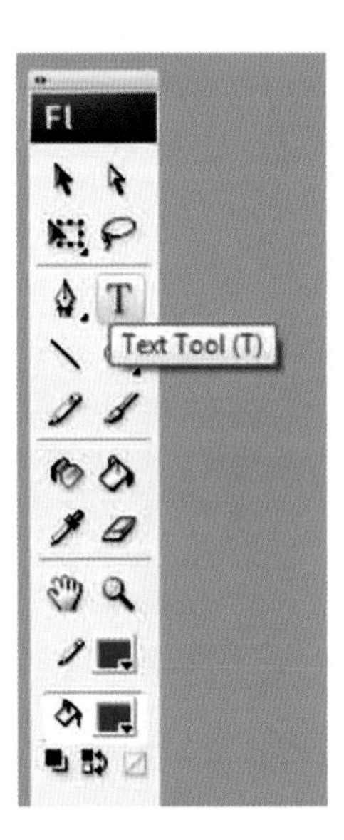

The text style, including the font, size and colour, is set in the properties panel at the bottom of the screen.

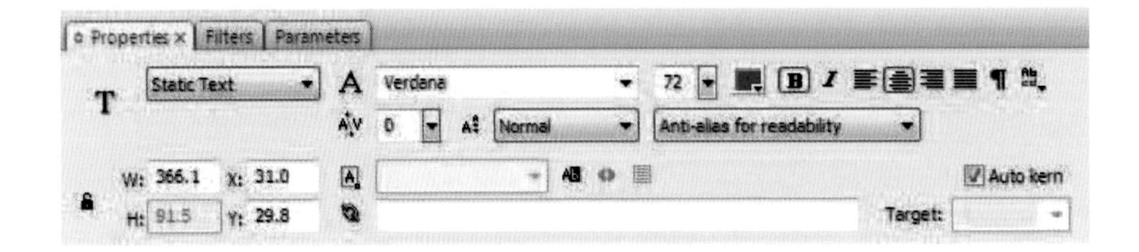

Type in the text and position it on the stage (or pasteboard) using the selection tool.

You can add keyframes and a motion tween to make the text 'fly in' from one side of the stage. In this example, the text will start at the right-hand side of the pasteboard. (Remember that the pasteboard is not visible in the final animated graphic. The only time any of the text is visible in the final graphic is when it passes over the stage.) As the animation progresses through the frames, the text will move across the stage from the right. All the movement will be complete by Frame 30. At this point the text will be positioned at the left-hand side of the pasteboard.

Note: using 30 frames at 12 frames per second, the animation will take two and a half seconds to complete the movement. You will need to make sure there is enough time to read the text as it moves.

The text should be positioned on the pasteboard as described below.

At Frame 1 (keyframe), the start of the animation, the text is positioned on the pasteboard at the right-hand side.

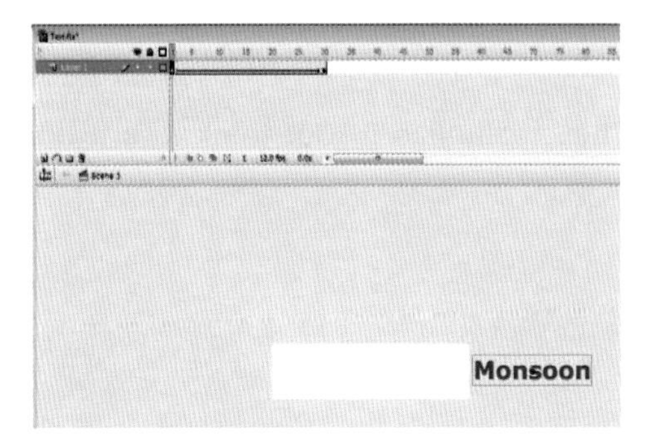

At Frame 15 (tweened frame), half-way through the animation, the motion tween has moved the text to the middle of the stage. (This frame is created by Flash as part of the tween.)

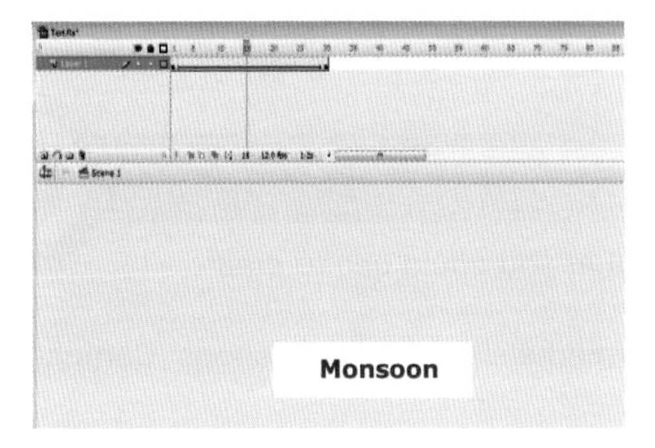

At Frame 30 (keyframe), the end of the animation, the text is positioned on the pasteboard at the left-hand side.

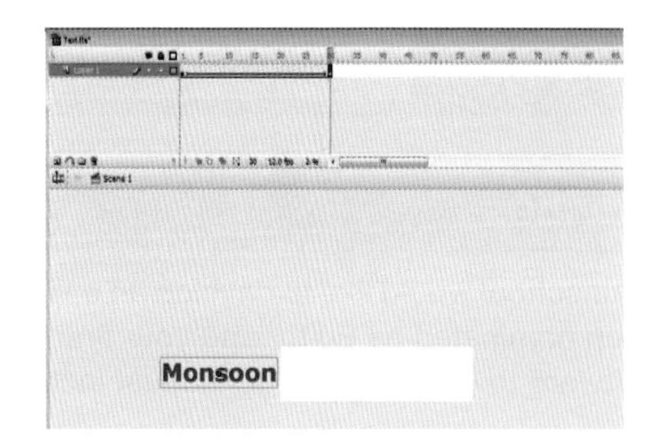

This animated text effect can now be used as a scrolling banner across a web page. To make the text scroll continuously from right to left, the animation needs to be looped in Flash before publishing.

The control menu is used to loop the playback.

Control Debug Window Help

Menu item	Shortcut
Play	Enter
Rewind	Ctrl+Alt+R
Go To End	
Step Forward One Frame	.
Step Backward One Frame	,
Test Movie	Ctrl+Enter
Test Scene	Ctrl+Alt+Enter
Test Project	Ctrl+Alt+P
Delete ASO Files	
Delete ASO Files and Test Movie	
✓ Loop Playback	
Play All Scenes	
Enable Simple Frame Actions	Ctrl+Alt+F
Enable Simple Buttons	Ctrl+Alt+B
✓ Enable Live Preview	
Mute Sounds	Ctrl+Alt+M

Test the playback of the animated text by pressing the Enter key. When everything is working, publish the animation from the File menu. You can choose a range of different file formats for the animation; .gif and .swf are the most suitable for this type of work.

Let's go!

Activities

1. Your school would like to develop an online newsletter which will be operated by the pupils. You have been nominated as Editor and your first task is to create a home page, using appropriate web page software to create the page. It must include the school logo and motto.
2. You have invited pupils from different year groups to write articles about various topics for the newsletter. Year Seven are really keen and have already submitted their information about their experience for the first half-term.
   a) Create a page for Year Seven within your website.
   b) Hyperlink the Year Seven page to the home page.
   c) Give the Year Seven page an appropriate title.
3. You have shown the home page to a panel of pupils. They really like it, but think it is a bit dull, because the information is static.
   a) Animate the school name.
   b) Select a section of text and animate it.
   c) Animate the school logo.

Summary

- Creating your own web page is not as difficult as it may first appear. People from all walks of life can make their own website pages including text, graphics, sound and video. There are many different programs you can use to create web pages, for example Microsoft FrontPage 2000 and Dreamweaver. Your web page does not have to be very complicated.

Give me five

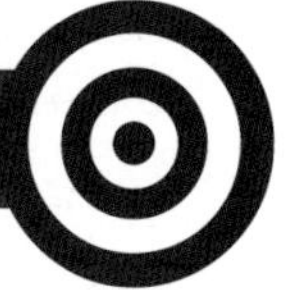

1. Use the internet to compare different types of software that you could use to create web pages.
2. Look at two websites with similar content, e.g. two supermarkets or two music shops. Compare the websites. Which do you like most? Why?
3. Why might you ask a web designer to create your website instead of doing it yourself?
4. What advice would you give to someone planning their own website?
5. Plan and create a website of your own choice, perhaps about a hobby or something that interests you.

Key words

HTML – programming language that is used to create web pages.

Hyperlink – a word, picture or other object that moves you to another page or even another website when you click on it.

Flash – a program that can be used to develop animations and graphics for websites.

Home page – the first page you come to when viewing a website.

Website – a collect of linked web pages.

Web page – a single page, usually one of a number of pages that make up a website.

Site plan – the structure of how your website will work.

Rollover/mouse over – a graphic on a web page that will change when a mouse passes over it. Sometimes used as a way of linking pages or sites.

Navigation – the way in which you move around within a website.

Timeline – the line which represents the passing of time.

Stage – the white area on the centre of the screen.

Work area – the grey area around the stage.

Keyframes – specific points on the timeline where something changes in the animation.

Tweening – the process used to work out what the animation will look like 'in be**tween**' the keyframes.

Exam style questions

You have just started a band, and you have decided to create your own website so that more people can hear and read about what you are up to and the gigs you have planned for the future.

1 You have been asked to submit the first two pages of your website to a local agency for them to consider whether they want to take you on to their books or not. Remember that your band is aimed at 13–16 year olds and your pages will need to include the following:
   - Details of a competition to win free tickets to your next gig
   - The fact that there are four members of the band, three boys and one girl
   - A couple of places where you have played and possibly a gig review
   - A contact telephone number
   - The name of the band and the type of music that you play. (15 marks)

2 The agency is quite interested in your band but wants more details about the members of the band. Create four pages with details of each band member; this could be similar to a Curriculum Vitae or you could base it on another website about band members. You will need to create a hyperlink from the home page to each band member's page and include a picture. (10 marks)

3 A friend has asked for some advice on setting up their own website. Point out the benefits as well as the pitfalls of creating a website. (6 marks)

ASSESSMENT

Preparing for assessment

Preparing for assessment

In this chapter you will learn:

- about the type of examinations you will be sitting
- what the controlled assessment will be like
- how to increase your chances of success.

Getting started

The GCSE Business and Communications qualification is made up of three units:

- Unit 8, ICT Systems in Business, is assessed by a one-hour written paper. The examination will be marked out of 80 marks, which is approximately 40 per cent of the final marks.
- Unit 9, ICT in Business, is assessed by a practical paper lasting one and a half hours. The examination will be marked out of 60 marks, which is approximately 35 per cent of the final marks.
- Unit 10, Investigating ICT in Business, is a **controlled assessment**. The controlled assessment will be marked out of 40 marks, which is approximately 25 per cent of the final marks.

What you need to know

Unit 8, ICT Systems in Business

This unit introduces you to the importance of business and communication systems, which contribute to the success of a business in achieving its objectives. You will be asked questions about how ICT systems affect the way people work and how they improve communications. You will need to be able to explain how ICT helps a business, and also the potential problems caused by data insecurity and health and safety issues.

The sections of the specification you will need to revise are:

- The business environment
- Business administration
- Workplace organisation
- Health and Safety at work
- ICT systems in business
- Security of data
- Recruitment and selection of staff
- Training
- Rewarding staff
- Employment rights and responsibilities
- The purpose of communication
- Communication systems
- The importance of ICT in business communications
- The internet and e-commerce.

You will be asked questions of varying length, usually worth between one and nine marks each.

The one or two mark questions may ask you to state the meaning of a term, so it is important that you learn the key words from the chapters. Here are two examples of this type of question:

State what is meant by the term stakeholder. (2 marks)

Identify two ways that Sarah could advertise for a new employee. (2 marks)

The mark scheme for this type of question is:

- Level 2: two valid methods or clear understanding, 2 marks
- Level 1: one valid method or some understanding, 1 mark
- Level 0: no valid response, 0 marks.

These questions will most usually be testing assessment objective (AO) 1: the ability to recall, select and communicate your knowledge and understanding of concepts, issues and terminology in business communications.

There will also be some longer questions, worth between two and six marks, which may test a combination of AO1 and AO2. AO2 is the ability to apply the skills, knowledge and understanding in a variety of contexts and in planning and carrying out tasks.

Here is an example of this sort of question:

State two reasons why the Music Shop might advertise for staff on the internet and explain how this would benefit the business. (6 marks)

There will also be some questions worth nine marks which are designed to assess AO3: the ability to analyse and evaluate evidence, make reasoned judgements and present appropriate conclusions. These questions will often ask you to recommend to someone what they should do about a specific problem and to give reasons for your recommendations by discussing all the possible options you have been given or know about. To get the full marks you will need to discuss each option and come to a conclusion.

Remember to answer all the questions and to write clearly so that the examiner can read your answers. You will be allowed to bring a calculator into the examination and you must write in black pen.

Unit 9, Using ICT in Business

This unit introduces you to a range of software applications that are used in different functional areas of a business. It will help you understand how a business uses software to capture, store, retrieve and analyse data in order to meet its requirements.

The sections of the specification you will need to revise are:

- The selection and use of appropriate software for business purposes
- Using word processing software
- Using spreadsheet software
- Using database software
- Using software to produce graphics
- Using presentation software
- Using web authoring software.

You will probably be asked to complete three or more tasks which may be integrated or stand alone: for example, you may be asked to produce a newsletter or a presentation containing a graph and a logo, or to create a business report.

You may be asked to annotate your finished documents to explain the choices you have made. AO3 will also be assessed by the appropriateness of the documents you produce for the intended audience.

Your teacher or examinations officer will tell you when you will take this examination; the actual date and sessions will not appear on your examination timetable.

Unit 10, Investigating ICT in Business

This controlled assessment assesses the subject content of Unit 9, Using ICT in Business:

- The selection and use of appropriate software for business purposes
- Using word processing software
- Using spreadsheet software

- Using database software
- Using software to produce graphics
- Using presentation software
- Using web authoring software.

Before the controlled assessment takes place, you will receive a sheet from AQA with details of the scenario and the research and planning you need to do in order to complete the assessment.

The research and planning should be carried out in between five and eight hours, and your teacher may give you guidance and feedback. You may do your research in groups, as long as the final task is all your own work.

The final task must be completed in no more than four hours. It is recommended that you spend the full four hours on completing the task and checking your work before you submit it.

As in Unit 9, you will probably be asked to complete several tasks which may be integrated or stand alone; for example, you may be asked to produce a flyer or a presentation and an accompanying business letter.

You may be asked to annotate your finished documents to explain the choices you have made. AO3 will also be assessed by the appropriateness of the documents you produce for the intended audience.

Your teacher or examinations officer will tell you when you will take this examination; the actual date and sessions will not appear on your examination timetable.

Examination advice

- A number of candidates lose marks because they do not provide what the examination question asks for, so it is very important to read the question through at least twice before you begin. You need to answer the question, not what you want the question to be!
- It is useful to underline or highlight important parts of the question: for example, if the question calls for different fonts and sizes, highlight those words and then make sure that you have used at least two fonts and sizes in your work. (In this example, three would be better; if one is not correct, then you have alternatives.)
- Work out the time you should spend completing each question according to the marks available. If there are 60 marks in a one-hour paper (as in Unit 8) then you should allow one minute per mark, including reading and checking time.
- Save your work as you go through the examination. If you make a mistake and delete something then it is easier to go back without having to start from the beginning.
- Attempt all the questions: if you do not then you are likely to lose valuable marks. Even if you are not sure how to do the question, try it – you can probably gain some marks.
- Check your work carefully and make sure that you place all printed sheets carefully away from the rest of your work so that you do not write on the back of the sheet or throw it away by accident.
- Check your folder of work carefully at the end of the examination – it is very sad to watch candidates throw away two years' work because they rush out of the examination room to be first in the lunch queue!
- Make sure that your name and candidate number are on every single sheet of paper that you print out. If your name is not on a piece of work, the invigilator may not be able to count it in your marks, because they have no proof you have done it. During the course, get into the habit of using headers and footers on every piece of work that you produce.
- Enjoy the examinations: they are your opportunities to show the examiner what you have learned and what you are capable of doing. The examination is not designed to trip you up or show what you don't know. If you have covered the specification then you can do the examination. Do your best: that is all anyone can ask.
- Use the AQA website to look at the specification, if your teacher has not given you a copy of it, and look at any specimen or past papers as they become available. Also look for mark schemes and any reports that the principal examiners may have written. In these reports, examiners point out common mistakes made by candidates, which can be very useful.

Make sure that you know when and where the examinations and controlled assessments are taking place: this can be complicated as some will need to take place in ICT rooms. Remember that examinations that take place in ICT rooms are still proper examinations, so arrive in plenty of time to settle yourself before they start. Take pens and rulers into all sessions, as you may be asked to annotate your work.

Finally, we will not wish you good luck because luck does not really come into examination success. Good preparation leads to good results!

Index